Oxford Paperback English Texts General Editor **John Buxton**

Sir Walter Scott

Selected Poems

Sir Walter Scott

Selected Poems

Edited by **Thomas Crawford**

1972 Clarendon Press: Oxford

Oxford University Press *Ely House, London W.1*

Glasgow New York Toronto Melbourne Wellington
Cape Town Ibadan Nairobi Dar es Salaam Lusaka Addis Ababa
Bombay Calcutta Madras Karachi Lahore Dacca Delhi
Kuala Lumpur Singapore Hong Kong Tokyo

Made and printed in Great Britain by
William Clowes & Sons, Limited
London, Beccles and Colchester

Contents

Introduction

Scott's earliest verses were nothing if not classical—translations from Virgil and Horace undertaken when he was about twelve years old for the Rector of the Royal High School in Edinburgh, three heroic couplets on a thunderstorm, and ten lines on the setting sun. But there is evidence that by his fifteenth or his sixteenth year he was writing in a more 'romantic' manner. The very themes of his lost works from that period point clearly in that direction—the love of an eleventh-century Norman adventurer, Robert Guiscard, for a certain Matilda, and a poem in four books on the Conquest of Granada.[1] And in his 1787 letters to his first love, 'Jessie from Kelso', he conveyed the impression of a youth who liked to pay his respects to every item in the cult of sentiment:

I have addressed the moon—that most be-rhimed of planets—so often I am ashamed to look her in the face. I have made odes to nightingales so numerous they might suffice for all that ever were hatched, and as for elegies, ballads, and sonnets and other small ware, truly I can assert their name is legion, for they are many.[2]

He sent her stilted love-songs of his own composition and popular ballads which he had touched up, thus showing how natural it was for him to combine the two main traditions of eighteenth-century Scottish lyric, the genteel and the folk. Scott often visited Jessie while she was tending an invalid aunt in Edinburgh. If he arrived when the old lady was awake, he had to hide in a cramped closet till the coast was clear:

Though tired of standing all this time
  I dare na stir a leg,
Though wishing sair to stretch my arms
  I canna move a peg.

The glasses tremble at my breath
  So close to me they stand,
Whilst jars are pressing at my feet
  And jugs at either hand.

('The Prisoner's Complaint', Sts. v–vi)[3]

This poem, like the 'Law versus Love' which is the other example of

[1] A. M. Clark, *Sir Walter Scott: the formative years*, Edinburgh 1969, pp. 21, 128.

[2] *Letters*, I. 3–4.

[3] *New Love Poems by Sir Walter Scott*, ed. D. Cook, Oxford 1932, p. 31.

Scott's juvenilia printed below, does not draw on any pallid 'pre-Romantic' style, but on the vigorous humour of popular lyric.

The strongest of all the influences which contributed to his development was that of the 'folk'. Although his ballad-collecting began perhaps as early as his sixth year, when he committed to memory a version of 'Lady Isabel and the Elf-Knight' (Child 4) and one of 'Lamkin' (Child 93), it was not until his twenty-second or twenty-third year that he began his regular expeditions to the Borders in search of ballad texts. German ballads for a time interested him as much as native ones, and became fused in his mind with the English ballad-imitations in Gregory Lewis's Gothic novel *The Monk* (1795). He injected this Germanic and 'Monkish' style into his own compositions, 'Glenfinlas' and 'The Eve of Saint John'. The first, unusually eclectic even for Scott in its use of supernatural source-material, adds Welsh corpse-lights and Rosicrucian personages like 'The Lady of the Flood' and 'The Monarch of the Mine' to a Highland oral tale of two hunters, alone in a hut, who are visited by two beautiful women in green. A hunter leaves with one of the women; his companion, who remains steadfastly behind, finds only his bones in the morning. 'The Eve of Saint John', set in the Borders, has always been more popular than 'Glenfinlas', at least in Scotland. In their context lines 185–92 (see below, p. 21) raise a *frisson* seldom aroused by Gothic-supernatural verse.

'Cadyow Castle', written in 1802, looks forward to the rather simple-minded delight in physical action found in so much of Scott's later poetry. Three stanzas describing an almost symbolic Caledonian bull stand out as poetry of some quality:

Through the huge oaks of Evandale
  Whose limbs a thousand years have worn,
What sullen roar comes down the gale
  And draws the hunter's pealing horn?

Mightiest of all the beasts of chase
  That roam in woody Caledon,
Crashing the forest in his race,
  The Mountain Bull comes thundering on.

Fierce on the hunter's quivered band
  He rolls his eyes of swarthy glow,
Spurs with black hoof and horn the sand,
  And tosses high his mane of snow.

It is not, however, in these three imitations (all printed in *The Minstrelsy of the Scottish Border*) that Scott's best poetry of this

period is to be found, but rather in his creative editing of traditional ballads. Lines 133–36 and 149–52 of 'Jamie Telfer of the Fair Dodhead' and lines 121–24 of 'Kinmont Willie' are almost certainly his own work, and so is much of 'Katharine Janfarie'. The three parts of 'Thomas the Rhymer' are a kind of paradigm of Scott's relation to the popular tradition. Part First is the product of his collecting and editorial method; it is 'from a copy obtained from a lady residing not far from Ercildoune', but 'corrected and enlarged' from the manuscript version supplied by Mrs. Brown of Falkland which forms Professor Child's A text.[1] That is to say, it is a *creative* running together of two different traditional versions. In the Second Part Scott arranges prophetic verses ascribed to Thomas of Ercildoune and printed by Andro Hart in 1615 into what must surely be regarded as an original composition. Part Third, avowedly described as 'Modern—By W. Scott', tells of Thomas's Arthurian lays and of his ultimate return to Fairy Land: as Scott himself says, it 'would have been placed with greater propriety among the class of Modern Ballads, had it not been for its immediate connexion with the first and second parts of the same story'.[2] Part First is archetypal rather than narrowly local, for Huntlie Bank and the Eildon Tree are as much part of a poetic world as Xanadu or Prospero's Island; Part Two, in contrast, is national in inspiration, taking the whole history of Scotland for its subject-matter, from the death of Alexander III in 1286 to Bannockburn, Flodden, and the Union of the Crowns; Part Three moves from the immediate vicinity of the Borders to the romantic atmosphere of Arthurian legend, dealing with Avalon, Merlin, and Sir Tristrem, then forward again to the local particularity of Learmont's tower, Leader Stream, and Soutra's mountains. Such a mingling of the local, the national, and the European is typical of Scott at all periods of his life; he passes from creative editing to original composition within the three parts of a single work just as in his career he moved from ballad-collecting and romance-editing to the creation of original ballads and romances.

The Lay of the Last Minstrel, written at the suggestion of the Countess of Dalkeith, was originally intended to be another ballad imitation of the kind already published in the *Minstrelsy*. In what is perhaps the first mention of *The Lay* in his correspondence, he thinks of his subject as 'a Legend'; his raw materials were not so much words or even scenes, as 'traditions' (*Letters*, I. 175, 237). The poem has often been criticized as a *mélange* of heterogeneous elements,

[1] Child, I. 317–29. [2] *PW*, IV. 158.

yet it is unified both thematically and rhetorically. The theme is formulated in Canto I, lines 178–80, when the Mountain Spirit, in dialogue with the River Spirit, states that though he cannot clearly read the decrees of the stars, he can see at least one thing with certainty, that they will not deign to shower any kind of influence

> On Teviot's tide and Branksome's tower,
> Till pride be quelled and love be free.

The mother learns to subdue her own pride when her daughter's lover, a family enemy, secures her son's release by impersonating the wounded Buccleuch Champion in single combat with the English Champion. The simple narrative line of the poem is enclosed within a frame, and each of the cantos is itself framed, by the direct comments of the Minstrel, 'last of his race', who chants the poem to Anne, Duchess of Buccleuch.

Such framing involves a triple time-scheme. The poem is sung in 1690 about events that took place around 1560. Scott is writing for a particular audience in and outside classical Edinburgh during the first decade of the nineteenth century. He sees the action through the prejudices and tastes of that audience, who are as it were his 'optic glass'. He puts before their eyes the last decade of the seventeenth century, when Minstrelsy and at least one Scottish way of life was dead; and beyond that, he portrays the time and world of the story, which are on one level the Border of 1560 and on another a fictive world that seems richer in colour and romance, as well as more feudal and more Catholic than the real Scotland of the early Reformation. Not for nothing did Scott term the inhabitants of the poem 'Gothic Borderers';[1] they are hybrids formed of Border 'manners' and fanciful chivalry, of Froissart and Horace Walpole's *The Castle of Otranto*. At the same time, his framing device creates a parallel between his own relationship as modern Minstrel to the Countess of Dalkeith, for whom he wrote the poem, and the narrator's to *his* patron, the seventeenth-century Duchess of Buccleuch. There is even irony and ambiguity in the parallel: does Scott see himself in 1802–5 as the last Minstrel of *his* Scotland?

Within its triple time-scheme, *The Lay's* structure is relatively loose and episodic. Its theoretical justification is implied in Scott's review of Southey's *Amadis of Gaul* in the *Edinburgh Review* for October 1803, where he admires prose romances which were linked together more firmly than the old 'rhapsodies' since they were meant to be read and not heard, but which were nevertheless loose enough to

[1] To G. Ellis, 21 Aug. 1804, *Letters*, I. 226–7.

permit inclusion of wide variation of matter and manner.[1] *The Lay* employs the flashbacks and violent transitions of the popular ballad in a broader scheme. As the *Critical Review* put it in 1805, 'Mr. Scott sets out, with every intention of diversifying his journey, by every variety of motion;' indeed this reviewer even went so far as to speak of 'the shock which the ear receives from violent and abrupt transitions', referring no doubt to the *Christabel*-like measure with which the poem begins, its contrast with the straight octosyllabics of later cantos, and finally, the alternation between narrative and lyric in the first and sixth cantos.[2] Such transitions do not destroy the poem's coherence any more than 'montage' undermines the unity of a traditional ballad.

With a tighter but still faulty narrative structure, *Marmion* makes a bolder and more impressive use of a verse-form derived from late medieval romances, where octosyllabic couplets are repeated two, three, or even more times, then interrupted by a six-syllabled line, followed by another group of eights, then a second six, rhyming with the first. The effect of the three-stressed line has often been compared to the breaking and falling of a wave, evident even in such a purely visual passage as the celebrated description of Edinburgh, when Lord Marmion lets his eyes

> . . . mark the distant city glow
>   with gloomy splendour red;
> For on the smoke-wreaths, huge and slow,
> That round her sable turrets flow,
>   The morning beams were shed,
> And tinged them with a lustre proud,
> Like that which streaks a thunder-cloud.
>
> Such dusky grandeur clothed the height,
> Where the huge Castle holds its state,
>   And all the steep slope down,
> Whose ridgy back heaves to the sky,
> Piled deep and massy, close and high,
>   Mine own romantic town!
> But northward far, with purer blaze,
> On Ochil mountains fell the rays,

[1] *Miscellaneous Prose Works of Sir Walter Scott*, 28 vols., Edinburgh 1834–6, XVIII. 13–15.

[2] *PW*, VI. 38. Scott owed his knowledge of *Christabel* (not published until 1816) to John Stoddart, who had visited Wordsworth and Coleridge at Grasmere, and recited parts of that poem to Scott at Lasswade in 1800, two years before *The Lay* was begun (see *PW*, VI. 23, 26–7).

And as each heathy top they kissed,
It gleamed a purple amethyst.
Yonder the shores of Fife you saw;
Here Preston Bay and Berwick-Law:
  And, broad between them rolled,
The gallant Frith the eye might note,
Whose islands on its bosom float,
  Like emeralds chased in gold.

(*Marmion.* Canto IV, lines 6–28)

The breaker-like effect is particularly striking when allied to the sound and turmoil of battle. It is perhaps no longer possible to claim *Marmion* as Scott's poetical masterpiece. Its interest lies in the strong delineation of individual scenes, such as the Gothic chiaroscuro of the trial and immuring of Constance; in the vigour and narrative skill of the battle sequence in Canto VI; in incidental felicities of characterization and dialogue, as when Lady Heron coyly declines to perform before she is finally prevailed upon to sing 'Lochinvar'; and above all in the flawed central character, at one and the same time a self-seeking schemer and a gallant fighter. Byron put it well in *English Bards and Scotch Reviewers*:

Now forging scrolls, now foremost in the fight,
Not quite a Felon, yet but half a Knight;
The gibbet or the field prepared to grace,
A mighty mixture of the great and base.

(lines 167–70)

The introductory epistles to Scott's friends which separate the cantos are at once a highly competent display of occasional octosyllabics and a delightful expression of Scott's personality. Though written in English, they have affinities with a type of Scottish poem, whose greatest successes are in the vernacular, in the verse letters of Ramsay[1] and Burns.

Just as Burns regarded *Tam o' Shanter* as his 'standard performance in the Poetical line',[2] so Scott held that 'in point of interest of story' *The Lady of the Lake* was 'the best of my efforts'.[3] His earliest notion of the poem was that its central core should be realistic and antiquarian, that it should not give an imaginary account of the Highlander's 'manners', but rather 'a vivid and exact description of that

[1] Allan Ramsay (1686–1758) the poet, and father of the painter of the same name, was the first important figure in the Scottish vernacular revival of the eighteenth century.

[2] Burns, *Letters*, ed. J. de Lancey Ferguson, 2 vols., Oxford 1931, II. 68.

[3] To Lady Abercorn, 14 Apr. 1810, *Letters*, II. 324.

remarkable race as they actually existed at no very distant period'.[1] Oral tales were among his sources—'I have been spending some time on the banks of Loch Lomond lately, where I have heard so many stories of raids, feuds and creaghs, that they have almost unchained the devil of the rhyme in my poor noddle.'[2] Another source was the Highland landscape itself—'the sight of our beautiful Mountains and lakes . . . and your Ladyship's kind exhortations have set me to threading verses together with what success I am yet uncertain.'[3] From such intentions as these one would surely expect a poem firmly anchored to everyday reality, displaying what (adapting Roger Langbaum) might be called 'the poetry of *historical* experience'. How is it, then, that *The Lady of the Lake* has impressed so many readers as 'pure airy romance, getting its effects as swiftly and surely as a fairy-tale'?[4]

The poem embodies a type of romance perfectly consonant with Scott's most abiding inspiration, the traditions of popular art; it has, that is to say, the reality that lies behind the wish-fulfilment dreams of ordinary men and women. The main situation, that of a disguised monarch wandering among his people, is a favourite one of broadside balladry; so is the happily-ever-after ending with the bestowal of 'fetters and warden'—the golden chain of matrimony and a virtuous wife—upon the rebel, Graeme. What Scott does is to fuse romance with the everyday, so that reality *is* fairy-like both in the poem's world and in the natural and social world which it reflects. As in *The Lay*, the whole poem is 'framed'—in this case by the Harp of the North, long strangled by symbolic ivy. The Harp symbolizes the past glories of Scottish and Celtic poetry, which were in Scott's view essentially 'romantic'. (See Canto I, lines 1–29, where some of the key words are 'witch-elm', 'minstrelsy', 'knighthood', 'wizard note', 'Enchantress', or Canto VI, where one finds 'Spirit of the Air', 'Fairy's frolic wing', 'witch-note', and 'spell'.)

The descriptive set piece that opens Canto I owes its individuality in large part to the way in which the fantastic-picturesque of the real Trossachs is compared to a humanized and medievalized landscape with buildings and artefacts. Stanza xi for example contains 'turret', 'dome', 'battlement', 'cupola', 'minaret', 'pagod', 'mosque', 'banner', and 'streamers green', while Stanza xiii makes rare poetry out of the simile of a castle and the metaphor of parenthood:

[1] To R. Heber, 15 July 1806, *Letters*, XII. 286–7.
[2] To R. Surtees, 17 Sept. 1809, *Letters*, II. 246–7.
[3] To Lady Aberdeen, 14 Sept. 1809, *Letters*, II. 239.
[4] J. Buchan, *Sir Walter Scott*, London 1932, p. 112.

The shaggy mounds no longer stood,
Emerging from entangled wood,
But, wave-encircled, seemed to float,
Like castle girdled with its moat;
Yet broader floods extending still
Divide them from their parent hill,
Till each, retiring, claims to be
An islet in an inland sea.

(St. xiii, lines 11–18)

Scott's landscape is thus naturally and instinctively linked to and contrasted with the customary 'props' of the literary man's feudal society—towers, lady's bowers, a cloister grey, and the conventional hoary hermit's lonely cell (St. xv). Ellen Douglas compares her sire's 'tall form' to Ferragus and Ascabart, heroes of medieval Rome. The refugees' luxurious bower in the lake has more than a hint of the pastoral world of the late Shakespearian tragi-comedies. There is a Harper within the tale, parallel to but different from the Harper of the frame, with an instrument which, though not Aeolian, nevertheless produces strains other than those consciously willed by the musician—strains dictated by Fate (Canto II, St. vii). Other figures of romance appear, such as Brian the lone seer who beholds the River Demon (Canto III, St. vii), the pre-Byronic bandit, Roderick Dhu, and the prophetic spaewife Blanche of Devan (Canto IV, Sts. xxiii–xxvii).

Reality is assured not only by the description ('a light, glittering summary of relevant features') but by the dialogue, the narrative pace (e.g. Canto V, St. xvi), and above all by that expert creation of historical models which was later to characterize the Waverley novels. The contrast between the anti-monarchical magnates and the citizenry allied to the Crown in Canto V, St. xxi is a perfect instance; another is the debate between Roderick and Fitzjames in Canto V, Sts. vii–viii, where Scott, like Dryden before him, proves an adept at reasoning in verse. Romance and realism are synthesized in the hand-to-hand fight between the King and Roderick (Canto V, St. xiv–xvi); it is at one and the same time an exciting conflict in technicolor as it were, and a paradigm of the historical struggle between Highlander and Lowlander. Unity is provided by narrative line and, as in *The Lay*, by image-patterns. For example, the stag is identified with a warrior or a king in the first five cantos, and Ellen Douglas is associated with such flowers as the rose and the pressed harebell. One must agree, of course, that the poem does not yield the same sort of pleasure as a concentrated lyric or a philosophically structured

epic like *Paradise Lost*; Scott's diffuse octosyllabics render scenes and tell a story rather than create a *verbal* experience. Detailed analysis, however, does not substantiate Coleridge's scornful dismissal:

In short, what I felt in *Marmion,* I feel still more in *The Lady of the Lake*—viz. that a man accustomed to cast words in metre and familiar with descriptive Poets & Tourists himself a Picturesque Tourist, must be troubled with a mental Strangury, if he could not lift up his leg six times at six different Corners, and each time p—— a canto.[1]

If for most of the time Scott gives us verse rather than poetry, that does not mean to say that his work is worthless, but merely that its value resides in what lies *behind* the verse and what it bodies forth.

In *The Bridal of Triermain* the tension between reality and 'fairy-land' that underlies *The Lady of the Lake* is expressed in the contrast between the poem's 'frame' and the Tale itself. In the 'frame', consisting of the Introductions to Cantos I and III, and the conclusions to Cantos II and III and to the whole poem, a contemporary narrator pays court to a flesh and blood Lucy, satirizing his real and possible rivals, such as the fop

> Who comes in foreign trashery
>   Of tinkling chain and spur,
> A walking haberdashery,
>   Of feathers, lace and fur:
> In Rowley's antiquated phrase,
> Horse-milliner of modern days.

(Conclusion to Canto II, St. iii, lines 19–24)

The Cantos themselves consist of a 'Lovers' Tale' that takes the form of an Arthurian Romance about how Roland de Vaux, Lord of Triermain, frees Gyneth from a spell laid upon her by Merlin. Much of the effect of *Triermain,* as of *The Lay of the Last Minstrel,* is derived from the deployment and telescoping of three time-scales; these are a contemporary love-dialogue, King Arthur's seduction of Gyneth's mother in the legendary past, and de Vaux's rescue of her spell-bound daughter no less than five hundred years later. Reality is not confined to the early nineteenth-century dialogue with Lucy; it comes into the Arthurian fantasy by the back door, since the conventions of Arthurian romance enable Scott to hint at sensual love and to treat of adultery and illegitimacy with a frankness hardly seen

[1] Coleridge to Wordsworth, 1810, in J. O. Hayden, ed., *Scott: the Critical Heritage*, London 1970, p. 70.

in his novels. *Triermain* is in some ways a 'pre-Victorian' poem—a precursor of *Locksley Hall*, *Maud*, and even *Great Expectations*;[1] the 'ruined' Gwendolen's hatred of men resembles Miss Havisham's, and Gyneth's cruelty is like Estella's. The 'frame' of *Triermain* is to the other long poems as *St Ronan's Well* is to the rest of the Waverley novels—an interesting and oddly stimulating experiment in the contemporary that does not quite come off. In contrast, the main body of the poem exhibits less surface realism and a more consistently 'romantic' supernaturalism than the ballad epics. *Rokeby* was begun in September 1812 and finished on 31 December, and was in part a response to the competition of *Childe Harold* Cantos I and II (published in March 1812). Deliberately catering for English taste, it celebrates the scenery of Yorkshire as *The Lay* and *The Lady of the Lake* did the topography of the Borders and the Trossachs; the place references are equally detailed; and there is a similar attempt to fuse national feeling (English, or 'all-British') with an emotional response to landscape. Although the historical period is the less recondite one of the Civil Wars, the impression conveyed (as in *The Lay*) is of a feudal rather than an early modern society, into which a high-minded trio of early nineteenth-century sentimentalists—the noble and beautiful Matilda, the chivalrous soldier Redmond, and the poetical milksop Wilfrid—have unaccountably strayed. Scott introduces a band of *déclassé* robbers, deserters from both Cromwell and the King, who live on the banks of the Greta and are more operatic than even Roderick Dhu's clansmen; and his villain, the ex-pirate Bertram of Risingham, fits in very well with the taste that Byron was creating at the same time. To a contemporary critic in *The Monthly Review*, Bertram raised almost the same issues as Milton's Satan posed for readers of the Romantic generation:

> We do not here enter into the question as to the good taste of an author who employs his utmost strength of description on a compound of bad qualities; but we must observe . . . that something must be wrong where poetical effect and moral approbation are so much at variance. . . . Powerful indeed must be the genius of the poet who, out of such materials as those above mentioned, can form an interesting whole. This, however, is the fact; and Bertram at times so overcomes hatred with admiration that he (or rather his painter) is almost pardonable for his energy alone.[2]

Rokeby's plot is more tightly constructed than any before; interest is even more strongly centred on character-contrast, situation and

[1] C. O. Parsons, *Witchcraft and Demonology in Scott's Fiction*, Edinburgh and London 1964, p. 64.

[2] Quoted in *PW*, IX. 304.

narrative line; one cannot but feel that below the verse-surface of *Rokeby* a Waverley novel is struggling to be born.

The Lord of the Isles (1815), begun before *Rokeby* though finished later, is a tighter narrative still. The first stirrings of the idea are found in a letter to the Revd. E. Berwick of 8 Oct. 1810: 'I should like before I hang my harp on the willows for ever to try an Irish tale mixed with something of our own Hebrides.'[1] Among his motives is deliberate tourism: 'My principal employment for the autumn will be reducing the knowledge I have acquired of the Islands into scenery and stage-room for *The Lord of the Isles*';[2] and he can refer to it light-heartedly and even cynically as 'Scottified up to the Teeth'.[3] On to a straightforward account of Bruce's landing in Carrick in 1307, and the struggle for Scotland's independence up to 1314, considerably doctored in the interests of plot and aesthetic effect, Scott grafts the sentimental tale of Edith of Lorn's love for Ronald, Lord of the Isles. Despite Ronald's attachment to Bruce's sister Isabel, Edith wins him in the end after following him to the war in the guise of a mute page-boy. Most contemporary reviewers saw the poem as inferior to its predecessors, but from our present vantage-point it is the most epic-seeming of all Scott's poems, if only because of its heroic treatment of the Bruce. The chivalric abnegation shown by the women is reminiscent of Redmond and Wilfrid in *Rokeby*. Isabel refuses to listen to Ronald's suit unless Edith first releases him from his vow; the disguised Edith then conveys his ring and other tokens to Isabel; Isabel voluntarily relinquishes him to Edith.

The most remarkable feature of *The Lord of the Isles* is its achievement of a violent anti-poetry of action superior to the more conventional heroics for which Scott is famous. One example is where Bruce slays a murderer with a brand snatched from the fire:

> The spattered brain and bubbling blood
> Hissed on the half-extinguished wood,
> The miscreant gasped and fell!
>
> (Canto III, St. xxix, lines 6–8)

Another occurs during the battle of Bannockburn when d'Argentine pierced Colonsay's 'bloody tartans', whereupon

> Nailed to the earth, the mountaineer
> Yet writhed him up against the spear,
> And swung his broadsword round!

[1] *Letters*, II. 387.
[2] To J. B. S. Morritt, 14 Sept. [1814], *Letters*, III. 498.
[3] To Morritt, 21 Jan. 1815, *Letters*, IV. 18.

—Stirrup, steel-boot and cuish gave way,
Beneath that blows tremendous sway
  The blood gushed from the wound;
And the grim Lord of Colonsay
  Hath turned him on the ground,
And laughed in death-pang, that his blade,
The mortal thrust so well repaid.

(Canto VI, St. xxiii, lines 20–9)

In *The Lord of the Isles* Scott's poetic style seems more austere than in earlier poems, thanks perhaps to his use of Barbour's *Brus* as source material. He borrows from Barbour the concept that Scotland under Bruce was fighting for the freedom of all the people, commons and serfs as well as lords, and develops to an almost ridiculous extent Barbour's notion of a chivalrous Bruce, generous to defeated Englishmen. As Jeffrey put it at the time, the poem is

> not sufficiently national—and breathes nothing either of that animosity towards England, or that exultation over her defeat, which must have animated all Scotland at the period to which he refers; and ought, consequently, to have been the ruling passion of his poem. Mr. Scott, however, not only dwells fondly on the valour and generosity of the invaders, but actually makes an elaborate apology to the English for having ventured to select for his theme a story which records their disasters.[1]

Jeffrey here draws attention to a conflict in Scott's mind between his feeling for the Scots nation and his loyalty to the idea of Britain—a conflict which undoubtedly limits the epic quality of *The Lord of the Isles*.

What is most individual in Scott's longer poems is his unique synthesis of national sentiment and a feeling for landscape, supported by the concrete particularity of his antiquarian detail, whereby the mere listing of places and persons lends a remarkable solidity to the poems in which they occur; by this means 'background' becomes the poet's real subject. A revealing comparison with Wordsworth can be made at this point. Scott was irritated by these lines in 'Yarrow Unvisited':

Let beeves and home-bred kine partake
The sweets of Burn-mill meadow;
The swan on still St. Mary's lake
Floats double, swan and shadow.

He wrote to Wordsworth: 'We have Broad-meadow upon Yarrow which with the addition of green or fair or any other epithet of one syllable will give truth to the locality & supply the place of Burnmill

[1] Quoted in *PW*, X. 266–7.

meadow which we have not.'[1] For Scott truth to locality is a primary value, whereas Wordsworth's conception of poetic truth is satisfied by an euphonious and atmospheric *invented* place-name. On the other hand Scott is prepared quite mechanically to advise the choice of any commonplace adjective in order that the demands of literal truth and particularity of place should be satisfied—a procedure which would not have commended itself to Wordsworth.

Since much of even the narrative poetry of the early nineteenth century was lyric and inward-looking in spirit, and since Scott's long poems often read like expanded lyrics or ballads which are on the point of turning into novels, it is perhaps hardly surprising that his greatest successes are either occasional poems, or songs. The 'Epilogue to the Drama founded on "St. Ronan's Well"' shows what he could do in the vernacular tradition of Allan Ramsay and that greater laureate of Edinburgh's streets, Robert Fergusson; one wishes he had written more in Scots. Scott claimed he had no ear for a tune, but an excellent sense of time.[2] Be that as it may, 'MacGregor's Gathering', 'Pibroch of Donuil Dhu', 'March, march, Ettrick and Teviotdale', 'Donald Caird's come again', and 'Bonny Dundee' are excellent examples of the traditional Scottish game of setting words to music; in each case, Scott had a definite tune in mind. Like many of Burns's songs ('My luve she's but a lassie yet', 'Tam Glen', 'Thou has left me ever, Jamie'), Scott's most memorable lyrics are of the dramatic type, sung by an imaginary character ('Rebecca's Hymn', 'I'm Madge of the Country'); in addition, they are often impregnated by the spirit of the larger work in which they appear ('The Fight of Grace', 'Look not thou on Beauty's charming') and are deliberate exercises in the style of a bygone age. They are most individual when they express robust action, elegiac sadness, extreme and even stark poignancy, and the sublime (as in the Coronach 'He is gone on the mountain' in *The Lady of the Lake* Canto III, p. 195 below, and 'Rebecca's Hymn' in *Ivanhoe*, p. 36 below). Scott is unduly neglected even as a novelist; as a poet he is under a cloud. Yet he is, after Blake, the finest lyric poet in Britain between Burns and Shelley.[3]

[1] *Letters*, I. 241.
[2] To Mrs. Scott of Lochore, 29 Dec. 1825, in *Letters*, IX. 356.
[3] See H. J. C. Grierson, 'The Man and the Poet,' in *Sir Walter Scott Lectures 1940–1948*, ed. W. L. Renwick, Edinburgh 1950, pp. 15–17.

Chronological Table

In compiling this table I have consulted the similar table in A. M. Clark, *Sir Walter Scott: the formative years*, Edinburgh 1969.

1770 or 1771	Born in College Wynd, Edinburgh (15 August). His father, a prudent lawyer, was directly descended from the cattle-raiding Wat of Harden in *The Lay of the Last Minstrel* (Canto IV, lines 120–44), and that other Walter Scott (known in Teviotdale as 'Beardie') who refused to cut his beard after the Stuarts were banished in 1688. His mother, Anne Rutherford, a physician's daughter, introduced him to art, poetry, folk ballads, and tales.
1772 or 1773	Contracts (?) poliomyelitis, which lames him for life.
1773–6	Stays mostly at Sandyknowe, 40 miles from Edinburgh, with intermediate stay at Bath.
1776	Returns to his family at George Square, Edinburgh.
1776–9	Preliminary schooling.
1779–83	Attends High School of Edinburgh.
1783–6	Attends classes at Edinburgh University.
1785	First lessons in sketching.
1785–6	Suffers haemorrhage and long convalescence.
1786	Begins as apprentice Writer to the Signet.
1787	Falls in love with 'Jessie from Kelso', and writes poems for her. First journeys in Borders and to Highlands.
1789	Decides to become an Advocate.
1789–92	Attends classes at Edinburgh University.
1792	Formally becomes an Advocate (11 July). Begins collecting ballads in Liddesdale. Falls in love with Williamina Belsches.
1792–1800	Translates German poems and plays.
1796	Publishes anonymously *The Chase*, and *William and Helen*, translations from Bürger. Jilted by Williamina Belsches.
1797	Marries Margaret Charlotte Carpenter (24 December).
1798	Resides at 39 Castle Street, Edinburgh.
1799	Publishes under his own name a translation of Goethe's *Goetz von Berlichingen*. His father dies. Takes cottage at Lasswade as country house. Contributes to *Tales of Terror* (Kelso). Daughter (Charlotte Sophia) born. Appointed Sheriff-Depute of Selkirkshire (16 December).
1800	*The Eve of Saint John*.

1801 Contributes to M. G. Lewis's *Tales of Wonder*.
Son (Walter) born.

1802 *Minstrelsy of the Scottish Border* (Kelso), Vols. I and II.

1803 Daughter (Anne) born.
Minstrelsy of the Scottish Border, Vol. III.

1804 Edits Romance of *Sir Tristrem*.
Takes country house at Ashestiel.

1805 *The Lay of the Last Minstrel*.
Becomes a partner in James Ballantyne & Co., Printers.
Son (Charles) born.

1806 Becomes one of Principal Clerks of Session.
Ballads and Lyrical Pieces.

1807 Made Secretary to Parliamentary Commission for Improvement of Scottish Jurisprudence.

1808 *Marmion*.
Edits *The Works of John Dryden . . . with Notes, . . . and a Life of the Author*.
Takes part in formation of *Quarterly Review* (first published 1810).
Becomes a partner in John Ballantyne & Company, booksellers and publishers.

1810 *The Lady of the Lake*.
Edits *English Minstrelsy*.
Edits *The Poetical Works of Anna Seward*.

1811 Buys Clarty Hole, out of which Abbotsford estate grew.
The Vision of Don Roderick.

1812 Moves from Ashestiel to Abbotsford.

1813 *Rokeby*.
The Bridal of Triermain.
John Ballantyne & Co. face financial trouble; help sought from Archibald Constable & Co.
Adds to Abbotsford estate.
Declines Poet Laureateship.
Made Freeman of City of Edinburgh.

1814 Edits *The Works of Jonathan Swift . . . with Notes and a Life of the Author*.
Waverley.
Contributes essays on 'Chivalry' and on 'Drama' to *Encyclopaedia Britannica*.

1814–17 *The Border Antiquities of England and Scotland*.

1815 *The Lord of the Isles*.
Guy Mannering.
First visit to continent (Waterloo, Paris).
The Field of Waterloo (poem).

1816 *Paul's Letters to his Kinsfolk*.

The Antiquary.
Tales of my Landlord, 1st Series (i.e., *The Black Dwarf* and *Old Mortality*).
Contributes Songs to *Albyn's Anthology*, ed. A. Campbell, Vol. I (with music).

1817 *Harold the Dauntless* (poem).
First serious stomach trouble.
Adds to Abbotsford estate.

1818 *Rob Roy.*
Tales of My Landlord, 2nd series (i.e., *The Heart of Midlothian*).
Accepts Baronetcy (gazetted 30 March 1820).
Contributes Songs to *Albyn's Anthology*, ed. A. Campbell, Vol. II (with music).

1819 Stomach cramps recur.
Tales of my Landlord, 3rd series (i.e., *The Bride of Lammermoor* and *A Legend of Montrose*).
His mother dies.
Ivanhoe.

1819–26 *The Provincial Antiquities of Scotland.*

1820 *The Monastery.*
Marriage of elder daughter Sophia to J. G. Lockhart.
The Abbot.
Becomes President of Royal Society of Edinburgh.

1821 *Kenilworth.*

1821–4 Writes *Lives of the Novelists* for Ballantyne's Novelist's Library.

1822 *The Pirate.*
The Fortunes of Nigel.
Halidon Hill (drama).
Active socially in George IV's visit to Scotland.
Contributes essay on 'Romance' to *Encyclopaedia Britannica.*
Peveril of the Peak.

1823 First symptoms of apoplexy.
Founder and first president of the (antiquarian) Bannatyne Club.
Quentin Durward.
Macduff's Cross (drama).

1824 *St. Ronan's Well.*
Redgauntlet.

1825 *Tales of the Crusaders* (i.e., *The Betrothed* and *The Talisman*).
Begins *Journal.*

1826 Bankruptcy following collapse of John Ballantyne & Co., Archibald Constable & Co., and Hurst & Robinson.

	Gives up 39 Castle Street.
	Lady Scott dies.
	Member of Royal Commission on Scottish Universities.
	Woodstock.
	Second continental visit (Paris).
1827	Publicly admits authorship of Waverley Novels (23 February).
	Life of Napoleon Buonaparte.
	Chronicles of the Canongate, 1st series (i.e., *The Highland Widow, The Two Drovers, The Surgeon's Daughter*).
1828	*Tales of a Grandfather*, 1st series.
	Chronicles of the Canongate, 2nd series (i.e., *The Fair Maid of Perth*).
1829	*Anne of Geierstein.*
	Tales of a Grandfather, 2nd series.
1829–30	*History of Scotland* (for *Lardner's Cabinet Cyclopaedia*).
1830	*Tales of a Grandfather*, 3rd series.
	The Doom of Devorgoil, A melodrama.
	Auchindrane; or the Ayrshire tragedy.
	Essays on Ballad Poetry added to 1830 edition of *Minstrelsy of the Scottish Border.*
	Paralytic attack.
	Resigns Clerkship of Court of Session.
	Apoplectic attack.
	Letters on Demonology and Witchcraft.
1831	*Tales of a Grandfather*, 4th series.
	Apoplectic paralysis.
	Voyage to Mediterranean on *H.M.S. Barham.*
1832	*Tales of my Landlord*, 4th series (i.e., *Count Robert of Paris, Castle Dangerous*).
	Returns from Italy (via the Rhine).
	Dies at Abbotsford (21 September).

Note on the Text

For the longer poems and the lyrics taken from the Waverley Novels, the text used in this selection has been based on the original Oxford Standard Authors Edition, edited in 1894 by J. Logie Robertson, and collated with Lockhart's edition of 1833 which itself formed Logie Robertson's copy text. Punctuation has occasionally been based on that of MSS or the first or other editions published in Scott's own lifetime. For the ballads printed in the *Minstrelsy of the Scottish Border* my copy text has been Volumes I–IV of Lockhart's edition, collated with the first and second editions of the *Minstrelsy*; and for 'Law versus Love', I have gone to Davidson Cook's *New Love Poems of Sir Walter Scott*, Oxford 1932.

Except for Scots poems the text has been modernized in conformity with the principles adopted for the series. In the case of place-names, Scott's own spellings have generally been preferred in the text. Modern orthography, however, has been used in the maps and in editorial material—e.g. *Branksome*, *Soltra* (Scott), Branxholm, Soutra (editorial).

Where a gloss or note contains a quotation followed by (S), the reference is to a note by Scott himself as printed in the edition of 1833. Where a quotation is followed by (L), the reference is to a note by Lockhart in the edition of 1833.

Any point in the text on which there is a Note at the end of the book is marked with a superior 'n'.

Abbreviations used in the Introduction, Glosses, and Notes

A.L.	*Poetical Works of Sir Walter Scott, Bart.*, selected and ed. A. Lang, with introduction and notes (2 vols., London and Edinburgh, 1895).
Child	*The English and Scottish Popular Ballads*, ed. F. J. Child, 5 vols., New York 1965, repr. from original edition of 1882–98. When followed not by a reference to volume and page, but by a number only, the reference is to the ballad as numbered by Child—e.g. Child 58 is *Sir Patrick Spens*.
Henderson	*The Minstrelsy of the Scottish Border*, ed. T. F. Henderson (4 vols., Edinburgh, 1932), repr. from original edition of 1902.
Jamieson	*Jamieson's Dictionary of the Scottish Language, abridged by J. Johnstone, revised and enlarged by J. Longmuir* (Edinburgh, 1895).
Letters	*Letters of Sir W. Scott*, ed. H. J. C. Grierson and others (12 vols., London, 1932).
Minstrelsy 1802	*Minstrelsy of the Scottish Border* (2 vols., Kelso, 1802).
Minstrelsy 1833	*Poetical Works of Sir Walter Scott, Bart.*, ed. J. G. Lockhart (Vols. I–IV, Edinburgh, 1833).
O.E.D.	*Oxford English Dictionary* (12 vols., Oxford, 1933).
O.G.S.	*Ordinance Gazetteer of Scotland: A Survey of Scottish Topography*, ed. F. H. Groome (6 vols., Edinburgh, 1884).
Parsons	C. O. Parsons, *Witchcraft and Demonology in Scott's Fiction* (Edinburgh and London, 1964).
PW	*The Poetical Works of Sir Walter Scott, Bart.*, ed. J. G. Lockhart (12 vols., Edinburgh, 1833–4).
Satchells	W. Scott (of Satchells), *Metrical History of the Honourable Families of Scot and Elliot in the Shires of Roxburgh and Selkirk*, 1688: repr. for the Scottish Literary Club (2 pts., Edinburgh, 1892).
Stuart	*Scott's Lady of the Lake*, ed. G. H. Stuart, with introduction and notes (London, 1891).
Stuart and Elliot	*Scott's Lay of the Last Minstrel*, edd. G. H. Stuart and E. H. Elliot, with introduction and notes (London, 1891).

Reading List

The works indicated in the Abbreviations should be consulted, as well as the following:

EARLY EDITIONS

The Lay of the Last Minstrel (1805; 1806 (3 edns.)).

The Lady of the Lake (Edinburgh, 1810 (8 edns.)).

Miscellaneous Prose Works (3 vols., Edinburgh, 1847).

Waverley Novels, Dryburgh edition (25 vols., London: A. & C. Black, 1892–4).

MODERN EDITIONS

Poetical Works, ed. J. L. Robertson (Oxford, 1894, etc.).

Poems and Plays, Everyman edition (2 vols., London, 1905, etc.).

Songs and Lyrics of Sir Walter Scott, ed. H. J. C. Grierson (Edinburgh, 1942).

The Journal of Sir Walter Scott, edd. J. G. Tait and W. M. Parker (3 vols., Edinburgh 1939–46; 1 vol. 1950).

IMPORTANT BOOKS

BRADLEY, A. C., *Oxford Lectures on Poetry* (London, 1911).

BUCHAN, J., *Sir Walter Scott* (London, 1932).

CLARK, A. M., *Sir Walter Scott: the formative years*, Edinburgh, 1969.

COOK, DAVIDSON, *New Love Poems of Sir Walter Scott* (Oxford, 1932).

CRAWFORD, T., *Scott*, (Writers & Critics Series, Edinburgh, 1965).

DEVLIN, D. D., *Walter Scott: Modern Judgements* (London, 1968).

GRIERSON, H. J. C., *Sir Walter Scott, Bart.* (London, 1938).

HAYDEN J. O. (ed.), *Scott: the Critical Heritage* (London, 1970).

JEFFARES, A. N. (ed.), *Scott's Mind and Art* (Edinburgh, 1969).

JOHNSON, E., *Sir Walter Scott, the Great Unknown* (2 vols., London, 1970).

KROEBER, K., *Romantic Narrative Art* (Madison, Wis., 1960).

LOCKHART, J. G., *The Life of Sir Walter Scott* (10 vols., Edinburgh, 1902–3).

MUIR, E., *Scott and Scotland* (London, 1936).

IMPORTANT ARTICLES

BLUNDEN, E., 'The Poetry of Scott', *Queen's Quarterly*, XXIX (1932), 593–602.

DAVIE, D., 'The Poetry of Sir Walter Scott', *Proceedings of the British Academy*, XLVII (1961), 60–75.

DOBIE, M. R., 'The Development of Scott's Minstrelsy', *Transactions of the Edinburgh Bibliographical Society*, II (Pt. I 1940), 65–87.

GRIERSON, H. J. C., 'The Man and the Poet' in *Sir Walter Scott Lectures 1940–1948*, ed. W. L. Renwick (Edinburgh, 1950), 3–30.

MONTGOMERIE, W., 'Sir Walter Scott as Ballad Editor', *Review of English Studies*, n.s. VII (1956), 158–63.

NOYES, A., 'Scott's Poetry', *Quarterly Review*, CCXC (1952), 211–25.

OLIVER, J. W., 'Scottish Poetry in the Earlier Nineteenth Century' in *Scottish Poetry: a Critical Survey*, ed. J. Kinsley (London, 1955), 212–30.

RUFF, W., 'A Bibliography of the Poetical Works of Sir Walter Scott 1796–1832', *Transactions of the Edinburgh Bibliographical Society*, I (1935–38), 101–239.

NICHOL SMITH, D., 'The Poetry of Sir Walter Scott', *University of Edinburgh Journal*, X (1945–51), 63–80.

I. Ballads, Lyrics, and Shorter Pieces

Jamie Telfer

Of the Fair Dodhead[n]

It fell about the Martinmas tide,
  Whan our Border steeds get corn and hay,
The Captain of Bewcastle hath bound him to ryde,
  And he's ower to Tividale to drive a prey.

The first ae guide that they met wi',
  It was high up in Hardhaughswire;
The second guide that they met wi',
  It was laigh down in Borthwick water.

'What tidings, what tidings, my trusty guide?'—
  'Nae tidings, nae tidings, I hae to thee;
But gin ye'll gae to the fair Dodhead,
  Mony a cow's cauf I'll let thee see.'—

And whan they cam to the fair Dodhead,
  Right hastily they clam the peel;
They loosed the kye out, ane and a',
  And ranshackled the house right weel.

Now Jamie Telfer's heart was sair,
  The tear aye rowing in his ee;
He pled wi' the Captain to hae his gear,
  Or else revenged he wad be.

The Captain turned him round and leugh;
  Said—'Man, there's naething in thy house,
But ae auld sword without a sheath,
  That hardly now would fell a mouse.'—

3 *Bewcastle*: village and parish in N. Cumberland 15 miles NE. of Carlisle.
4 *Tividale:* Teviotdale. 4 *drive a prey*: seize booty. 5 *first ae*: very first.
6 *Hardhaughswire*: pass from Liddesdale to the head of Teviotdale (S).
8 *laigh*: low.
8 *Borthwick water*: stream which falls into the Teviot three miles above Hawick (S).
10 *nae*: no. 10 *hae*: have. 12 *cauf*: calf.
13 *Dodhead*: near Singlee in the county of Selkirk.
14 *clam*: climbed. 14 *peel*: tower. 15 *kye*: cattle.
18 *rowing*: rolling. 21 *leugh*: laughed. 23 *ae*: one.

The sun wasna up, but the moon was down,
  It was the gryming of a new-fa'n snaw,
Jamie Telfer has run ten myles a-foot,
  Between the Dodhead and the Stobs's Ha'.

And whan he cam to the fair tower yate,
  He shouted loud, and cried weel hie,
Till out bespak auld Gibby Elliot—
  'Whae's this that brings the fray to me?'—

'It's I, Jamie Telfer o' the fair Dodhead,
  And a harried man I think I be!
There's naething left at the fair Dodhead,
  But a waefu' wife and bairnies three.'—

'Gae seek your succour at Branksome Ha',
  For succour ye'se get nane frae me!
Gae seek your succour where ye paid black-mail,
  For, man, ye ne'er paid money to me.'—

Jamie has turned him round about,
  I wat the tear blinded his ee—
'I'll ne'er pay mail to Elliot again,
  And the fair Dodhead I'll never see.

My hounds may a' rin masterless,
  My hawks may fly frae tree to tree,
My lord may grip my vassal lands,
  For there again maun I never be!'—

He has turned him to the Tiviot side,
  E'en as fast as he could drie,
Till he cam to the Coultart Cleugh,
  And there he shouted baith loud and hie.

26 *gryming*: sprinkling.
28 *Stobs's Ha'*: Stobs Castle in Cavers parish, Roxburgh, on the right bank of Siltrig Water.
29 *yate*: gate. 30 *hie*: high. 34 *harried*: plundered.
36 *waefu'*: woeful. 36 *bairnies*: children.
37 *Branksome Ha'*: Branxholm, ancient family seat of the Scotts of Buccleuch, 3 miles SW. of Hawick, on the Teviot in Selkirkshire.
39 *black-mail*: protection money.
42 *I wat*: assuredly. 50 *drie*: do it.
51 *Coultart Cleugh*: Coltherds cleugh, 'opposite to Carlinrig, on the road between Hawick and Mosspaul' (S). A cleugh is a hollow between steep banks or a narrow valley.

Then up bespak him auld Jock Grieve—
  'Whae's this that brings the fray to me?'—
'It's I, Jamie Telfer o' the fair Dodhead,
  A harried man I trow I be.

There's naething left in the fair Dodhead,
  But a greeting wife and bairnies three,
And sax poor ca's stand in the sta',
  A' routing loud for their minnie.'—

'Alack a wae!' quo' auld Jock Grieve,
  'Alack! my heart is sair for thee!
For I was married on the elder sister,
  And you on the youngest of a' the three.'

Then he has ta'en out a bonny black,
  Was right weel fed with corn and hay,
And he's set Jamie Telfer on his back,
  To the Catslockhill to tak the fray.

And whan he cam to the Catslockhill,
  He shouted loud, and cried weel hie,
Till out and spak him William's Wat—
  'O whae's this brings the fray to me?'—

'It's I, Jamie Telfer o' the fair Dodhead,
  A harried man I think I be!
The Captain o' Bewcastle has driven my gear;
  For God's sake rise, and succour me!'—

'Alas for wae!' quo' William's Wat,
  'Alack, for thee my heart is sair!
I never cam by the fair Dodhead,
  That ever I fand thy basket bare.'—

He's set his twa sons on coal-black steeds,
  Himsell upon a freckled gray,
And they are on wi' Jamie Telfer,
  To Branksome Ha' to tak the fray.

And whan they cam to Branksome Ha',
  They shouted a' baith loud and hie,
Till up and spak him auld Buccleuch,
  Said—'Whae's this brings the fray to me?'—

58 *greeting*: weeping. 59 *ca's*: calves. 59 *sta'*: stall.
60 *routing*: lowing. 60 *minnie*: mother.
68 *Catslockhill*: this place-name, from Yarrow, seems to be misplaced (Child, V. 518).

'It's I, Jamie Telfer o' the fair Dodhead,
  And a harried man I think I be!
There's nought left in the fair Dodhead,
  But a greeting wife and bairnies three.'—

'Alack for wae!' quoth the gude auld lord,
  'And ever my heart is wae for thee.
But fye gar cry on Willie, my son,
  And see that he come to me speedilie!

Gar warn the water, braid and wide,
  Gar warn it sune and hastilie!
They that winna ride for Telfer's kye,
  Let them never look in the face o' me!

Warn Wat o'Harden, and his sons,
  Wi' them will Borthwick Water ride;
Warn Gaudilands, and Allanhaugh,
  And Gilmanscleugh, and Commonside.

Ride by the gate at Priesthaughswire,
  And warn the Currors o' the Lee;
As ye come down the Hermitage Slack,
  Warn doughty Willie o'Gorrinberry.'—

The Scotts they rade, the Scotts they ran,
  Sae starkly and sae steadilie!
And aye the ower-word o' the thrang
  Was—'Rise for Branksome readilie!'—

The gear was driven the Frostylee up,
  Frae the Frostylee unto the plain,
Whan Willie has looked his men before,
  And saw the kye right fast drivand.

95 *fye*: expletive. 95 *gar cry on*: cause (him) to be summoned.
97 *water*: all who dwell on the river's banks.
101–4: 'The estates mentioned here belonged to families of the name of Scott residing upon the waters of Borthwick and Teviot, near the castle of their chief' (S).
105–8: 'The pursuers seem to have taken the road through the hills of Liddesdale, in order to collect forces, and intercept the forayers at the passage of the Liddel, on their return to Bewcastle' (S).
Priesthaughswire: pass slightly to the S. of Penchryst Pen, near Brankholm.
Hermitage: stream in Castleton parish, Liddesdale.
Slack: a pass.
Willie o' Gorrinberry: an Elliot, who took part in the rescue of Kinmont Willie. Gorrinberry is in Castleton parish.
111 *ower-word*: refrain. 111 *thrang*: company.
113 *Frostylee*: a stream joining the Teviot near Mosspaul.

'Whae drives thir kye?' can Willie say,
  'To make an outspeckle o' me?'—
'It's I, the Captain o' Bewcastle, Willie;
  I winna layne my name for thee.'—

'O will ye let Telfer's kye gae back?
  Or will ye do aught for regard o' me?
Or, by the faith of my body,' quo' Willie Scott,
  'I'se ware my dame's cauf skin on thee!'—

'I winna let the kye gae back,
  Neither for thy love, nor yet thy fear;
But I will drive Jamie Telfer's kye,
  In spite of every Scott that's here.'—

'Set on them, lads!' quo' Willie than,
  'Fye, lads, set on them cruellie!
For ere they win to the Ritterford,
  Mony a toom saddle there sall be!'—

Then til't they gaed wi' heart and hand,
  The blows fell thick as bickering hail;
And mony a horse ran masterless,
  And mony a comely cheek was pale.

But Willie was stricken ower the head,
  And through the knapscap the sword has gane;
And Harden grat for very rage,
  When Willie on the grund lay slane.

But he's taen aff his gude steel cap,
  And thrice he's waved it in the air—
The Dinlay snaw was ne'er mair white
  Nor the lyart locks of Harden's hair.

'Revenge! revenge!' auld Wat can cry,
  'Fye, lads, lay on them cruellie!
We'll ne'er see Tiviotside again,
  Or Willie's death revenged sall be.'—

117 *thir*: those. 117 *can*: did.
118 *outspeckle*: laughing-stock. 120 *layne*: conceal.
124 *ware—thee*: apply my wife's (mother's) whip to you.
131 *Ritterford*: ford on the river Liddel.
132 *toom*: empty. 133 *til*: to.
138 *knapscap*: headpiece. 139 *grat*: wept.
141–4: this stanza is almost certainly not traditional, and is probably Scott's own.
143 *Dinlay*: 'a mountain in Liddesdale' (S).
144 *nor*: than. 144 *lyart*: grey.

O mony a horse ran masterless,
  The splintered lances flew on hie;
But or they wan to the Kershope ford,
  The Scotts had gotten the victory.

John o'Brigham there was slane,
  And John o'Barlow, as I heard say;
And thirty mae o' the Captain's men
  Lay bleeding on the grund that day.

The Captain was run through the thick of the thigh,
  And broken was his right leg bane;
If he had lived this hundred years,
  He had never been loved by woman again.

'Hae back the kye!' the Captain said;
  'Dear kye, I trow, to some they be!
For gin I suld live a hundred years,
  There will ne'er fair lady smile on me.'—

Then word is gane to the Captain's bride,
  Even in the bower where that she lay,
That her lord was prisoner in enemy's land,
  Since into Tividale he had led the way.

'I wad lourd have had a winding-sheet,
  And helped to put it ower his head,
Ere he had been disgraced by the Border Scot,
  Whan he ower Liddel his men did lead!'—

There was a wild gallant amang us a',
  His name was Watty wi' the Wudspurs,
Cried—'On for his house in Stanegirthside,
  If ony man will ride with us!'

Whan they cam to the Stanegirthside,
  They dang wi' trees, and burst the door;
They loosed out a' the Captain's kye,
  And set them forth our lads before.

151 *or*: before.
151 *Kershope ford*: on the Kershope burn a tributary of the Liddel.
153 *Brigham*: 'perhaps Brougham in Cumberland' (S).
169 *lourd*: rather.
174 *Wudspurs*: 'Hotspur, or Madspur' (S).
177 *Stanegirthside*: 'A house belonging to the Foresters, situated on the English side of the Liddel' (S).
178 *dang*: beat.

There was an auld wife ayont the fire,
  A wee bit o' the Captain's kin—
'Whae dar loose out the Captain's kye,
  Or answer to him and his men?'—

'It's I, Watty Wudspurs, loose the kye!
  I winna layne my name frae thee!
And I will loose out the Captain's kye,
  In scorn of a' his men and he.'—

Whan they cam to the fair Dodhead,
  They were a welcome sight to see!
For instead of his ain ten milk kye,
  Jamie Telfer has gotten thirty and three.

And he has paid the rescue shot,
  Baith wi' goud and white monie;
And at the burial o' Willie Scott,
  I wat was mony a weeping ee.

181 *ayont*: beyond.

Kinmont Willie[n]

O have ye na heard o' the fause Sakelde?
O have ye na heard o' the keen Lord Scroope?
How they hae ta'en bauld Kinmont Willie,
On Haribee to hang him up?

Had Willie had but twenty men,
But twenty men as stout as he,
Fause Sakelde had never the Kinmont ta'en,
Wi' eight score in his companie.

They band his legs beneath the steed,
They tied his hands behind his back;
They guarded him fivesome on each side,
And they brought him ower the Liddel-rack.

They led him through the Liddel-rack,
And also through the Carlisle sands;
They brought him to Carlisle castell,
To be at my Lord Scroope's commands.

'My hands are tied, but my tongue is free!
And whae will dare this deed avow?
Or answer by the Border law?
Or answer to the bauld Buccleuch?'—

'Now haud thy tongue, thou rank reiver!
There's never a Scot shall set thee free:
Before ye cross my castle yate,
I trow ye shall take farewell o' me.'—

1 *Sakelde*: 'a gentleman within the west-Wardenry' and Scroope's deputy (who was probably Sheriff of Cumberland at this time (S).

2 *Scroope*: warden of the west Marches of England.

3 *Kinmont Willie*: William Armstrong of Kinmonth, cited in a list of border clans in 1597 as a leader of a band of Armstrongs called Sandies Barnes, inhabiting the Debateable Land between Scotland and England (S).

4 *Haribee*: place of execution at Carlisle.

12 *Liddel-rack*: ford on the Liddel, which for a few miles before it joins the Esk, forms the boundary between England and Scotland.

21 *reiver*: robber.

23 *yate*: gate.

'Fear na ye that, my lord,' quo' Willie:
  'By the faith o' my bodie, Lord Scroope,' he said,
'I never yet lodged in a hostelrie,
  But I paid my lawing before I gaed.'—

Now word is gane to the bauld Keeper,
  In Branksome Ha' where that he lay,
That Lord Scroope has ta'en the Kinmont Willie,
  Between the hours of night and day.

He has ta'en the table wi' his hand,
  He garred the red wine spring on hie—
'Now Christ's curse on my head,' he said,
  'But avenged of Lord Scroope I'll be!

O is my basnet a widow's curch?
  Or my lance a wand of the willow-tree?
Or my arm a ladye's lilye hand,
  That an English lord should lightly me!

And have they ta'en him, Kinmont Willie,
  Against the truce of Border tide?
And forgotten that the bauld Buccleuch
  Is Keeper here on the Scottish side?

And have they e'en ta'en him, Kinmont Willie,
  Withouten either dread or fear?
And forgotten that the bauld Buccleuch
  Can back a steed, or shake a spear?

O were there war between the lands,
  As well I wot that there is none,
I would slight Carlisle castell high,
  Though it were builded of marble stone.

I would set that castell in a low,
  And sloken it with English blood!
There's nevir a man in Cumberland,
  Should ken where Carlisle castell stood.

But since nae war's between the lands,
  And there is peace, and peace should be;
I'll neither harm English lad or lass,
  And yet the Kinmont freed shall be!'

28 *lawing*: reckoning. 30 *Branksome*: see above, p. 4, line 37.
34 *garred*: caused. 37 *basnet*: helmet. 37 *curch*: coif.
40 *lightly*: scorn. 53 *low*: flame. 54 *sloken*: quench.

He has called him forty Marchmen bauld,
  I trow they were of his ain name,
Except Sir Gilbert Elliot, called
  The Laird of Stobs, I mean the same.

He has called him forty Marchmen bauld,
  Were kinsmen to the bauld Buccleuch;
With spur on heel, and splent on spauld,
  And gleuves of green, and feathers blue.

There were five and five before them a',
  Wi' hunting-horns and bugles bright:
And five and five came wi' Buccleuch,
  Like warden's men, arrayed for fight.

And five and five, like a mason gang,
  That carried the ladders lang and hie;
And five and five, like broken men;
  And so they reached the Woodhouselee.

And as we crossed the Bateable Land,
  When to the English side we held,
The first o' men that we met wi',
  Whae sould it be but fause Sakelde?

'Where be ye gaun, ye hunters keen?'
  Quo' fause Sakelde; 'come tell to me!'—
'We go to hunt an English stag,
  Has trespassed on the Scots countrie.'—

'Where be ye gaun, ye marshal men?'
  Quo' fause Sakelde; 'come tell me true!'—
'We go to catch a rank reiver,
  Has broken faith wi' the bauld Buccleuch.'—

'Where are ye gaun, ye mason lads,
  Wi' a' your ladders, lang and hie?'—
'We gang to herry a corbie's nest,
  That wons not far frae Woodhouselee.'—

61 *Marchmen*: borderers. 64 *Stobs*: see above, p. 4, line 28.
67 *splent*: armour (of overlapping plates).
67 *spauld*: shoulder. 68 *gleuves*: sword-decorations.
76 *Woodhouselee*: a house on the border, 'belonging to Buccleuch' (S).
91 *corbie*: raven. 92 *wons*: dwells.

'Where be ye gaun, ye broken men?'
Quo' fause Sakelde, 'come tell to me!'
Now Dickie of Dryhope led that band,
And the nevir a word of lear had he.

'Why trespass ye on the English side?
Row-footed outlaws, stand!' quo' he;
The nevir a word had Dickie to say,
Sae he thrust the lance through his fause bodie.

Then on we held for Carlisle toun,
And at Staneshaw-bank the Eden we crossed;
The water was great and meikle of spait,
But the nevir a horse nor man we lost.

And when we reached the Staneshaw-bank,
The wind was rising loud and hie;
And there the Laird garred leave our steeds,
For fear that they should stamp and nie.

And when we left the Staneshaw-bank,
The wind began full loud to blaw;
But 'twas wind and weet, and fire and sleet,
When we came beneath the castle wa'.

We crept on knees, and held our breath,
Till we placed the ladders against the wa';
And sae ready was Buccleuch himsell
To mount the first before us a'.

He has ta'en the watchman by the throat,
He flung him down upon the lead—
'Had there not been peace between our lands,
Upon the other side thou hadst gaed!'

'Now sound out, trumpets!' quo' Buccleuch;
'Let's waken Lord Scroope right merrilie!'
Then loud the warden's trumpet blew—
O wha dare meddle wi' me?

95 *Dickie o' Dryhope*: 'one of the Mangerton Armstrongs' (Henderson, II. 69).
96 *lear*: learning. 98 *row-footed*: rough-footed.
102 *Staneshaw-bank*: 'the Stony Bank', below Carlisle Bridge.
102 *Eden*: river which passes N. of Carlisle.
103 *meikle*: great. 103 *spait*: flood. 108 *nie*: neigh.
111 *fire and sleet*: ?'flyand sleet' (L). But 'fire' is probably lightning (Henderson, II. 63).
124 *O wha dare*, etc.: 'name of a Border tune' (S).

Then speedilie to wark we gaed,
 And raised the slogan ane and a',
And cut a hole through a sheet of lead,
 And so we wan to the castle ha'.

They thought King James and a' his men
 Had won the house wi' bow and spear;
It was but twenty Scots and ten,
 That put a thousand in sic a stear!

Wi' coulters, and wi' forehammers,
 We garred the bars bang merrilie,
Until we came to the inner prison,
 Where Willie o' Kinmont he did lie.

And when we cam to the lower prison,
 Where Willie o' Kinmont he did lie—
'O sleep ye, wake ye, Kinmont Willie,
 Upon the morn that thou's to die?'—

'O I sleep saft, and I wake aft;
 It's lang since sleeping was fleyed frae me!
Gie my service back to my wife and bairns,
 And a' gude fellows that speir for me.'

Then Red Rowan has hent him up,
 The starkest man in Teviotdale—
'Abide, abide now, Red Rowan,
 Till of my Lord Scroope I take farewell.

Farewell, farewell, my gude Lord Scroope!
 My gude Lord Scroope, farewell!' he cried—
'I'll pay you for my lodging maill,
 When first we meet on the Border side.'

Then shoulder high, with shout and cry,
 We bore him down the ladder lang;
At every stride Red Rowan made,
 I wot the Kinmont's airns played clang!

126 *slogan*: war-cry. 132 *stear*: stir.
142 *fleyed*: frightened. 144 *speir*: ask.
145 *Red Rowan*: 'Probably Thomas Armstrong of Rowanburne, who is mentioned, 16 Nov. 1692 (in the *Border Papers*) as taking part in a raid with the Kinmont Armstrongs' (Henderson, II. 69).
145 *hent*: lifted. 151 *lodging maill*: rent. 156 *airns*: irons.

'O mony a time,' quo' Kinmont Willie,
'I have ridden horse baith wild and wood;
But a rougher beast than Red Rowan
I ween my legs have ne'er bestrode.

And mony a time,' quo' Kinmont Willie,
'I've pricked a horse out oure the furs;
But since the day I backed a steed,
I never wore sic cumbrous spurs!'—

We scarce had won the Staneshaw-bank,
When a' the Carlisle bells were rung,
And a thousand men on horse and foot,
Cam wi' the keen Lord Scroope along.

Buccleuch has turned to Eden Water,
Even where it flowed frae bank to brim,
And he has plunged in wi' a' his band,
And safely swam them through the stream.

He turned him on the other side,
And at Lord Scroope his glove flung he—
'If ye like na my visit in merry England,
In fair Scotland come visit me!'

All sore astonished stood Lord Scroope,
He stood as still as rock of stane;
He scarcely dared to trew his eyes,
When through the water they had gane.

'He is either himsell a devil frae hell,
Or else his mother a witch maun be;
I wadna have ridden that wan water
For a' the gowd in Christentie.'

158 *wood*: mad. 162 *furs*: furrows. 179 *trew*: believe.

The Eve of Saint John[n]

THE Baron of Smaylho'me rose with day,
He spurred his courser on,
Without stop or stay, down the rocky way,
That leads to Brotherstone.

He went not with the bold Buccleuch,
His banner broad to rear;
He went not 'gainst the English yew
To lift the Scottish spear.

Yet his plate-jack was braced, and his helmet was laced,
And his vaunt-brace of proof he wore;
At his saddle-gerthe was a good steel sperthe,
Full ten pound weight and more.

The Baron returned in three days' space,
And his looks were sad and sour;
And weary was his courser's pace,
As he reached his rocky tower.

He came not from where Ancrum Moor
Ran red with English blood;
Where the Douglas true and the bold Buccleuch
'Gainst keen Lord Evers stood.

Yet was his helmet hacked and hewed,
His acton pierced and tore,
His axe and his dagger with blood imbrued,—
But it was not English gore.

4 *Brotherstone*: hamlet on the road from Smailholm to Melrose.
5 *Buccleuch*: Sir Walter Scott, to whose conduct the historians Pitscottie and Buchanan ascribe 'the success of the engagement at Ancrum Moor' (S).
9 *plate-jack*: coat-armour. 10 *vaunt-brace*: body-armour.
11 *sperthe*: battle-axe.
17 *Ancrum Moor*: site of a Scottish victory against an invading English force under Lord Evers and Sir Brian Latoun in 1545.
18 *Douglas*: Archibald Douglas seventh Earl of Angus, commander of the Scottish force at Ancrum Moor.
22 *acton*: stuffed jacket.

He lighted at the Chapellage,
He held him close and still;
And he whistled thrice for his little foot-page,
His name was English Will.

'Come thou hither, my little foot-page,
Come hither to my knee;
Though thou art young, and tender of age,
I think thou art true to me.

Come, tell me all that thou has seen,
And look thou tell me true!
Since I from Smaylho'me tower have been,
What did thy lady do?'—

'My lady each night sought the lonely light
That burns on the wild Watchfold;
For from height to height, the beacons bright
Of the English foemen told.

The bittern clamoured from the moss,
The wind blew loud and shrill;
Yet the craggy pathway she did cross
To the eerie Beacon Hill.

I watched her steps, and silent came
Where she sat her on a stone;
No watchman stood by the dreary flame,
It burned all alone.

The second night I kept her in sight
Till to the fire she came,
And by Mary's might! an armed Knight
Stood by the lonely flame.

And many a word that warlike lord
Did speak to my lady there;
But the rain fell fast, and loud blew the blast,
And I heard not what they were.

The third night there the sky was fair,
And the mountain-blast was still,
As again I watched the secret pair
On the lonesome Beacon Hill.

And I heard her name the midnight hour,
And name this holy eve,
And say "Come this night to thy lady's bower;
Ask no bold Baron's leave.

He lifts his spear with the bold Buccleuch;
His lady is all alone;
The door she'll undo to her knight so true
On the eve of good Saint John."—

"I cannot come, I must not come,
I dare not come to thee;
On the eve of Saint John I must wander alone,
In thy bower I may not be."—

"Now out on thee, fainthearted knight!
Thou shouldst not say me nay;
For the eve is sweet, and when lovers meet
Is worth the whole summer's day.

And I'll chain the blood-hound, and the warder shall not sound,
And rushes shall be strewed on the stair;
So by the black rood-stone, and by holy Saint John,
I conjure thee, my love, to be there!"

"Though the blood-hound be mute, and the rush beneath my foot,
And the warder his bugle should not blow,
Yet there sleepeth a priest in the chamber to the east,
And my footstep he would know"—

"O fear not the priest, who sleepeth to the east,
For to Dryburgh the way he has ta'en;
And there to say mass, till three days do pass,
For the soul of a knight that is slayne."—

He turned him around, and grimly he frowned,
Then he laughed right scornfully—
"He who says the mass-rite for the soul of that knight
May as well say mass for me:

79 *rood-stone*: 'The black rood of Melrose was a crucifix of black marble, and of superior sanctity' (S).
86 *Dryburgh*: abbey on R. Tweed.

At the lone midnight hour, when bad spirits have power,
  In thy chamber will I be."
With that he was gone, and my lady left alone,
  And no more did I see.'

Then changed, I trow, was that bold Baron's brow,
  From the dark to the blood-red high—
'Now tell me the mien of the knight thou hast seen,
  For, by Mary, he shall die!'—

'His arms shone full bright in the beacon's red light;
  His plume it was scarlet and blue;
On his shield was a hound in a silver leash bound,
  And his crest was a branch of the yew.'—

'Thou liest, thou liest, thou little foot-page,
  Loud dost thou lie to me!
For that knight is cold, and low laid in the mould,
  All under the Eildon-tree.'—

'Yet hear but my word, my noble lord!
  For I heard her name his name;
And that lady bright, she called the knight
  Sir Richard of Coldinghame.'—

The bold Baron's brow then changed, I trow,
  From high blood-red to pale—
'The grave is deep and dark, and the corpse is stiff and stark,
  So I may not trust thy tale.

Where fair Tweed flows round holy Melrose,
  And Eildon slopes to the plain,
Full three nights ago, by some secret foe,
  That gay gallant was slain.

The varying light deceived thy sight,
  And the wild winds drowned the name;
For the Dryburgh bells ring and the white monks[n] do sing
  For Sir Richard of Coldinghame!'

He passed the court-gate, and he oped the tower-grate,
  And he mounted the narrow stair
To the bartizan-seat, where, with maids that on her wait
  He found his lady fair.

108 *Eildon-tree*: The spot, on the Eildon hills near Melrose, where Thomas the Rhymer was said to have uttered his prophecies (S).
127 *bartizan*: battlemented parapet.

That lady sat in mournful mood,
Looked over hill and vale,
Over Tweed's fair flood and Mertoun's wood
And all down Teviotdale.

'Now hail, now hail, thou lady bright!'—
'Now hail, thou Baron true!
What news, what news from Ancrum fight?
What news from the bold Buccleuch?'—

'The Ancrum Moor is red with gore,
For many a southron fell;
And Buccleuch has charged us evermore
To watch our beacons well.'

The lady blushed red, but nothing she said;
Nor added the Baron a word.
Then she stepped down the stair to her chamber fair,
And so did her moody lord.

In sleep the lady mourned, and the Baron tossed and turned,
And oft to himself he said,
'The worms around him creep, and his bloody grave is deep—
It cannot give up the dead!'

It was near the ringing of matin-bell,
The night was wellnigh done,
When a heavy sleep on that Baron fell,
On the eve of good Saint John.

The lady looked through the chamber fair,
By the light of a dying flame;
And she was aware of a knight stood there—
Sir Richard of Coldinghame!

'Alas! away, away!' she cried,
'For the holy Virgin's sake!'—
'Lady, I know who sleeps by thy side;
But, lady, he will not awake.

By Eildon-tree, for long nights three,
In bloody grave have I lain;
The mass and the death-prayer are said for me,
But, lady, they are said in vain.

131 *Mertoun*: Tweedside parish in SW. Berwickshire.

By the Baron's brand, near Tweed's fair strand,
  Most foully slain I fell;
And my restless sprite on the beacon's height
  For a space is doomed to dwell.

At our trysting-place, for a certain space,
  I must wander to and fro;
But I had not had power to come to thy bower
  Had'st thou not conjured me so.'

Love mastered fear; her brow she crossed—
  'How, Richard, hast thou sped?
And art thou saved, or art thou lost?'
  The vision shook his head!

'Who spilleth life shall forfeit life;
  So bid thy lord believe:
That lawless love is guilt above,
  This awful sign receive.'

He laid his left palm on an oaken beam,
  His right upon her hand—
The lady shrunk, and fainting sunk,
  For it scorched like a fiery brand.

The sable score of fingers four
  Remains on that board impressed;
And for evermore that lady wore
  A covering on her wrist.

There is a nun in Dryburgh bower,
  Ne'er looks upon the sun;
There is a monk in Melrose tower,
  He speaketh word to none.

That nun who ne'er beholds the day,
  That monk who speaks to none—
That nun was Smaylho'me's Lady gay,
  That monk the bold Baron.

Lochinvar[n]

O, young Lochinvar is come out of the west,
Through all the wide Border his steed was the best;
And save his good broadsword he weapons had none,
He rode all unarmed, and he rode all alone.
So faithful in love, and so dauntless in war,
There never was knight like the young Lochinvar.

He stayed not for brake, and he stopped not for stone,
He swam the Eske river where ford there was none;
But ere he alighted at Netherby gate,
The bride had consented, the gallant came late:
For a laggard in love, and a dastard in war,
Was to wed the fair Ellen of brave Lochinvar.

So boldly he entered the Netherby Hall,
Among bride's-men, and kinsmen, and brothers, and all:
Then spoke the bride's father, his hand on his sword,
(For the poor craven bridegroom said never a word,)
'O come ye in peace here, or come ye in war,
Or to dance at our bridal, young Lord Lochinvar?'

'I long wooed your daughter, my suit you denied;—
Love swells like the Solway, but ebbs like its tide—
And now am I come, with this lost love of mine,
To lead but one measure, drink one cup of wine.
There are maidens in Scotland more lovely by far,
That would gladly be bride to the young Lochinvar.'

The bride kissed the goblet: the knight took it up,
He quaffed off the wine, and he threw down the cup.
She looked down to blush, and she looked up to sigh,
With a smile on her lips, and a tear in her eye.
He took her soft hand, ere her mother could bar,—
'Now tread we a measure!' said young Lochinvar.

9 *Netherby*: hamlet in Cumberland on R. Esk, adjacent to the boundary with Scotland. Netherby Hall is the seat of the Cumberland Grahams.

So stately his form, and so lovely her face,
That never a hall such a galliard did grace;
While her mother did fret, and her father did fume,
And the bridegroom stood dangling his bonnet and plume;
And the bride-maidens whispered, ''Twere better by far,
To have matched our fair cousin with young Lochinvar.'

One touch to her hand, and one word in her ear,
When they reached the hall-door, and the charger stood near;
So light to the croupe the fair lady he swung,
So light to the saddle before her he sprung!
'She is won! we are gone, over bank, bush, and scaur;
They'll have fleet steeds that follow,' quoth young Lochinvar.

There was mounting 'mong Græmes of the Netherby clan;
Forsters, Fenwicks, and Musgraves, they rode and they ran:
There was racing and chasing on Cannonbie Lee,
But the lost bride of Netherby ne'er did they see.
So daring in love, and so dauntless in war,
Have ye e'er heard of gallant like young Lochinvar?

39 *croupe*: hindquarters of an animal.
41 *scaur*: 'precipitous bank of earth' (S).
45 *Cannonbie*: border village and parish of Eskdale, S. Dumfriesshire.

The Battle of Harlaw[n]

Now haud your tongue, baith wife and carle,
  And listen, great and sma',
And I will sing of Glenallan's Earl
  That fought on the red Harlaw.[n]

The cronach's cried on Bennachie,
  And doun the Don and a',
And hieland and lawland may mournfu' be
  For the sair field of Harlaw.

They saddled a hundred milk-white steeds,
  They hae bridled a hundred black,
With a chafron of steel on each horse's head,
  And a good knight upon his back.

They hadna ridden a mile, a mile,
  A mile, but barely ten,
When Donald came branking down the brae
  Wi' twenty thousand men.

Their tartans they were waving wide,
  Their glaives were glancing clear,
The pibrochs rung frae side to side,
  Would deafen ye to hear.

The great Earl in his stirrups stood,
  That Highland host to see;
Now here a knight that's stout and good
  May prove a jeopardie:

'What would'st thou do, my squire so gay,
  That rides beside my reyne,
Were ye Glenallan's Earl the day,
  And I were Roland Cheyne?

5 *cronach*: coronach.
5 *Bennachie*: mountain (1,698 ft.) in Garioch region of Aberdeenshire.
6 *Don*: river in S. Aberdeenshire.
11 *chafron*: chevron.
15 *branking*: making a show.

To turn the rein were sin and shame,
To fight were wondrous peril;
What would ye do now, Roland Cheyne,
Were ye Glenallan's Earl?'—

'Were I Glenallan's Earl this tide,
And ye were Roland Cheyne,
The spur should be in my horse's side,
And the bridle upon his mane.

If they hae twenty thousand blades,
And we twice ten times ten,
Yet they hae but their tartan plaids,
And we are mail-clad men.

My horse shall ride through ranks sae rude,
As through the moorland fern,—
Then ne'er let the gentle Norman blude
Grow cauld for Highland kerne.'

Law versus Love[n]

AWAY with parchments, warrants, bills—
Come fairies, brownies, knights and giants:
Avaunt all stupid books of Law,
Shakespeare and Spenser are my clients.

Heineccius to your shelf return
With brother Erskine's dryer labours,
For I have to supply your place—
Romance and Love those pleasant neighbours.

Heaven keep your slumbers undisturbed
You weary dreary dull civilians!
Love's are the only Institutes—
His Pandects are the laws of millions.

44 *kerne*: a poor Highland foot-soldier.

5 *Heineccius*, (J.G.): *Analysis of the Institutes and Pandects* (Davidson Cook, ed. cit.).

6 *Erskine*, (John): *An Institute of the Law of Scotland*, Edinburgh 1773. 'These are two law books he was at that time studying which are often mentioned by him in his familiar letters of the same period, as insufferably tedious' (Cook, ed. cit.).

Glad as I 'scape from thy dull rule
  A fresher air seems breaking o'er me;
There towers a castle strong and high,
  Here blooms a fair pleasaunce before me.

A lady's bower mine eye invites,
  My feet gang there in willing duty;
I enter, and amid its flowers
  I find a flower of matchless beauty.

There sits my peerless queen enthroned
  And whilst in haste my joy I'm proving,
I'm roused by Tom who sharply cries
  'Hey Wattie, man! Ye're unco loving!'

The dingy boards again transform
  To mother nature's verdant bosom;
The inkstands turn to goodly trees
  And all the pens begin to blossom.

Our shabby cloth and corduroy
  Now change to richest silk and satin,
And nought but fairy music sounds
  'Stead of broad Scotch or musty Latin.

But greater changes still ensue,
  (I fear that I'm non compos mentis,)
I spy a horrid Saracen
  In every yawning gowk apprentice.

These paynims vile I fierce assault,
  Till stopped by cry of snoring dolour,
I find by Allan's bloody pate
  I've cracked his noddle with the ruler.

Where shall the Lover rest[n]

WHERE shall the lover rest,
  Whom the fates sever
From his true maiden's breast,
  Parted for ever?

36 *gowk*: half-witted.

Where, through groves deep and high,
  Sounds the far billow,
Where early violets die,
  Under the willow.

Chorus

Eleu loro, &c. Soft shall be his pillow.

There, through the summer day,
  Cool streams are laving;
There, while the tempests sway,
  Scarce are boughs waving;
There, thy rest shalt thou take,
  Parted for ever,
Never again to wake,
  Never, O never!

Chorus

Eleu loro, &c. Never, O never!

Where shall the traitor rest,
  He, the deceiver,
Who could win maiden's breast,
  Ruin, and leave her?
In the lost battle,
  Borne down by the flying,
Where mingles war's rattle
  With groans of the dying.

Chorus

Eleu loro, &c. There shall he be lying.

Her wing shall the eagle flap
  O'er the false-hearted;
His warm blood the wolf shall lap,
  Ere life be parted.
Shame and dishonour sit
  By his grave ever;
Blessing shall hallow it,
  Never, O never!

Chorus

Eleu loro, &c. Never, O never!

9 *Eleu loro*, &c.: meaningless Gaelic refrain; perhaps the syllables are derived from traditional names of musical notes.

False Love and hast thou played me this[n]

FALSE love, and hast thou played me this
  In summer among the flowers?
I will repay thee back again
  In winter among the showers.
Unless again, again, my love,
  Unless you turn again;
As you with other maidens rove,
  I'll smile on other men.

Young Men will love thee[n]

YOUNG men will love thee more fair and more fast;
  Heard ye so merry the little bird sing?
Old men's love the longest will last,
  And the throstle-cock's head is under his wing.

The young man's wrath is like light straw on fire;
  Heard ye so merry the little bird sing?
But like red-hot steel is the old man's ire,
  And the throstle-cock's head is under his wing.

The young man will brawl at the evening board;
  Heard ye so merry the little bird sing?
But the old man will draw at the dawning the sword,
  And the throstle-cock's head is under his wing.

Birth Song[n]

CANNY moment, lucky fit;
Is the lady lighter yet?
Be it lad, or be it lass,
Sign wi' cross, and sain wi' mass.

'Birth Song' 1 *canny*: propitious. 1 *fit*: muscular movement.

Trefoil, vervain, John's-wort, dill,
Hinders witches of their will;
Weel is them, that weel may
Fast upon Saint Andrew's day.

Saint Bride and her brat,
Saint Colme and his cat,
Saint Michael and his spear,
Keep the house frae reif and wear.

Dirge[n]

WASTED, weary, wherefore stay,
Wrestling thus with earth and clay?
From the body pass away;—
        Hark! the mass is singing.

From thee doff thy mortal weed,
Mary Mother be thy speed,
Saints to help thee at thy need;—
        Hark! the knell is ringing.

Fear not snowdrift driving fast,
Sleet, or hail, or levin blast;
Soon the shroud shall lap thee fast,
And the sleep be on thee cast
        That shall ne'er know waking.

Haste thee, haste thee, to be gone,
Earth flits fast, and time draws on,—
Gasp thy gasp, and groan thy groan,
        Day is near the breaking.

        Open locks, end strife,
        Come death, and pass life.

9 *brat*: mantle (one of the saint's emblems).
10 *Colme*: Columba. 12 *reif*: robbery. 12 *wear*: violence.

Gin by Pailfuls[n]

Gin by pailfuls, wine in rivers,
Dash the window-glass to shivers,
For three wild lads were we, brave boys,
And three wild lads were we;
Thou on the land, and I on the sand,
And Jack on the gallows-tree!

Jock of Hazeldean[n]

'Why weep ye by the tide, ladie?
Why weep ye by the tide?
I'll wed ye to my youngest son,
And ye sall be his bride:
And ye sall be his bride, ladie,
Sae comely to be seen'—
But aye she loot the tears down fa'
For Jock of Hazeldean.

'Now let this wilfu' grief be done,
And dry that cheek so pale;
Young Frank is chief of Errington,
And lord of Langley-dale;
His step is first in peaceful ha',
His sword in battle keen'—
But aye she loot the tears down fa'
For Jock of Hazeldean.

'A chain of gold ye sall not lack,
Nor braid to bind your hair;
Nor mettled hound, nor managed hawk,
Nor palfrey fresh and fair;

Hazeldean: Hassendean in Minto Parish, Roxburghshire, 4 miles NNE. of Hawick.

7 *loot*: let.

11 *Errington*: village in Northumberland, 5 miles N. of Hexham.

12 *Langley-dale*: probably the area near Langley Castle, 8¾ miles WSW. of Hexham, rather than the parish of Langleydale, 5 miles N. of Barnard Castle in Co. Durham. The former is much closer to Errington.

And you, the foremost o' them a',
  Shall ride our forest queen'—
But aye she loot the tears down fa'
  For Jock of Hazeldean.

The kirk was decked at morning-tide,
  The tapers glimmered fair;
The priest and bridegroom wait the bride,
  And dame and knight are there.
They sought her baith by bower and ha';
  The ladie was not seen!
She's o'er the Border, and awa'
  Wi' Jock of Hazeldean.

MacGregor's Gathering[n]

THE moon's on the lake, and the mist's on the brae,
And the Clan has a name that is nameless by day;
  Then gather, gather, gather, Grigalach!
  Gather, gather, gather, &c.

Our signal for fight, that from monarchs we drew,
Must be heard but by night in our vengeful haloo!
  Then haloo, Grigalach! haloo, Grigalach!
  Haloo, haloo, haloo, Grigalach, &c.

Glen Orchy's proud mountains, Coalchuirn and her towers,
Glenstrae and Glenlyon no longer are ours;
  We're landless, landless, landless, Grigalach!
  Landless, landless, landless, &c.

But doomed and devoted by vassal and lord,
MacGregor has still both his heart and his sword!
  Then courage, courage, courage, Grigalach!
  Courage, courage, courage, &c.

9 *Glen Orchy*: Glenorchy (12 miles due W. of Glen Lochay) is in the Lorn district of Argyll, between Loch Awe and Loch Tulla.
9 *Coalchuirn*: Kilchurn Castle in Glenorchy.
10 *Glenstrae*: in Glenorchy parish, the main stronghold of the MacGregors up to 1604.
10 *Glenlyon*: long narrow glen in the Breadalbane district of Perthshire.

If they rob us of name, and pursue us with beagles,
Give their roofs to the flame, and their flesh to the eagles!
Then vengeance, vengeance, vengeance, Grigalach!
Vengeance, vengeance, vengeance, &c.

While there's leaves in the forest, and foam on the river,
MacGregor, despite them, shall flourish for ever!
Come then, Grigalach, come then, Grigalach,
Come them, come then, come then, &c.

Through the depths of Loch Katrine the steed shall
career,
O'er the peak of Ben Lomond the galley shall steer,
And the rocks of Craigroyston like icicles melt,
Ere our wrongs be forgot, or our vengeance unfelt!
Then gather, gather, gather, Grigalach!
Gather, gather, gather, &c.

Pibroch of Donuil Dhu[n]

PIBROCH of Donuil Dhu,
Pibroch of Donuil,
Wake thy wild voice anew,
Summon Clan-Conuil.
Come away, come away,
Hark to the summons!
Come in your war array,
Gentles and commons.

Come from deep glen, and
From mountain so rocky,
The war-pipe and pennon
Are at Inverlochy.
Come every hill-plaid, and
True heart that wears one,
Come every steel blade, and
Strong hand that bears one.

27 *Craigroyston*: 'Rob Roy's Cave' at E. side of Loch Lomond, N. by W. of Inversnaid.

Leave untended the herd,
  The flock without shelter;
Leave the corpse uninterred,
  The bride at the altar;
Leave the deer, leave the steer,
  Leave nets and barges:
Come with your fighting gear,
  Broadswords and targes.

Come as the winds come, when
  Forests are rended,
Come as the waves come, when
  Navies are stranded:
Faster come, faster come,
  Faster and faster,
Chief, vassal, page and groom,
  Tenant and master.

Fast they come, fast they come;
  See how they gather!
Wide waves the eagle plume,
  Blended with heather.
Cast your plaids, draw your blades,
  Forward, each man, set!
Pibroch of Donuil Dhu,
  Knell for the onset!

The Aged Carle[n]

'WHY sit'st thou by that ruined hall,
  Thou aged carle so stern and grey?
Dost thou its former pride recall,
  Or ponder how it passed away?'—

'Know'st thou not me?' the Deep Voice cried;
  'So long enjoyed, so oft misused –
Alternate, in thy fickle pride,
  Desired, neglected, and accused!

Before my breath, like blazing flax,
Man and his marvels pass away!
And changing empires wane and wax,
Are founded, flourish, and decay.

Redeem mine hours—the space is brief—
While in my glass the sand-grains shiver,
And measureless thy joy or grief
When TIME and thou shall part for ever!'

Dredging Sang[n]

THE herring loves the merry moonlight,
The mackerel loves the wind,
But the oyster loves the dredging sang,
For they come of a gentle kind.

I'm Madge of the Country[n]

I'M Madge of the country, I'm Madge of the town,
And I'm Madge of the lad I am blithest to own—
The Lady of Beever in diamonds may shine,
But has not a heart half so lightsome as mine.
I am Queen of the Wake, and I'm Lady of May,
And I lead the blithe ring round the May-pole to-day;
The wild-fire that flashes so fair and so free
Was never so bright, or so bonnie as me.

3 *Beever*: Belvoir Castle in Leicestershire, for many centuries the home of the Earls and Dukes of Rutland. 'Belvoir' is locally pronounced 'Beever'.

The Fight of Grace[n]

WHEN the fight of grace is fought,
When the marriage vest is wrought,
When Faith has chased cold Doubt away,
And Hope but sickens at delay,
When Charity, imprisoned here,
Longs for a more expanded sphere,—
Doff thy robes of sin and clay,
Christian, rise, and come away.

Proud Maisie[n]

PROUD Maisie is in the wood,
  Walking so early;
Sweet Robin sits on the bush,
  Singing so rarely.

'Tell me, thou bonny bird,
  When shall I marry me?'—
'When six braw gentlemen
  Kirkward shall carry ye.'—

'Who makes the bridal bed,
  Birdie, say truly?'—
'The grey-headed sexton
  That delves the grave duly.

The glow-worm o'er grave and stone
  Shall light thee steady.
The owl from the steeple sing,
  "Welcome, proud lady."'

Look not thou on Beauty's charming[n]

LOOK not thou on beauty's charming,
Sit thou still when kings are arming,
Taste not when the wine-cup glistens,
Speak not when the people listens,
Stop thine ear against the singer,
From the red gold keep thy finger;
Vacant heart and hand and eye,
Easy live and quiet die.

Rebecca's Hymn[n]

WHEN Israel, of the Lord beloved,
  Out from the land of bondage came,
Her fathers' God before her moved,
  An awful guide in smoke and flame.
By day, along the astonished lands
  The cloudy pillar glided slow;
By night, Arabia's crimsoned sands
  Returned the fiery column's glow.

There rose the choral hymn of praise,
  And trump and timbrel answered keen,
And Zion's daughters poured their lays,
  With priest's and warrior's voice between.
No portents now our foes amaze,
  Forsaken Israel wanders lone:
Our fathers would not know Thy ways,
  And Thou hast left them to their own.

But present still, though now unseen!
  When brightly shines the prosperous day,
Be thoughts of Thee a cloudy screen
  To temper the deceitful ray.
And oh, when stoops on Judah's path
  In shade and storm the frequent night,
Be Thou, long-suffering, slow to wrath,
  A burning and a shining light!

Our harps we left by Babel's streams,
The tyrant's jest, the Gentile's scorn;
No censer round our altar beams,
And mute are timbrel, harp, and horn.
But Thou hast said, The blood of goat,
The flesh of rams I will not prize;
A contrite heart, a humble thought,
Are mine accepted sacrifice.

March, march, Ettrick and Teviotdale[n]

MARCH, march, Ettrick and Teviotdale,
Why the deil dinna ye march forward in order?
March, march, Eskdale and Liddesdale,
All the Blue Bonnets are bound for the Border.
Many a banner spread,
Flutters above your head,
Many a crest that is famous in story.
Mount and make ready then,
Sons of the mountain glen,
Fight for the Queen and the old Scottish glory.

Come from the hills where your hirsels are grazing,
Come from the glen of the buck and the roe;
Come to the crag where the beacon is blazing,
Come with the buckler, the lance, and the bow.
Trumpets are sounding,
War-steeds are bounding,
Stand to your arms then, and march in good order;
England shall many a day
Tell of the bloody fray,
When the Blue Bonnets came over the Border.

1–3 *Ettrick . . . Liddesdale*: see map, p. 281.
4 *Blue Bonnets*: a broad round flat cap of blue wool, formerly in general use in Scotland and worn by common soldiers.
10 *Queen*: Mary, Queen of Scots.
11 *hirsels*: flocks, herds.

Donald Caird's come again[n]

Chorus

Donald Caird's come again!
Donald Caird's come again!
Tell the news in brugh and glen,
Donald Caird's come again!

Donald Caird can lilt and sing,
Blithely dance the Hieland fling,
Drink till the gudeman be blind,
Fleech till the gudewife be kind;
Hoop a leglin, clout a pan,
Or crack a pow wi' ony man;—
Tell the news in brugh and glen,
Donald Caird's come again.

Donald Caird's come again!
Donald Caird's come again!
Tell the news in brugh and glen,
Donald Caird's come again.

Donald Caird can wire a maukin,
Kens the wiles o' dun-deer staukin',
Leisters kipper, makes a shift
To shoot a muir-fowl in the drift;
Water-bailiffs, rangers, keepers,—
He can wauk when they are sleepers;
Not for bountith or rewaird
Dare ye mell wi' Donald Caird.

Donald Caird's come again!
Donald Caird's come again!
Gar the bagpipes hum amain,
Donald Caird's come again.

Donald Caird can drink a gill
Fast as hostler-wife can fill;
Ilka ane that sells gude liquor
Kens how Donald bends a bicker;

1 *Caird*: tinker. 3 *brugh*: burgh, town. 7 *gudeman*: husband.
8 *Fleech*: flatter. 9 *leglin*: milk-pail. 9 *clout*: hammer.
10 *pow*: head. 17 *wire a maukin*: trap a hare.
19 *Leisters kipper*: catches with a fish-spear salmon in the state of spawning.
24 *mell*: meddle. 27 *Gar*: cause (to). 32 *bicker*: bowl.

When he's fou he's stout and saucy,
Keeps the cantle o' the causey;
Hieland chief and Lawland laird
Maun gie room to Donald Caird!

Donald Caird's come again!
Donald Caird's come again!
Tell the news in brugh and glen,
Donald Caird's come again.

Steek the amrie, lock the kist,
Else some gear may weel be missed;
Donald Caird finds orra things
Where Allan Gregor fand the tings;
Dunts of kebbuck, taits o' woo,
Whiles a hen and whiles a sow,
Webs or duds frae hedge or yaird—
'Ware the wuddie, Donald Caird!

Donald Caird's come again!
Donald Caird's come again!
Dinna let the Shirra ken
Donald Caird's come again.

On Donald Caird the doom was stern,
Craig to tether, legs to airn;
But Donald Caird, wi' mickle study,
Caught the gift to cheat the wuddie;
Rings of airn, and bolts of steel,
Fell like ice frae hand and heel!
Watch the sheep in fauld and glen,
Donald Caird's come again!

Donald Caird's come again!
Donald Caird's come again!
Dinna let the Justice ken,
Donald Caird's come again.

34 *Keeps . . . causey*: keeps the crown of the street, i.e., acts like a man of substance.
41 *Steek*: shut. 41 *amrie*: large kitchen cupboard. 41 *kist*: chest.
43 *orra*: strange. 44 *Where . . . tings*: at the fireside.
45 *kebbuck*: cheese. 45 *taits o' woo*: small pieces of wool.
48 *wuddie*: hangman's rope.
51 *Shirra*: Sheriff (in Scotland, the chief local judge in a county).
54 *Craig*: neck. 54 *airn*: iron.

Epilogue[n]

TO THE DRAMA FOUNDED ON 'ST. RONAN'S WELL'

Enter MEG DODDS, *encircled by a crowd of unruly boys, whom a town's-officer is driving off.*

THAT'S right, friend—drive the gaitlings back,
And lend yon muckle ane a whack;
Your Embro' bairns are grown a pack,
    Sae proud and saucy,
They scarce will let an auld wife walk
    Upon your causey.

I've seen the day they would been scaur'd,
Wi' the Tolbooth, or wi' the Guard,
Or maybe wud hae some regard
    For Jamie Laing—
The Water-hole was right weel wared
    On sic a gang.

But whar's the gude Tolbooth gane now?
Whar's the auld Claught, wi' red and blue?
Whar's Jamie Laing? and whar's John Doo?
    And whar's the Weigh-house?
Deil hae't I see but what is new,
    Except the Playhouse!

Yoursells are changed frae head to heel,
There's some that gar the causeway reel
With clashing hufe and rattling wheel,
    And horses canterin',
Wha's fathers daunder'd hame as weel
    Wi' lass and lantern.

1 *gaitlings*: children.   2 *muckle*: large.   3 *Embro'*: Edinburgh.
6 *causey*: street.
8 *Tolbooth*: the prison pulled down in 1817, known as 'The Heart of Midlothian'.
10 *Laing*: a much-feared police official, d. 1806.
11 *Water-hole*: police cell.   11 *wared*: bestowed.
14 *Claught*: the 'Clutchers', or Town Guard, finally disbanded 1817.
15 *John Doo*: a fearsome-looking member of the Town Guard.
16 *Weigh-house*: at the head of the West Bow, demolished 1822 in order to make way for the royal procession to the Castle.
23 *daunder'd*: strolled.

Mysell being in the public line,
I look for howfs I kenn'd lang syne,
Whar gentles used to drink gude wine,
And eat cheap dinners;
But deil a soul gangs there to dine,
Of saints or sinners!

Fortune's and Hunter's gane, alace!
And Bayle's is lost in empty space;
And now if folk would splice a brace,
Or crack a bottle,
They gang to a new-fangled place
They ca' a Hottle.

The deevil hottle them for Meg!
They are sae greedy and sae gleg,
That if ye're served but wi' an egg,
(And that's puir pickin',)
In comes a chiel and makes a leg,
And charges chicken!

'And wha may ye be,' gin ye speer,
'That brings your auld-warld clavers here?'
Troth, if there's onybody near
That kens the roads,
I'll haud ye Burgundy to beer,
He kens Meg Dodds.

I came a piece frae west o' Currie;
And, since I see you're in a hurry,
Your patience I'll nae langer worry,
But be sae crouse
As speak a word for ane Will Murray,
That keeps this house.

25 *public*: innkeeping. 26 *howfs*: inns.
31 *Fortune's*: a tavern on the W. side of the Old Stamp Office Close, High Street.
31 *Hunter's*: a tavern in Writer's Court, Royal Exchange.
32 *Bayle's*: a tavern and coffee-house removed when Waterloo Place was built.
38 *gleg*: cunning. 41 *chiel*: fellow.
43 *speer*: ask. 44 *clavers*: chatter.
49 *Currie*: village near Edinburgh. 52 *crouse*: bold.
53 *Murray*: manager of the theatre.

Plays are auld-fashion'd things, in truth,
And ye've seen wonders mair uncouth;
Yet actors shouldna suffer drouth,
    Or want of dramock,
Although they speak but wi' their mouth,
    Not with their stamock.

But ye tak care of a' folk's pantry;
And surely to hae stooden sentry
Ower this big house (that's far frae rent-free),
    For a lone sister,
Is claims as gude's to be a ventri—
    How'st ca'd—loquister.

Weel, sirs, gude'en, and have a care
The bairns mak fun o' Meg nae mair;
For gin they do, she tells you fair,
    And without failzie,
As sure as ever ye sit there,
    She'll tell the Bailie.

58 *dramock*: meal and water. 70 *failzie*: fail ('z' pronounced 'y').
72 *Bailie*: magistrate.

Bonny Dundee[n]

To the Lords of Convention 'twas Claver'se who spoke,
'Ere the King's crown shall fall there are crowns to be broke;
So let each Cavalier who loves honour and me,
Come follow the bonnet of Bonny Dundee.

'Come fill up my cup, come fill up my can,
Come saddle your horses, and call up your men;
Come open the West Port, and let me gang free,
And it's room for the bonnets of Bonny Dundee!'

Dundee he is mounted, he rides up the street,
The bells are rung backward, the drums they are beat;
But the Provost, douce man, said, 'Just e'en let him be,
The Gude Town is weel quit of that Deil of Dundee.'

Come fill up my cup, &c.

As he rode down the sanctified bends of the Bow,
Ilk carline was flyting and shaking her pow;
But the young plants of grace they looked couthie and slee,
Thinking, 'Luck to thy bonnet, thou Bonny Dundee!'

Come fill up my cup, &c.

With sour-featured Whigs the Grassmarket was crammed
As if half the West had set tryst to be hanged;
There was spite in each look, there was fear in each e'e,
As they watched for the bonnets of Bonny Dundee.

Come fill up my cup, &c.

1 *Lords of Convention*: Convention of Scottish Estates which proclaimed William and Mary as King and Queen of Scotland in April 1689.
1 *Claver'se*: John Graham of Claverhouse, Viscount Dundee (1649–89).
14 *Bow*: the West Bow, or street in Edinburgh.
15 *flyting*: scolding.
16 *couthie*: affable.
16 *slee*: sly.
19 *Whigs*: Presbyterians. *Grassmarket*: place of public execution in Edinburgh.

These cowls of Kilmarnock had spits and had spears,
And lang-hafted gullies to kill Cavaliers;
But they shrunk to close-heads, and the causeway was free,
At the toss of the bonnet of Bonny Dundee.

Come fill up my cup, &c.

He spurred to the foot of the proud Castle rock,
And with the gay Gordon he gallantly spoke;
'Let Mons Meg and her marrows speak twa words or three,
For the love of the bonnet of Bonny Dundee.'

Come fill up my cup, &c.

The Gordon demands of him which way he goes—
'Where'er shall direct me the shade of Montrose!
Your Grace in short space shall hear tidings of me,
Or that low lies the bonnet of Bonny Dundee.

Come fill up my cup, &c.

'There are hills beyond Pentland, and lands beyond Forth,
If there's lords in the Lowlands, there's chiefs in the North;
There are wild Duniewassals, three thousand times three,
Will cry *hoigh!* for the bonnet of Bonny Dundee.

Come fill up my cup, &c.

'There's brass on the target of barkened bull-hide;
There's steel in the scabbard that dangles beside;
The brass shall be burnished, the steel shall flash free,
At a toss of the bonnet of Bonny Dundee.

Come fill up my cup, &c.

'Away to the hills, to the caves, to the rocks—
Ere I own an usurper, I'll couch with the fox;
And tremble, false Whigs, in the midst of your glee,
You have not seen the last of my bonnet and me!'

Come fill up my cup, &c.

24 *cowls of Kilmarnock*: covenanters from West of Scotland.
25 *gullies*: knives.
26 *to close-heads*: into passages of tenement houses. 26 *causeway*: street.
30 *Gordon*: George, First Duke of Gordon (1643–1716) who held Edinburgh Castle for James till June 1689.
31 *Mons Meg*: a cannon in Edinburgh castle. 31 *marrows*: companions.
35 *Montrose*: James Graham, Marquis of Montrose (1612–50) who fought for Charles I in Scotland, 1644–5.
41 *Duniewassals*: gentlemen of secondary rank (Jamieson).
44 *barkened*: tanned.

He waved his proud hand, and the trumpets were blown,
The kettle-drums clashed, and the horsemen rode on,
Till on Ravelston's cliffs and on Clermiston's lee,
Died away the wild war-notes of Bonny Dundee.

Come fill up my cup, come fill up my can,
Come saddle the horses and call up the men,
Come open your gates, and let me gae free,
For it's up with the bonnets of Bonny Dundee!

56 *Ravelston, Clermiston*: estates in Corstorphine parish, Midlothian; now suburbs of Edinburgh.

II. Romances

The Lay of the Last Minstrel

Introduction

THE way was long, the wind was cold,
The Minstrel was infirm and old;
His withered cheek, and tresses gray,
Seemed to have known a better day;
The harp, his sole remaining joy,
Was carried by an orphan boy.
The last of all the Bards was he,
Who sung of Border chivalry;
For, welladay! their date was fled,
His tuneful brethren all were dead;
And he, neglected and oppressed,
Wished to be with them, and at rest.
No more, on prancing palfrey borne,
He carolled, light as lark at morn;
No longer courted and caressed,
High placed in hall, a welcome guest,
He poured to lord and lady gay
The unpremeditated lay:
Old times were changed, old manners gone,
A stranger filled the Stuarts' throne;
The bigots of the iron time
Had called his harmless art a crime.[n]
A wandering Harper, scorned and poor,
He begged his bread from door to door,
And tuned, to please a peasant's ear,
The harp a king had loved to hear.

He passed where Newark's stately tower[n]
Looks out from Yarrow's birchen bower:
The Minstrel gazed with wishful eye—
No humbler resting-place was nigh;
With hesitating step at last
The embattled portal arch he passed,
Whose ponderous grate and massy bar
Had oft rolled back the tide of war,

28 *Yarrow*: a tributary of Ettrick water, Selkirkshire.

But never closed the iron door
Against the desolate and poor.
The Duchess marked his weary pace,
His timid mien, and reverend face,
And bade her page the menials tell
That they should tend the old man well:
For she had known adversity,
Though born in such a high degree;
In pride of power, in beauty's bloom,
Had wept o'er Monmouth's bloody tomb!

When kindness had his wants supplied,
And the old man was gratified,
Began to rise his minstrel pride:
And he began to talk anon
Of good Earl Francis, dead and gone,
And of Earl Walter, rest him God!
A braver ne'er to battle rode;
And how full many a tale he knew
Of the old warriors of Buccleuch:
And, would the noble Duchess deign
To listen to an old man's strain,
Though stiff his hand, his voice though weak,
He thought even yet, the sooth to speak,
That, if she loved the harp to hear,
He could make music to her ear.

The humble boon was soon obtained;
The aged Minstrel audience gained.
But, when he reached the room of state,
Where she with all her ladies sate,
Perchance he wished his boon denied:
For when to tune his harp he tried,
His trembling hand had lost the ease,
Which marks security to please;
And scenes long past, of joy and pain,
Came wildering o'er his aged brain—
He tried to tune his harp in vain!
The pitying Duchess praised its chime,
And gave him heart, and gave him time,

44 *Monmouth*: see below p. 280, end-note to line 27.
49 *Earl Francis*: the Duchess's father.
50 *Earl Walter*: her grandfather. 67 *security*: confidence.

Till every string's according glee
Was blended into harmony.
And then, he said, he would full fain
He could recall an ancient strain
He never thought to sing again.
It was not framed for village churls,
But for high dames and mighty earls;
He had played it to King Charles the Good,
When he kept court in Holyrood;
And much he wished, yet feared, to try
The long-forgotten melody.
Amid the strings his fingers strayed,
And an uncertain warbling made—
And oft he shook his hoary head.
But when he caught the measure wild,
The old man raised his face, and smiled;
And lightened up his faded eye
With all a poet's ecstasy!
In varying cadence, soft or strong,
He swept the sounding chords along:
The present scene, the future lot,
His toils, his wants, were all forgot;
Cold diffidence, and age's frost,
In the full tide of song were lost.
Each blank, in faithless memory void,
The poet's glowing thought supplied;
And, while his harp responsive rung,
'Twas thus the LATEST MINSTREL sung.

Canto First

I

THE feast was over in Branksome tower,
And the Ladye had gone to her secret bower;
Her bower that was guarded by word and by spell,
Deadly to hear, and deadly to tell—
Jesu Maria, shield us well![n]
No living wight, save the Ladye alone,
Had dared to cross the threshold stone.

80 *Charles*: Charles I. 81 *Holyrood*: palace in Edinburgh.
1 *Branksome*: see p. 4, line 37.

II

The tables were drawn, it was idlesse all;
  Knight, and page, and household squire,
Loitered through the lofty hall,
  Or crowded round the ample fire:
The stag-hounds, weary with the chase,
  Lay stretched upon the rushy floor,
And urged, in dreams, the forest race
  From Teviot-stone to Eskdale-moor.

III

Nine-and-twenty knights[n] of fame
  Hung their shields in Branksome hall;
Nine-and-twenty squires of name
  Brought them their steeds to bower from stall;
    Nine-and-twenty yeomen tall
    Waited, duteous, on them all:
    They were all knights of mettle true,
    Kinsmen to the bold Buccleuch.

IV

Ten of them were sheathed in steel,
With belted sword, and spur on heel:
They quitted not their harness bright,
Neither by day, nor yet by night:
    They lay down to rest,
    With corslet laced,
Pillowed on buckler cold and hard;
    They carved at the meal
    With gloves of steel,
And they drank the red wine through the helmet barred.[n]

V

Ten squires, ten yeomen, mail-clad men,
Waited the beck of the warders ten:
Thirty steeds, both fleet and wight,
Stood saddled in stable day and night,

8 *drawn*: to the side of the hall, after evening meal.
17 *hung . . . shields*: i.e., always dwelt there.
36 *wight*: strong.

Barbed with frontlet of steel, I trow,
And with Jedwood-axe at saddlebow;
A hundred more fed free in stall:
Such was the custom of Branksome Hall.

VI

Why do these steeds stand ready dight?
Why watch these warriors, armed, by night?
They watch to hear the blood-hound baying:
They watch to hear the war-horn braying;
To see St. George's red cross streaming,
To see the midnight beacon gleaming:
They watch against Southern force and guile,
Lest Scroop, or Howard, or Percy's[n] powers,
Threaten Branksome's lordly towers,
From Warkworth, or Naworth, or merry Carlisle.

VII

Such is the custom of Branksome Hall.
Many a valiant knight is here;
But he, the chieftain of them all,
His sword hangs rusting on the wall,
Beside his broken spear.
Bards long shall tell
How Lord Walter[n] fell!
When startled burghers fled, afar,
The furies of the Border war;
When the streets of high Dunedin
Saw lances gleam, and falchions redden,
And heard the slogan's deadly yell—
Then the Chief of Branksome fell.

VIII

Can piety the discord heal,
Or stanch the death-feud's enmity?
Can Christian lore, can patriot zeal,
Can love of blessed charity?

38 *barbed*: protected (with armour).
39 *Jedwood-axe*: a kind of partisan or 'long-handled spear, the blade having one or more lateral projections' (*O.E.D.*).
46 *St. George's . . . cross*: flag of England.
47 *beacon*: to warn of invasion. 61 *Dunedin*: Edinburgh.
62 *falchion*: curved sword, convex-edged.
63 *slogan*: war-cry.

No! vainly to each holy shrine,
  In mutual pilgrimage[n] they drew;
Implored in vain the grace divine
  For chiefs their own red falchions slew.
While Cessford[n] owns the rule of Carr,
  While Ettrick[n] boasts the line of Scott,
The slaughtered chiefs, the mortal jar,
The havoc of the feudal war,
  Shall never, never be forgot!

IX

In sorrow o'er Lord Walter's bier
  The warlike foresters had bent;
And many a flower and many a tear
  Old Teviot's maids and matrons lent:
But o'er her warrior's bloody bier
The Ladye dropped nor flower[n] nor tear!
Vengeance, deep-brooding o'er the slain,
  Had locked the source of softer woe;
And burning pride and high disdain[n]
  Forbade the rising tear to flow;
Until, amid his sorrowing clan,
  Her son lisped from the nurse's knee—
'And if I live to be a man
  My father's death revenged shall be!'
Then fast the mother's tears did seek
To dew the infant's kindling cheek.

X

All loose her negligent attire,
    All loose her golden hair,
Hung Margaret o'er her slaughtered sire,
  And wept in wild despair.
But not alone the bitter tear
  Had filial grief supplied;
For hopeless love and anxious fear
  Had lent their mingled tide:
Nor in her mother's altered eye
Dared she to look for sympathy.

73 *Carr*: Kerr. 81 *lent*: gave.

Her lover, 'gainst her father's clan,
  With Carr in arms had stood,
When Mathouse-burn to Melrose ran
  All purple with their blood;
And well she knew, her mother dread,
Before Lord Cranstoun[n] she should wed,
Would see her on her dying bed.

XI

Of noble race the Ladye came;
Her father was a clerk of fame,
  Of Bethune's line of Picardie:[n]
He learned the art that none may name,
  In Padua, far beyond the sea.
Men said he changed his mortal frame
  By feat of magic mystery;
For when, in studious mood, he paced
  St. Andrew's cloistered hall,
His form no darkening shadow traced
  Upon the sunny wall![n]

XII

And of his skill, as bards avow,
  He taught that Ladye fair,
Till to her bidding she could bow
  The viewless forms of air.[n]
And now she sits in secret bower,
In old Lord David's western tower,
And listens to a heavy sound
That moans the mossy turrets round.
Is it the roar of Teviot's tide,
That chafes against the scaur's red side?
Is it the wind that swings the oaks?
Is it the echo from the rocks?
What may it be, the heavy sound,
That moans old Branksome's turrets round?[n]

106 *Mathouse-burn*: Malthouse burn, a stream in Melrose parish, N. Roxburghshire, to S. of the Tweed.
115 *Padua*: in legend, 'The principal school of necromancy' (S).
119 *St. Andrews*: a monastic and university town.
127 *Lord David*: 'Branksome Castle was enlarged and strengthened by Sir David Scott the grandson of Sir William, its first possessor' (S).
131 *scaur*: 'precipitous bank of earth' (S).

XIII

At the sullen, moaning sound,
  The ban-dogs bay and howl;
And, from the turrets round,
  Loud whoops the startled owl.
In the hall, both squire and knight
  Swore that a storm was near,
And looked forth to view the night;
  But the night was still and clear!

XIV

From the sound of Teviot's tide,
Chafing with the mountain's side,
From the groan of the wind-swung oak,
From the sullen echo of the rock,
From the voice of the coming storm,
  The Ladye knew it well!
It was the Spirit of the Flood that spoke,
  And he called on the Spirit of the Fell.

XV

RIVER SPIRIT

'Sleep'st thou, brother?'

MOUNTAIN SPIRIT

'Brother, nay—
On my hills the moon-beams play.
From Craikcross to Skelfhill-pen,
By every rill, in every glen,
  Merry elves their morris pacing,
    To aërial minstrelsy,
  Emerald rings on brown heath tracing,
    Trip it deft and merrily.
  Up, and mark their nimble feet!
  Up, and list their music sweet!'

137 *ban-dogs*: dogs held in bands (chains).
149 *knew . . . well*: could distinguish from.
150 *spirit*: see below p. 282, end-note to line 125.
151 *Fell*: hillside.
154 *Craikcross, Skelfhill-pen*: hills on opposite sides of the Teviot.
158 *rings*: supposedly made by fairy feet.

XVI

RIVER SPIRIT

'Tears of an imprisoned maiden
  Mix with my polluted stream;
Margaret of Branksome, sorrow-laden,
  Mourns beneath the moon's pale beam.
Tell me, thou, who view'st the stars,
When shall cease these feudal jars?
What shall be the maiden's fate?
Who shall be the maiden's mate?'

XVII

MOUNTAIN SPIRIT

'Arthur's slow wain his course doth roll
In utter darkness round the pole;
The Northern Bear lowers black and grim;
Orion's studded belt is dim;
Twinkling faint, and distant far,
Shimmers through mist each planet star;
  Ill may I read their high decree!
But no kind influence deign they shower
On Teviot's tide and Branksome's tower
  Till pride be quelled and love be free.'

XVIII

The unearthly voices ceast,
  And the heavy sound was still;
It died on the river's breast,
  It died on the side of the hill.
But round Lord David's tower
  The sound still floated near;
For it rung in the Ladye's bower
  And it rung in the Ladye's ear.
She raised her stately head,
  And her heart throbbed high with pride:
'Your mountains shall bend,
And your streams ascend,
Ere Margaret be our foeman's bride!'

170 *Arthur's slow wain*: Charles's wain in the Great Bear.
171 *utter*: outer.

XIX

The Ladye sought the lofty hall,
  Where many a bold retainer lay,
And with jocund din, among them all,
  Her son pursued his infant play.
A fancied moss-trooper, the boy
  The truncheon of a spear bestrode,
And round the hall, right merrily,
  In mimic foray rode.
Even bearded knights, in arms grown old,
  Share in his frolic gambols bore,
Albeit their hearts of rugged mould
  Were stubborn as the steel they wore.
For the gray warriors prophesied
  How the brave boy, in future war,
Should tame the Unicorn's pride,
  Exalt the Crescent and the Star.

XX

The Ladye forgot her purpose high,
  One moment, and no more;
One moment gazed with a mother's eye,
  As she paused at the arched door:
Then from amid the armed train,
She called to her William of Deloraine.[n]

XXI

A stark moss-trooping Scott was he,
As e'er couched Border lance by knee:
Through Solway sands, through Tarras moss,
Blindfold, he knew the paths to cross;
By wily turns, by desperate bounds,
Had baffled Percy's best blood-hounds;
In Esk, or Liddel,[n] fords were none,
But he would ride them one by one;
Alike to him was time or tide,
December's snow, or July's pride;
Alike to him was tide or time,
Moonless midnight, or matin prime:

198 *truncheon*: shaft.
207 *Unicorn*: heraldic emblem of the Cessford Kerrs.
208 *Crescent*, *Star*: emblems of the Buccleuch Scotts.
217 *Tarras*: trout stream in Eskdale, E. Dumfriesshire.

Steady of heart, and stout of hand,
As ever drove prey from Cumberland;
Five times outlawed had he been,
By England's King, and Scotland's Queen.

XXII

'Sir William of Deloraine, good at need,
Mount thee on the wightest steed;
Spare not to spur, nor stint to ride,
Until thou come to fair Tweedside;
And in Melrose's holy pile
Seek thou the Monk of St. Mary's aisle.
  Greet the Father well from me;
    Say that the fated hour is come,
  And to-night he shall watch with thee,
    To win the treasure of the tomb:
For this will be St. Michael's night,
And though stars be dim, the moon is bright;
And the Cross, of bloody red,
Will point to the grave of the mighty dead.

XXIII

What he gives thee, see thou keep;
Stay not thou for food or sleep:
Be it scroll, or be it book,
Into it, Knight, thou must not look;
If thou readest, thou art lorn!
Better had'st thou ne'er been born.'—

XXIV

'O swiftly can speed my dapple-grey steed,
  Which drinks of the Teviot clear;
Ere break of day,' the Warrior 'gan say,
  'Again will I be here:
And safer by none may thy errand be done,
  Than, noble dame, by me;
Letter nor line know I never a one,
  Were't my neck-verse at Hairibee.'[n]

232 *wightest*: strongest.
235 *Melrose's holy pile*: abbey in N. Roxburghshire, between the Eildon Hills and the Tweed, was founded in 1136 by David I, 'a sore saint for the crown'.
241 *St. Michael's night*: Michaelmas (29 Sept.).
249 *lorn*: lost.

XXV

Soon in his saddle sate he fast,
And soon the steep descent he passed,
Soon crossed the sounding barbican,
And soon the Teviot side he won.
Eastward the wooded path he rode,—
Green hazels o'er his basnet nod;
He passed the Peel of Goldiland,
And crossed old Borthwick's roaring strand;
Dimly he viewed the Moat-hill's mound,
Where Druid shades still flitted round;
In Hawick twinkled many a light;
Behind him soon they set in night;
And soon he spurred his courser keen
Beneath the tower of Hazeldean.

XXVI

The clattering hoofs the watchmen mark:
'Stand, ho! thou courier of the dark.'
'For Branksome, ho!' the knight rejoined,
And left the friendly tower behind.
  He turned him now from Teviotside,
    And, guided by the tinkling rill,
  Northward the dark ascent did ride,
    And gained the moor at Horsliehill;
Broad on the left before him lay,
For many a mile, the Roman way.

XXVII

A moment now he slacked his speed,
A moment breathed his panting steed;
Drew saddle-girth and corslet-band,
And loosened in the sheath his brand.

261 *barbican*: double tower over a castle's outer gate or bridge.
264 *basnet*: light globular steel headpiece closed in front with a visor.
265 *Peel*: Border tower.
266 *Borthwick*: tributary of the Teviot.
267 *Moat-hill*: 'a round, artificial mount near Hawick' (S).
272 *Hazeldean*: i.e., Hassendean, an estate in Roxburghshire situated some 4 miles NNE. of Hawick, which was once owned by a family of Scotts.
280 *Horsliehill*: in Roxburghshire, SW. of Hassendean.
282 *Roman way*: 'ancient Roman road' (S).
285 *drew*: i.e., tighter, against possible attack.

On Minto-crags the moonbeams glint,
Where Barnhill[n] hewed his bed of flint;
Who flung his outlawed limbs to rest,
Where falcons hang their giddy nest,
Mid cliffs, from whence his eagle eye
For many a league his prey could spy;
Cliffs doubling, on their echoes borne,
The terrors of the robber's horn;
Cliffs which, for many a later year,
The warbling Doric reed[n] shall hear,
When some sad swain shall teach the grove,[n]
Ambition is no cure for love!

XXVIII

Unchallenged, thence passed Deloraine,
To ancient Riddel's[n] fair domain,
  Where Aill, from mountains freed,
Down from the lakes did raving come;
Each wave was crested with tawny foam,
  Like the mane of a chestnut steed.
In vain! no torrent, deep or broad,
Might bar the bold moss-trooper's road.

XXIX

At the first plunge the horse sunk low,
And the water broke o'er the saddle-bow;
Above the foaming tide, I ween,
Scarce half the charger's neck was seen;
For he was barded from counter to tail,
And the rider was armed complete in mail:
Never heavier man and horse
Stemmed a midnight torrent's force.
The warrior's very plume, I say,
Was daggled by the dashing spray;
Yet through good heart, and Our Ladye's grace,
At length he gained the landing-place.

301 *Aill*: a tributary of the Teviot.
311 *barded*: from Fr. *barde* horse-armour.
311 *counter*: horse's chest.
316 *daggled*: wet.

XXX

Now Bowden Moor the march-man won,
And sternly shook his plumed head,
As glanced his eye o'er Halidon:
For on his soul the slaughter red
Of that unhallowed morn arose
When first the Scott and Carr were foes;
When royal James beheld the fray;
Prize to the victor of the day;
When Home and Douglas, in the van,
Bore down Buccleuch's retiring clan,
Till gallant Cessford's heart-blood dear
Reeked on dark Elliot's Border spear.

XXXI

In bitter mood he spurred fast,
And soon the hated heath was past;
And far beneath, in lustre wan,
Old Melros' rose, and fair Tweed ran:
Like some tall rock with lichens grey,
Seemed dimly huge the dark Abbaye.
When Hawick he passed, had curfew rung,
Now midnight lauds[n] were in Melrose sung.
The sound upon the fitful gale,
In solemn wise did rise and fail,
Like that wild harp whose magic tone
Is wakened by the winds alone.
But when Melrose he reached, 'twas silence all:
He meetly stabled his steed in stall,
And sought the convent's lonely wall.

HERE paused the harp; and with its swell
The Master's fire and courage fell;
Dejectedly and low he bowed,
And, gazing timid on the crowd,
He seemed to seek in every eye
If they approved his minstrelsy;

319 *Bowden*: parish in NW. Roxburghshire.
319 *march-man*: borderer.
321 *Halidon*: a seat of the Cessford Kerrs. 'Skirmish Field', site of a battle between the Kerrs and the Scotts, lies ¼ mile to the north.
334 *Melros'*: Melrose abbey. 341 *harp*: the Aeolian harp.

And, diffident of present praise,
Somewhat he spoke of former days,
And how old age and wandering long
Had done his hand and harp some wrong.
The Duchess and her daughters fair,
And every gentle lady there,
Each after each in due degree,
Gave praises to his melody;
His hand was true, his voice was clear,
And much they longed the rest to hear.
Encouraged thus, the aged man,
After meet rest, again began.

Canto Second

I

If thou would'st view fair Melrose aright,
Go visit it by the pale moonlight;
For the gay beams of lightsome day
Gild, but to flout, the ruins grey.
When the broken arches are black in night,
And each shafted oriel glimmers white;
When the cold light's uncertain shower
Streams on the ruined central tower;
When buttress and buttress, alternately,
Seem framed of ebon and ivory;
When silver edges the imagery,
And the scrolls that teach thee to live and die;
When distant Tweed is heard to rave,
And the owlet to hoot o'er the dead man's grave,
Then go—but go alone the while—
Then view St. David's[n] ruined pile;
And, home returning, soothly swear,
Was never scene so sad and fair!

II

Short halt did Deloraine make there;
Little recked he of the scene so fair:
With dagger's hilt, on the wicket strong,
He struck full loud, and struck full long.

4 *flout*: mock, by highlighting its ruins.
12 *scrolls*: containing spiritual texts.
16 *St. David's*: see I. 235. 17 *soothly*: with truth.

The porter hurried to the gate—
'Who knocks so loud, and knocks so late?'
'From Branksome I,' the warrior cried;
And straight the wicket opened wide:
For Branksome's Chiefs had in battle stood,
  To fence the rights of fair Melrose;
And lands and livings, many a rood,
  Had gifted the shrine for their souls' repose.

III

Bold Deloraine his errand said;
The porter bent his humble head;
With torch in hand, and feet unshod,
And noiseless step, the path he trod:
The arched cloister, far and wide,
Rang to the warrior's clanking stride,
Till, stooping low his lofty crest,
He entered the cell of the ancient priest,
And lifted his barred aventayle,
To hail the Monk of St. Mary's aisle.

IV

'The Ladye of Branksome greets thee by me;
  Says, that the fated hour is come,
And that to-night I shall watch with thee,
  To win the treasure of the tomb.'
From sackcloth couch the Monk arose,
  With toil his stiffened limbs he reared;
A hundred years had flung their snows
  On his thin locks and floating beard.

V

And strangely on the Knight looked he,
  And his blue eyes gleamed wild and wide;
'And darest thou, Warrior! seek to see
  What heaven and hell alike would hide?
My breast, in belt of iron pent,[n]
  With shirt of hair and scourge of thorn;
For threescore years, in penance spent,
  My knees those flinty stones have worn;

28 *fence*: defend. 39 *aventayle*: visor.

Yet all too little to atone
For knowing what should ne'er be known.
  Would'st thou thy every future year
    In ceaseless prayer and penance drie,
  Yet wait thy latter end with fear—
    Then, daring Warrior, follow me!'

VI

'Penance, father, will I none;
Prayer know I hardly one;
For mass or prayer can I rarely tarry,
Save to patter an Ave Mary,
When I ride on a Border foray.
Other prayer can I none;
So speed me my errand, and let me be gone.'

VII

Again on the Knight looked the Churchman old,
And again he sighed heavily;
For he had himself been a warrior bold,
And fought in Spain and Italy.
And he thought on the days that were long since by,
When his limbs were strong, and his courage was high:
Now, slow and faint, he led the way,
Where, cloistered round, the garden lay;
The pillared arches were over their head,
And beneath their feet were the bones of the dead.

VIII

Spreading herbs and flowerets bright,
Glistened with the dew of night;
Nor herb nor floweret glistened there,
But was carved in the cloister-arches as fair.
  The Monk gazed long on the lovely moon,
    Then into the night he looked forth;
  And red and bright the streamers light[n]
    Were dancing in the glowing north.
  So had he seen, in fair Castile,
    The youth in glittering squadrons start,
  Sudden the flying jennet wheel,
    And hurl the unexpected dart.[n]

60 *drie*: endure. 68 *can*: know.
83 *But*: that not. 90 *jennet*: small Spanish horse.

He knew, by the streamers that shot so bright,
That spirits were riding the northern light.

IX

By a steel-clenched postern door,
They entered now the chancel tall;
The darkened roof rose high aloof
On pillars lofty and light and small:
The key-stone, that locked each ribbed aisle,
Was a fleur-de-lys, or a quatre-feuille;
The corbels were carved grotesque and grim;
And the pillars, with clustered shafts so trim,
With base and with capital flourished around,
Seemed bundles of lances which garlands had bound.

X

Full many a scutcheon and banner riven,
Shook to the cold night-wind of heaven,
Around the screened altar's pale;
And there the dying lamps did burn,
Before thy low and lonely urn,
O gallant Chief of Otterburne![n]
And thine, dark Knight of Liddesdale![n]
O fading honours of the dead!
O high ambition, lowly laid!

XI

The moon on the east oriel shone
Through slender shafts of shapely stone,
By foliaged tracery combined;
Thou would'st have thought some fairy's hand
'Twixt poplars straight the ozier wand,
In many a freakish knot, had twined;
Then framed a spell, when the work was done,
And changed the willow-wreaths to stone.[n]
The silver light, so pale and faint,
Shewed many a prophet and many a saint,

99 *quatre-feuille*: carved floral ornaments at intersection of the ribs of a vaulted arch.
100 *corbels*: projections supporting the arches.

Whose image on the glass was dyed;
Full in the midst, his Cross of Red
Triumphant Michael brandished,
And trampled the Apostate's pride.
The moonbeam kissed the holy pane,
And threw on the pavement a bloody stain.

XII

They sate them down on a marble stone
(A Scottish monarch slept below):
Thus spoke the Monk, in solemn tone:
'I was not always a man of woe;
For Paynim countries I have trod,
And fought beneath the Cross of God:
Now, strange to my eyes thine arms appear,
And their iron clang sounds strange to my ear.

XIII

In these far climes it was my lot
To meet the wondrous Michael Scott;[n]
A wizard, of such dreaded fame,
That when, in Salamanca's cave,
Him listed his magic wand to wave,
The bells would ring in Notre Dame!
Some of his skill he taught to me;
And, Warrior, I could say to thee
The words that cleft Eildon hills in three[n],
And bridled the Tweed with a curb of stone:
But to speak them were a deadly sin;
And for having but thought them my heart within,
A treble penance must be done.

XIV

When Michael lay on his dying bed,
His conscience was awakened:
He bethought him of his sinful deed,
And he gave me a sign to come with speed.
I was in Spain when the morning rose,
But I stood by his bed ere evening close.

125 *Michael*: the archangel, triumphant over Satan.
130 *Scottish monarch*: Alexander II (1214–49).
140 *Salamanca's cave*: Spain was traditionally infested with magicians.
141 *him listed*: it pleased him.

The words may not again be said,
That he spoke to me, on death-bed laid;
They would rend this Abbaye's massy nave,
And pile it in heaps above his grave.

XV

I swore to bury his Mighty Book,
That never mortal might therein look;
And never to tell where it was hid,
Save at his Chief of Branksome's need:
And when that need was past and o'er,
Again the volume to restore.
I buried him on St. Michael's night,
When the bell tolled one, and the moon was bright,
And I dug his chamber among the dead,
When the floor of the chancel was stained red,
That his patron's cross might over him wave,
And scare the fiends from the Wizard's grave.

XVI

It was a night of woe and dread,
When Michael in the tomb I laid!
Strange sounds along the chancel passed,
The banners waved without a blast'—
—Still spoke the Monk, when the bell tolled one!—
I tell you, that a braver man
Than William of Deloraine, good at need,
Against a foe ne'er spurred a steed;
Yet somewhat was he chilled with dread,
And his hair did bristle upon his head.

XVII

'Lo, Warrior! now, the Cross of Red
Points to the grave of the mighty dead;
Within it burns a wondrous light,[n]
To chase the spirits that love the night:
That lamp shall burn unquenchably,
Until the eternal doom shall be.'

166 *St. Michael's night*: Michaelmas, 29 Sept. 170 *patron*: St. Michael.
175 *blast*: i.e., of wind. 187 *eternal doom*: Day of Judgement.

Slow moved the Monk to the broad flag-stone,
Which the bloody cross was traced upon:
He pointed to a secret nook;
An iron bar the Warrior took;
And the Monk made a sign with his withered hand,
The grave's huge portal to expand.

XVIII

With beating heart to the task he went;
His sinewy frame o'er the grave-stone bent;
With bar of iron heaved amain,
Till the toil-drops fell from his brows, like rain.
It was by dint of passing strength,
That he moved the massy stone at length.
I would you had been there, to see
How the light broke forth so gloriously,
Streamed upward to the chancel roof,
And through the galleries far aloof!
No earthly flame blazed e'er so bright:
It shone like heaven's own blessed light,
  And, issuing from the tomb,
Showed the Monk's cowl, and visage pale,
Danced on the dark-browed Warrior's mail,
  And kissed his waving plume.

XIX

Before their eyes the Wizard lay,
As if he had not been dead a day,
His hoary beard in silver rolled,
He seemed some seventy winters old;
  A palmer's amice wrapped him round,
  With a wrought Spanish baldric bound,
    Like a pilgrim from beyond the sea:
  His left hand held his Book of Might;
  A silver cross was in his right;
    The lamp was placed beside his knee:
High and majestic was his look,
At which the fellest fiends had shook,
And all unruffled was his face:
They trusted his soul had gotten grace.[n]

214 *amice*: cap, hood or cape of religious orders.

XX

Often had William of Deloraine
Rode through the battle's bloody plain,
And trampled down the warriors slain,
  And neither known remorse nor awe;
Yet now remorse and awe he owned;
His breath came thick, his head swam round,
  When this strange scene of death he saw.
Bewildered and unnerved he stood,
And the priest prayed fervently and loud:
With eyes averted prayed he;
He might not endure the sight to see,
Of the man he had loved so brotherly.

XXI

And when the priest his death-prayer had prayed,
Thus unto Deloraine he said:—
'Now, speed thee what thou hast to do,
Or, Warrior, we may dearly rue;
For those thou mayest not look upon
Are gathering fast round the yawning stone!'
Then Deloraine, in terror, took
From the cold hand the Mighty Book,
With iron clasped, and with iron bound:
He thought, as he took it, the dead man frowned;
But the glare of the sepulchral light,
Perchance, had dazzled the warrior's sight.

XXII

When the huge stone sunk o'er the tomb,
The night returned in double gloom;
For the moon had gone down, and the stars were few,
And, as the Knight and Priest withdrew,
With wavering steps and dizzy brain,
They hardly might the postern gain.
'Tis said, as through the aisles they passed,
They heard strange noises on the blast;
And through the cloister-galleries small,
Which at mid-height thread the chancel wall,
Loud sobs, and laughter louder, ran,
And voices unlike the voice of man;

As if the fiends kept holiday,
Because these spells were brought to day.
I cannot tell how the truth may be;
I say the tale as 'twas said to me.

XXIII

'Now, hie thee hence,' the Father said,
'And when we are on death-bed laid,
O may our dear Ladye, and sweet St. John,
Forgive our souls for the deed we have done!'
  The Monk returned him to his cell,
    And many a prayer and penance sped;
  When the convent met at the noontide bell—
    The Monk of St. Mary's aisle was dead!
Before the cross was the body laid,
With hands clasped fast, as if still he prayed.

XXIV

The Knight breathed free in the morning wind,
And strove his hardihood to find:
He was glad when he passed the tombstones grey,
Which girdle round the fair Abbaye;
For the mystic Book, to his bosom pressed,
Felt like a load upon his breast;
And his joints, with nerves of iron twined,
Shook, like the aspen leaves in wind.
Full fain was he when the dawn of day
Began to brighten Cheviot grey;
He joyed to see the cheerful light,
And he said Ave Mary, as well as he might.

XXV

The sun had brightened Cheviot grey,
  The sun had brightened the Carter's side;
And soon beneath the rising day
  Smiled Branksome towers and Teviot's tide.
The wild birds told their warbling tale,
  And wakened every flower that blows;
And peeped forth the violet pale,
  And spread her breast the mountain rose.

261 *to day*: to daylight. 270 *convent*: company of monks.
287 *Carter*: Carter Fell above Jedburgh, one of the Cheviot hills, situated on the border itself.

And lovelier than the rose so red,
  Yet paler than the violet pale,
She early left her sleepless bed,
  The fairest maid of Teviotdale.

XXVI

Why does fair Margaret so early awake,
  And don her kirtle so hastilie;
And the silken knots, which in hurry she would make,
  Why tremble her slender fingers to tie;
Why does she stop, and look often around,
  As she glides down the secret stair;
And why does she pat the shaggy blood-hound,
  As he rouses him up from his lair;
And, though she passes the postern alone,
Why is not the watchman's bugle blown?

XXVII

The Ladye steps in doubt and dread,
Lest her watchful mother hear her tread;
The Ladye caresses the rough blood-hound,
Lest his voice should waken the castle round;
The watchman's bugle is not blown,
For he was her foster-father's son;
And she glides through the greenwood at dawn of light
To meet Baron Henry, her own true knight.

XXVIII

The Knight and Ladye fair are met,
And under the hawthorn's boughs are set.
A fairer pair were never seen
To meet beneath the hawthorn green.
He was stately, and young, and tall;
Dreaded in battle, and loved in hall:
And she, when love, scarce told, scarce hid,
Lent to her cheek a livelier red;
When the half sigh her swelling breast
Against the silken ribbon prest;
When her blue eyes their secret told,
Though shaded by her locks of gold—

311 *round*: adv., 'those in the castle who were sleeping around her'.
317 *are set*: have sat down.

Where would you find the peerless fair,
With Margaret of Branksome might compare!

XXIX

And now, fair dames, methinks I see
You listen to my minstrelsy;
Your waving locks ye backward throw,
And sidelong bend your necks of snow:
Ye ween to hear a melting tale,
Of two true lovers in a dale;
And how the Knight, with tender fire,
To paint his faithful passion strove;
Swore he might at her feet expire,
But never, never cease to love;
And how she blushed, and how she sighed,
And, half consenting, half denied,
And said that she would die a maid—
Yet, might the bloody feud be stayed,
Henry of Cranstoun, and only he,
Margaret of Branksome's choice should be.

XXX

Alas! fair dames, your hopes are vain!
My harp has lost the enchanting strain;
Its lightness would my age reprove:
My hairs are grey, my limbs are old,
My heart is dead, my veins are cold—
I may not, must not, sing of love.

XXXI

Beneath an oak, mossed o'er by eld,
The Baron's Dwarf[n] his courser held,
And held his crested helm and spear:
That Dwarf was scarce an earthly man,
If the tales were true that of him ran
Through all the Border, far and near.
'Twas said, when the Baron a-hunting rode
Through Reedsdale's glens, but rarely trod,
He heard a voice cry, 'Lost! lost! lost!'
And, like tennis-ball by racket tossed,

A leap, of thirty feet and three,
Made from the gorse this elfin shape,
Distorted like some dwarfish ape,
And lighted at Lord Cranstoun's knee.
Lord Cranstoun was some whit dismayed;
'Tis said that five good miles he rade,
To rid him of his company;
But where he rode one mile, the Dwarf ran four,
And the Dwarf was first at the castle door.

XXXII

Use lessens marvel, it is said:
This elvish Dwarf with the Baron stayed;
Little he ate, and less he spoke,
Nor mingled with the menial flock:
And oft apart his arms he tossed,
And often muttered 'Lost! lost! lost!'
He was waspish, arch, and litherlie,
But well Lord Cranstoun served he:[n]
And he of his service was full fain;
For once he had been ta'en or slain,
An it had not been for his ministry.
All between Home and Hermitage,[n]
Talked of Lord Cranstoun's Goblin-Page.

XXXIII

For the Baron went on pilgrimage,
And took with him this elvish Page,
To Mary's Chapel of the Lowes:
For there, beside our Ladye's lake,
An offering he had sworn to make,
And he would pay his vows.
But the Ladye of Branksome gathered a band
Of the best that would ride at her command:
The trysting place was Newark Lee.
Wat of Harden[n] came thither amain,
And thither came John of Thirlestane,
And thither came William of Deloraine;
They were three hundred spears and three.

377 *litherlie*: idle and mischievous. 381 *an*: if.
386 *Lowes*: Loch of the Lowes (lakes) adjoining St. Mary's Loch, Selkirkshire.
392 *trysting place*: rendezvous.
394 *Thirlestane*: on Ettrick Water, near Buccleuch. 395 *Deloraine*: see p. 284.

Through Douglas-burn, up Yarrow stream,
Their horses prance, their lances gleam.
They came to St. Mary's lake ere day;
But the chapel was void, and the Baron away.
They burned the chapel for very rage,
And cursed Lord Cranstoun's Goblin-Page.

XXXIV

And now, in Branksome's good green wood,
As under the aged oak he stood,
The Baron's courser pricks his ears,
As if a distant noise he hears.
The Dwarf waves his long lean arm on high,
And signs to the lovers to part and fly;
No time was then to vow or sigh.
Fair Margaret through the hazel grove,
Flew like the startled cushat-dove:
The Dwarf the stirrup held and rein;
Vaulted the Knight on his steed amain,
And, pondering deep that morning's scene,
Rode eastward through the hawthorns green.

WHILE thus he poured the lengthened tale,
The Minstrel's voice began to fail:
Full slyly smiled the observant page,
And gave the withered hand of age
A goblet, crowned with mighty wine
The blood of Velez' scorched vine.
He raised the silver cup on high,
And, while the big drop filled his eye,
Prayed God to bless the Duchess long,
And all who cheered a son of song.
The attending maidens smiled to see
How long, how deep, how zealously,
The precious juice the Minstrel quaffed;
And he, emboldened by the draught,
Looked gaily back to them, and laughed.

397 *Douglas-burn*: falls into Yarrow water below St. Mary's Loch.
411 *cushat-dove*: wood-pigeon.
421 *Velez*: in Malaga, Spain.

The cordial nectar of the bowl
Swelled his old veins, and cheered his soul;
A lighter, livelier prelude ran,
Ere thus his tale again began.

Canto Third

I

AND said I that my limbs were old,
And said I that my blood was cold,
And that my kindly fire was fled,
And my poor withered heart was dead,
  And that I might not sing of love?—
How could I to the dearest theme,
That ever warmed a minstrel's dream,
  So foul, so false a recreant prove!
How could I name love's very name,
Nor wake my heart to notes of flame!

II

In peace, Love tunes the shepherd's reed;
In war, he mounts the warrior's steed;
In halls, in gay attire is seen;
In hamlets, dances on the green.
Love rules the court, the camp, the grove,
And men below, and saints above;
For love is heaven, and heaven is love.

III

So thought Lord Cranstoun, as I ween,
While, pondering deep the tender scene,
He rode through Branksome's hawthorn green.
  But the Page shouted wild and shrill,
    And scarce his helmet could he don,
  When downward from the shady hill
    A stately knight came pricking on.
That warrior's steed, so dapple-grey,
Was dark with sweat, and splashed with clay;
  His armour red with many a stain;
He seemed in such a weary plight,
As if he had ridden the live-long night;
  For it was William of Deloraine.

3 *kindly*: natural.

IV

But no whit weary did he seem,
When, dancing in the sunny beam,
He marked the crane[n] on the Baron's crest;
For his ready spear was in his rest.
  Few were the words, and stern and high,
    That marked the foemen's feudal hate;
  For question fierce, and proud reply,
    Gave signal soon of dire debate.
Their very coursers seemed to know
That each was other's mortal foe,
And snorted fire, when wheeled around
To give each knight his vantage-ground.[n]

V

In rapid round the Baron bent;
  He sighed a sigh, and prayed a prayer:
The prayer was to his patron saint,
  The sigh was to his ladye fair.
Stout Deloraine nor sighed nor prayed,
Nor saint, nor ladye, called to aid;
But he stooped his head, and couched his spear,
And spurred his steed to full career.
The meeting of these champions proud
Seemed like the bursting thundercloud.

VI

Stern was the dint the Borderer lent!
The stately Baron backwards bent;
Bent backwards to his horse's tail,
And his plumes went scattering on the gale;
The tough ash spear, so stout and true,
Into a thousand flinders flew.
But Cranstoun's lance, of more avail,
Pierced through, like silk, the Borderer's mail;
Through shield, and jack, and acton, past,
Deep in his bosom broke at last.—
Still sate the warrior saddle-fast,
Till, stumbling in the mortal shock,
Down went the steed, the girthing broke,

34 *rest*: support for spear when in position for charge. 38 *debate*: contest.
61 *jack*: short coat worn under mail. 61 *acton*: stuffed jacket.
65 *girthing*: i.e., 'girth', strap passing under horse to secure saddle.

Hurled on a heap lay man and horse.
The Baron onward passed his course;
Nor knew—so giddy rolled his brain—
His foe lay stretched upon the plain.

VII

But when he reined his courser round,
And saw his foeman on the ground
Lie senseless as the bloody clay,
He bade his page to stanch the wound,
And there beside the warrior stay,
And tend him in his doubtful state,
And lead him to Branksome castle–gate:
His noble mind was inly moved
For the kinsman of the maid he loved.
'This shalt thou do without delay:
No longer here myself may stay;
Unless the swifter I speed away,
Short shrift will be at my dying day.'

VIII

Away in speed Lord Cranstoun rode;
The Goblin Page behind abode;
His lord's command he ne'er withstood,
Though small his pleasure to do good.
As the corslet off he took,
The Dwarf espied the Mighty Book!
Much he marvelled a knight of pride
Like a book-bosomed priest should ride:
He thought not to search or stanch the wound
Until the secret he had found.

IX

The iron band, the iron clasp,
Resisted long the elfin grasp:
For when the first he had undone,
It closed as he the next begun.
Those iron clasps, that iron band,
Would not yield to unchristened hand,
Till he smeared the cover o'er
With the Borderer's curdled gore;[n]

82 *shrift*: confession.

A moment then the volume spread,
And one short spell therein he read:
It had much of glamour might;
Could make a ladye seem a knight;
The cobwebs on a dungeon wall
Seem tapestry in lordly hall;
A nut-shell seem a gilded barge,
A shieling seem a palace large,
And youth seem age, and age seem youth—
All was delusion, nought was truth.

X

He had not read another spell,
When on his cheek a buffet fell,
So fierce, it stretched him on the plain
Beside the wounded Deloraine.
From the ground he rose dismayed,
And shook his huge and matted head;
One word he muttered, and no more,
'Man of age, thou smitest sore!'
No more the Elfin Page[n] durst try
Into the wondrous Book to pry;
The clasps, though smeared with Christian gore,
Shut faster than they were before.
He hid it underneath his cloak.
Now, if you ask who gave the stroke,
I cannot tell, so mot I thrive;
It was not given by man alive.

XI

Unwillingly himself he addressed,
To do his master's high behest:
He lifted up the living corse,
And laid it on the weary horse;
He led him into Branksome hall,
Before the beards of the warders all;
And each did after swear and say
There only passed a wain of hay.
He took him to Lord David's tower,
Even to the Ladye's secret bower;

103 *glamour*: magical delusion. 108 *shieling*: shepherd's hut.
125 *so . . . thrive*: as I hope to thrive.

And, but that stronger spells were spread,
And the door might not be opened,
He had laid him on her very bed.
Whate'er he did of gramarye
Was always done maliciously;
He flung the warrior on the ground,
And the blood welled freshly from the wound.

XII

As he repassed the outer court,
He spied the fair young child at sport:
He thought to train him to the wood;
For at a word, be it understood,
He was always for ill, and never for good.
Seemed to the boy, some comrade gay
Led him forth to the woods to play;
On the drawbridge the warders stout
Saw a terrier and lurcher passing out.

XIII

He led the boy o'er bank and fell,
  Until they came to a woodland brook;
The running stream[n] dissolved the spell,
  And his own elvish shape he took.
Could he have had his pleasure vilde,
He had crippled the joints of the noble child;
Or, with his fingers long and lean,
Had strangled him in fiendish spleen:
But his awful mother he had in dread,
And also his power was limited;
So he but scowled on the startled child,
And darted through the forest wild;
The woodland brook he bounding crossed,
And laughed, and shouted, 'Lost! lost! lost!'

XIV

Full sore amazed at the wondrous change,
  And frightened, as a child might be,
At the wild yell and visage strange,
  And the dark words of gramarye,

137 *but that*: if it were not that. 140 *gramarye*: magic.
146 *train*: draw. 157 *vilde*: vile.

The child, amidst the forest bower,
Stood rooted like a lily flower;
  And when at length, with trembling pace,
    He sought to find where Branksome lay,
  He feared to see that grisly face
    Glare from some thicket on his way.
Thus, starting oft, he journeyed on,
And deeper in the wood is gone,—
For aye the more he sought his way,
The farther still he went astray,—
Until he heard the mountains round
Ring to the baying of a hound.

XV

And hark! and hark! the deep-mouthed bark
  Comes nigher still, and nigher:
Bursts on the path a dark blood-hound;
His tawny muzzle tracked the ground,
  And his red eye shot fire.
Soon as the wildered child saw he,
He flew at him right furiouslie.
I ween you would have seen with joy
The bearing of the gallant boy,
When, worthy of his noble sire,
His wet cheek glowed 'twixt fear and ire!
He faced the blood-hound manfully,
And held his little bat on high;
So fierce he struck, the dog, afraid,
At cautious distance hoarsely bayed,
  But still in act to spring;
When dashed an archer through the glade,
And when he saw the hound was stayed,
  He drew his tough bow-string;
But a rough voice cried, 'Shoot not, hoy!
Ho! shoot not, Edward; 'tis a boy!'

XVI

The speaker issued from the wood,
And checked his fellow's surly mood,

177 *starting*: i.e., with fright.
188 *wildered*: lost in the wilds.

And quelled the ban-dog's ire:
He was an English yeoman good,
And born in Lancashire.
Well could he hit a fallow-deer
Five hundred feet him fro;
With hand more true, and eye more clear,
No archer bended bow.
His coal-black hair, shorn round and close,
Set off his sun-burned face:
Old England's sign, St. George's cross,
His barret-cap did grace;
His bugle-horn hung by his side,
All in a wolf-skin baldric tied;
And his short falchion, sharp and clear,
Had pierced the throat of many a deer.

XVII

His kirtle, made of forest green,
Reached scantly to his knee;
And, at his belt, of arrows keen
A furbished sheaf bore he;
His buckler, scarce in breadth a span,
No larger fence had he;
He never counted him a man
Would strike below the knee:
His slackened bow was in his hand,
And the leash that was his blood-hound's band.

XVIII

He would not do the fair child harm,
But held him with his powerful arm,
That he might neither fight nor flee;
For when the Red-Cross spied he,
The boy strove long and violently.
'Now, by St. George,' the archer cries,
'Edward, methinks we have a prize!
This boy's fair face, and courage free,
Show he is come of high degree.'—

206 *ban-dog*: mastiff (see I. 137). 216 *barret-cap*: flat archer's cap.
226 *fence*: shield.

XIX

'Yes! I am come of high degree,
  For I am the heir of bold Buccleuch;
And, if thou dost not set me free,
  False Southron, thou shalt dearly rue!
For Walter of Harden shall come with speed,
And William of Deloraine, good at need,
And every Scott from Esk to Tweed;
And, if thou dost not let me go,
Despite thy arrows and thy bow,
I'll have thee hanged to feed the crow!'

XX

'Gramercy for thy good-will, fair boy!
My mind was never set so high;
But if thou art chief of such a clan,
And art the son of such a man,
And ever comest to thy command,
  Our wardens had need to keep good order;
My bow of yew to a hazel wand,
  Thou'lt make them work upon the Border.
Meantime, be pleased to come with me,
For good Lord Dacre shalt thou see;
I think our work is well begun,
When we have taken thy father's son.'

XXI

Although the child was led away,
In Branksome still he seemed to stay,
For so the Dwarf his part did play;
And in the shape of that young boy,
He wrought the castle much annoy.
The comrades of the young Buccleuch
He pinched, and beat, and overthrew;
Nay, some of them he wellnigh slew.
He tore Dame Maudlin's silken tire,
And as Sym Hall stood by the fire,
He lighted the match of his bandolier,
And woefully scorched the hackbuteer.

255 *wardens*: guardians of the Border.
273 *hackbuteer*: harquebusier (type of musketeer).

It may be hardly thought or said,
The mischief that the urchin made,
Till many of the castle guessed,
That the young Baron was possessed!

XXII

Well I ween the charm he held
The noble Ladye had soon dispelled;
But she was deeply busied then
To tend the wounded Deloraine.
  Much she wondered to find him lie
    On the stone threshold stretched along;
  She thought some spirit of the sky
    Had done the bold moss-trooper wrong;
Because, despite her precept dread,
Perchance he in the Book had read;
But the broken lance in his bosom stood,
And it was earthly steel and wood.

XXIII

She drew the splinter from the wound,
  And with a charm she stanched the blood;
She bade the gash be cleansed and bound:
  No longer by his couch she stood;
But she has ta'en the broken lance,
  And washed it from the clotted gore,
  And salved the splinter[n] o'er and o'er.
William of Deloraine, in trance,
  Whene'er she turned it round and round,
  Twisted as if she galled his wound.
    Then to her maidens she did say
  That he should be whole man and sound
    Within the course of a night and day.
Full long she toiled; for she did rue
Mishap to friend so stout and true.

XXIV

So passed the day; the evening fell,
'Twas near the time of curfew bell;
The air was mild, the wind was calm,
The stream was smooth, the dew was balm;

E'en the rude watchman on the tower
Enjoyed and blessed the lovely hour.
Far more fair Margaret loved and blessed
The hour of silence and of rest.
On the high turret sitting lone,
She waked at times the lute's soft tone;
Touched a wild note, and all between
Thought of the bower of hawthorns green.
Her golden hair streamed free from band,
Her fair cheek rested on her hand,
Her blue eyes sought the west afar,
For lovers love the western star.

XXV

Is yon the star, o'er Penchryst Pen,
That rises slowly to her ken,
And, spreading broad its wavering light,
Shakes its loose tresses on the night?
Is yon red glare the western star?
O, 'tis the beacon-blaze of war!
Scarce could she draw her tightened breath,
For well she knew the fire of death!

XXVI

The Warder viewed it blazing strong,
And blew his war-note loud and long,
Till, at the high and haughty sound,
Rock, wood, and river rung around.
The blast alarmed the festal hall,
And startled forth the warriors all;
Far downward, in the castle-yard,
Full many a torch and cresset glared;
And helms and plumes, confusedly tossed,
Were in the blaze half-seen, half-lost;
And spears in wild disorder shook,
Like reeds beside a frozen brook.

XXVII

The Seneschal, whose silver hair
Was reddened by the torches' glare,

321 *Penchryst Pen*: hill not far from Branxholm, to the E. of the Teviot valley.

Stood in the midst with gesture proud,
And issued forth his mandates loud:
'On Penchryst glows a bale of fire,[n]
And three are kindling on Priesthaughswire;
    Ride out, ride out,
    The foe to scout!
Mount, mount for Branksome, every man!
Thou, Todrig, warn the Johnstone clan,
    That ever are true and stout—
Ye need not send to Liddesdale,
For when they see the blazing bale,
Elliots and Armstrongs never fail—
Ride, Alton, ride, for death and life!
And warn the Warden of the strife.
Young Gilbert, let our beacon blaze,
Our kin, and clan, and friends to raise.'

XXVIII

Fair Margaret from the turret head
Heard, far below, the coursers' tread,
  While loud the harness rung,
As to their seats, with clamour dread,
  The ready horsemen sprung:
And trampling hoofs, and iron coats,
And leaders' voices, mingled notes,
    And out! and out!
    In hasty rout,
  The horsemen galloped forth;
Dispersing to the south to scout,
  And east, and west, and north,
To view their coming enemies,
And warn their vassals and allies.

XXIX

The ready page, with hurried hand,
Awaked the need-fire's slumbering brand,
  And ruddy blushed the heaven:
For a sheet of flame from the turret high
Waved like a blood-flag on the sky,
  All flaring and uneven;

346 *Priesthaughswire*: slightly to the S. of Penchryst Pen.
349 *mount . . . Branksome*: the Scotts' gathering-word.
374 *need-fire*: beacon.

And soon a score of fires, I ween,
From height, and hill, and cliff, were seen;
Each with warlike tidings fraught;
Each from each the signal caught;
Each after each they glanced to sight,
As stars arise upon the night.
They gleamed on many a dusky tarn,
Haunted by the lonely earn;
On many a cairn's grey pyramid,
Where urns of mighty chiefs lie hid;
Till high Dunedin the blazes saw
From Soltra and Dumpender Law;
And Lothian heard the Regent's order
That all should bowne them for the Border.

XXX

The livelong night in Branksome rang
  The ceaseless sound of steel;
The castle-bell, with backward clang,[n]
  Sent forth the larum peal;
Was frequent heard the heavy jar,
Where massy stone and iron bar
Were piled on echoing keep and tower,
To whelm the foe with deadly shower;
Was frequent heard the changing guard,
And watch-word from the sleepless ward;
While, wearied by the endless din,
Blood-hound and ban-dog yelled within.

XXXI

The noble Dame, amid the broil,
Shared the grey Seneschal's high toil,
And spoke of danger with a smile;
  Cheered the young knights, and council sage
Held with the chiefs of riper age.
No tidings of the foe were brought,
Nor of his numbers knew they aught,

386 *earn*: eagle.
390 *Soltra*: Soutra Hill in E. Lothian, the most westerly ridge of the Lammermuir hills.
390 *Dumpender Law*: Traprain Law, in Prestonkirk parish, Haddington.
391 *Regent*: Mary of Guise, mother of Mary Queen of Scots.
392 *bowne*: prepare. 402 *ward*: guard.

Nor what in time of truce he sought.
  Some said that there were thousands ten;
And others weened that it was nought
  But Leven clans, or Tynedale men,
Who came to gather in black-mail;
And Liddesdale, with small avail,
  Might drive them lightly back again.
So passed the anxious night away,
And welcome was the peep of day.

CEASED the high sound—the listening throng
Applaud the Master of the Song;
And marvel much, in helpless age,
So hard should be his pilgrimage.
Had he no friend—no daughter dear,
His wandering toil to share and cheer;
No son to be his father's stay,
And guide him on the rugged way?
'Ay, once he had—but he was dead!'—
Upon the harp he stopped his head,
And busied himself the strings withal,
To hide the tear that fain would fall.
In solemn measure, soft and slow,
Arose a father's notes of woe.

Canto Fourth

I

SWEET Teviot! on thy silver tide
  The glaring bale-fires blaze no more;
No longer steel-clad warriors ride
  Along thy wild and willowed shore;
Where'er thou wind'st, by dale or hill,
All, all is peaceful, all is still,
  As if thy waves, since Time was born,
Since first they rolled upon the Tweed,
Had only heard the shepherd's reed,
  Nor started at the bugle-horn.

415 *Leven*: river in NW. Yorkshire.
415 *Tynedale*: in Northumberland.
416 *black-mail*: protection money. 2 *bale-fires*: beacons.

II

Unlike the tide of human time,
  Which, though it change in ceaseless flow,
Retains each grief, retains each crime
  Its earliest course was doomed to know;
And, darker as it downward bears,
Is stained with past and present tears.
  Low as that tide has ebbed with me,
It still reflects to Memory's eye
The hour my brave, my only boy
  Fell by the side of great Dundee.[n]
Why, when the volleying musket played
Against the bloody Highland blade,
Why was not I beside him laid!
Enough—he died the death of fame;
Enough—he died with conquering Græme.

III

Now over Border dale and fell
  Full wide and far was terror spread;
For pathless marsh, and mountain cell,
  The peasant left his lowly shed.
The frightened flocks and herds were pent
Beneath the peel's rude battlement;
And maids and matrons dropped the tear,
While ready warriors seized the spear.
From Branksome's towers, the watchman's eye
Dun wreaths of distant smoke can spy,
Which, curling in the rising sun,
Showed southern ravage was begun.

IV

Now loud the heedful gate-ward cried—
  'Prepare ye all for blows and blood!
Watt Tinlinn, from the Liddel-side,
  Comes wading through the flood.
Full oft the Tynedale snatchers knock
At his lone gate, and prove the lock;

37 *southern*: i.e., by southerners.
40 *Watt Tinlinn*: a retainer of the Buccleuchs.
42 *snatchers*: cattle-lifters. 43 *prove*: try.

It was but last St. Barnabright[n]
They sieged him a whole summer night,
But fled at morning; well they knew
In vain he never twanged the yew.
Right sharp has been the evening shower
That drove him from his Liddel tower;
And, by my faith,' the gate-ward said,
'I think 'twill prove a Warden-Raid.'

V

While thus he spoke, the bold yeoman
Entered the echoing barbican.
He led a small and shaggy nag,
That through a bog, from hag to hag,
Could bound like any Billhope stag.
It bore his wife and children twain;
A half-clothed serf was all their train;
His wife, stout, ruddy, and dark-browed,
Of silver brooch and bracelet proud,
Laughed to her friends among the crowd.
He was of stature passing tall,
But sparely formed, and lean withal;
A battered morion on his brow;
A leather jack, as fence enow,
On his broad shoulders loosely hung;
A border axe behind was slung;
His spear, six Scottish ells in length,
  Seemed newly dyed with gore;
His shafts and bow, of wondrous strength,
  His hardy partner bore.

VI

Thus to the Ladye did Tinlinn show
The tidings of the English foe:
'Belted Will Howard[n] is marching here,
And hot Lord Dacre[n], with many a spear,

47 *twanged*: bent his bow.
51 *Warden-Raid*: 'an inroad commanded by the warden in person' (S).
53 *barbican*: see I. 261. 55 *hag*: firm place in bog.
56 *Billhope*: place in Liddesdale, famous for game.
64 *morion*: open helmet. 65 *jack*: see III. 61.
68 *Scottish ell*: 37 inches.

And all the German hackbut-men,
Who have long lain at Askerten:
They crossed the Liddel at curfew hour,
And burned my little lonely tower:
The fiend receive their souls therefor!
It had not been burnt this year and more.
Barn-yard and dwelling, blazing bright,
Served to guide me on my flight;
But I was chased the livelong night.
Black John of Akeshaw and Fergus Græme[n]
Fast upon my traces came,
Until I turned at Priesthaugh Scrogg,
And shot their horses in the bog,
Slew Fergus with my lance outright—
I had him long at high despite:
He drove my cows last Fastern's night.'

VII

Now weary scouts from Liddesdale,
Fast hurrying in, confirmed the tale;
As far as they could judge by ken,
Three hours would bring to Teviot's strand
Three thousand armed Englishmen;
Meanwhile, full many a warlike band,
From Teviot, Aill, and Ettrick shade,
Came in, their Chief's defence to aid.
There was saddling and mounting in haste,
There was pricking o'er moor and lea;
He that was last at the trysting-place
Was but lightly held of his gay ladye.[n]

VIII

From fair St. Mary's silver wave,
From dreary Gamescleugh's[n] dusky height,
His ready lances Thirlestane brave
Arrayed beneath a banner bright.

76 *hackbut-men*: see III. 273.
77 *Askerten*: castle in Northumberland some 17 miles NE. of Carlisle.
87 *Priesthaugh*: see III. 346. 87 *Scrogg*: area of brushwood.
90 *had . . . despite*: hated.
91 *Fastern's night*: the evening before the fast (Lent), Shrove-Tuesday.
94 *ken*: observation.
98 *Teviot, Aill, Ettrick*: see map, p. 281.
101 *pricking*: spurring. 104 *St. Mary's*: see map, p. 281.

The tressured fleur-de-luce he claims
To wreathe his shield, since royal James,
Encamped by Fala's mossy wave,[n]
The proud distinction grateful gave,
  For faith 'mid feudal jars;
What time, save Thirlestane alone,
Of Scotland's stubborn barons none
  Would march to southern wars;
And hence, in fair remembrance worn,
Yon sheaf of spears his crest has borne;
Hence his high motto shines revealed—
'Ready, aye ready' for the field.

IX

An aged Knight, to danger steeled,
  With many a moss-trooper came on;
And azure in a golden field,
The stars and crescent graced his shield,
  Without the bend of Murdieston.[n]
Wide lay his lands round Oakwood[n] tower,
And wide round haunted Castle-Ower;
High over Borthwick's mountain flood
His wood-embosomed mansion stood;
In the dark glen, so deep below,
The herds of plundered England low—
His bold retainers' daily food,
And bought with danger, blows, and blood.
Marauding chief! his sole delight
The moonlight raid, the morning fight;
Not even the Flower of Yarrow's[n] charms,
In youth, might tame his rage for arms;
And still, in age, he spurned at rest,
And still his brows the helmet pressed,
Albeit the blanched locks below
Were white as Dinlay's spotless snow;

108 *tressured*: arranged in twisted border.
120 *aged Knight*: Walter Scott of Harden, a freebooting ancestor of the poet.
124 *bend* (herald.): space enclosed by diagonal parallel lines from top right to bottom left corner of the shield.
125 *Oakwood tower*: on the right bank of Ettrick Water, 4½ miles SW. of Selkirk.
126 *Castle-Ower*: a Roman camp in Eskdalemuir parish, NE. Dumfriesshire.
127 *Borthwick*: see I. 266. 140 *Dinlay*: hill in Liddesdale.

Five stately warriors drew the sword
Before their father's band;
A braver knight than Harden's lord
Ne'er belted on a brand.

X

Scotts of Eskdale, a stalwart band[n],
Came trooping down the Todshawhill;
By the sword they won their land,
And by the sword they hold it still.
Hearken, Ladye, to the tale,
How thy sires won fair Eskdale.

Earl Morton was lord of that valley fair;
The Beattisons were his vassals there.
The Earl was gentle, and mild of mood;
The vassals were warlike, and fierce, and rude;
High of heart, and haughty of word,
Little they recked of a tame liege lord.
The Earl into fair Eskdale came,
Homage and seigniory to claim:
Of Gilbert the Galliard a heriot he sought,
Saying, 'Give thy best steed, as a vassal ought.'—
'Dear to me is my bonny white steed,
Oft has he helped me at pinch of need;
Lord and Earl though thou be, I trow
I can rein Bucksfoot better than thou.'
Word on word gave fuel to fire,
Till so highly blazed the Beattison's ire,
But that the Earl the flight had ta'en,
The vassals there their lord had slain.
Sore he plied both whip and spur,
As he urged his steed through Eskdale muir;
And it fell down a weary weight,
Just on the threshold of Branksome gate.

XI

The Earl was a wrathful man to see,
Full fain avenged would he be.

146 *Todshawhill*: 1¼ miles NW. of Branxholm.
151 *Morton*: title assumed by the Lords Maxwell in 16th century.
159 *Galliard*: gay gallant.
159 *heriot*: render of best live beast on a tenant's decease.

In haste to Branksome's Lord he spoke,
Saying—'Take these traitors to thy yoke;
For a cast of hawks, and a purse of gold,
All Eskdale I'll sell thee, to have and hold:
Beshrew thy heart, of the Beattisons' clan
If thou leavest on Esk a landed man;
But spare Woodkerrick's[n] lands alone,
For he lent me his horse to escape upon.'
A glad man then was Branksome bold,
Down he flung him the purse of gold;
To Eskdale soon he spurred amain,
And with him five hundred riders has ta'en.
He left his merrymen in the mist of the hill,
And bade them hold them close and still;
And alone he wended to the plain,
To meet with the Galliard and all his train.
To Gilbert the Galliard thus he said:
'Know thou me for thy liege-lord and head;
Deal not with me as with Morton tame,
For Scotts play best at the roughest game.
Give me in peace my heriot due,
Thy bonny white steed, or thou shalt rue.
If my horn I three times wind,
Eskdale shall long have the sound in mind.'

XII

Loudly the Beattison laughed in scorn;
'Little care we for thy winded horn.
Ne'er shall it be the Galliard's lot
To yield his steed to a haughty Scott.
Wend thou to Branksome back on foot
With rusty spur and miry boot.'—
He blew his bugle so loud and hoarse,
That the dun deer started at fair Craikcross;
He blew again so loud and clear,
Through the grey mountain-mist there did lances appear;

177 *cast*: number of hawks let go at once from hand.
179 *beshrew*: may a curse fall on.
180 *Esk*: river of E. Dumfriesshire which finally passes off into Cumberland and flows into the head of the Solway Firth.
206 *Craikcross*: see I. 154.

And the third blast rang with such a din,
That the echoes answered from Pentoun-linn,
And all his riders came lightly in.
Then had you seen a gallant shock,
When saddles were emptied and lances broke!
For each scornful word the Galliard had said,
A Beattison on the field was laid.
His own good sword the chieftain drew,
And he bore the Galliard through and through;
Where the Beattisons' blood mixed with the rill,
The Galliard's Haugh men call it still.
The Scotts have scattered the Beattison clan,
In Eskdale they left but one landed man.
The valley of Esk, from the mouth to the source,
Was lost and won for that bonny white horse.—

XIII

Whitslade[n] the Hawk, and Headshaw came,
And warriors more than I may name;
From Yarrow-cleugh to Hindhaughswair,
  From Woodhouselie to Chester-glen,
Trooped man and horse, and bow and spear;
  Their gathering word was Bellenden.[n]
And better hearts o'er Border sod
To siege or rescue never rode.
  The Ladye marked the aids come in,
    And high her heart of pride arose:
  She bade her youthful son attend,
  That he might know his father's friend,
    And learn to face his foes.
  'The boy is ripe to look on war;
    I saw him draw a cross-bow stiff,
  And his true arrow struck afar
    The raven's nest upon the cliff;

210 *linn*: waterfall.
219 *Haugh*: flat land by river.
221 *one man*: i.e., Woodkerrick.
226 *cleugh*: (1) precipice, (2) narrow hollow between steep banks.
226 *swair*: descent of a hill.
227 *Woodhouselie*: a house on the border.
227 *Chester-glen*: in Ancrum parish, Roxburghshire.
229 *Bellenden*: Scott rendezvous near head of Borthwick water.

The red cross on a southern breast
Is broader than the raven's nest:
Thou, Whitslade, shalt teach him his weapon to wield,
And o'er him hold his father's shield.'

XIV

Well may you think the wily page
Cared not to face the Ladye sage.
He counterfeited childish fear,
And shrieked, and shed full many a tear,
And moaned and plained in manner wild.
The attendants to the Ladye told
Some fairy, sure, had changed the child,
That wont to be so free and bold.
Then wrathful was the noble dame;
She blushed blood-red for very shame:
'Hence! ere the clan his faintness view;
Hence with the weakling to Buccleuch!
Watt Tinlinn, thou shalt be his guide
To Rangleburn's lonely side.[n]
Sure some fell fiend has cursed our line,
That coward should e'er be son of mine!'

XV

A heavy task Watt Tinlinn had,
To guide the counterfeited lad.
Soon as the palfrey felt the weight
Of that ill-omened elfish freight,
He bolted, sprung, and reared amain,
Nor heeded bit, nor curb, nor rein.
It cost Wat Tinlinn mickle toil
To drive him but a Scottish mile;
But as a shallow brook they crossed,
The elf, amid the running stream,
His figure changed, like form in dream,
And fled, and shouted, 'Lost lost! lost!'
Full fast the urchin ran and laughed,
But faster still a cloth-yard shaft

262 *counterfeited*: i.e., counterfeit.
268 *Scottish mile*: nine English miles equalled eight Scottish miles.
270 see above, III. 155.
274 *shaft*: arrow as long as a yard for measuring cloth, shot from a long bow.

Whistled from startled Tinlinn's yew,
And pierced his shoulder through and through.
Although the imp might not be slain,
And though the wound soon healed again,
Yet, as he ran, he yelled for pain;
And Watt of Tinlinn, much aghast,
Rode back to Branksome fiery fast.

XVI

Soon on the hill's steep verge he stood,
That looks o'er Branksome's towers and wood;
And martial murmurs, from below,
Proclaimed the approaching southern foe.
Through the dark wood, in mingled tone,
Were Border pipes and bugles blown;
The coursers' neighing he could ken,
A measured tread of marching men;
While broke at times the solemn hum
The Almayn's sullen kettle-drum;
  And banners tall of crimson sheen
    Above the copse appear;
  And, glistening through the hawthorns green,
    Shine helm, and shield, and spear.

XVII

Light forayers, first, to view the ground,
Spurred their fleet coursers loosely round;
  Behind, in close array, and fast,
    The Kendal archers, all in green,
  Obedient to the bugle blast,
    Advancing from the wood were seen.
To back and guard the archer band,
Lord Dacre's bill-men were at hand:
A hardy race, on Irthing bred,
With kirtles white, and crosses red,

291 *Almayn*: German.
297 *loosely*: in loose formation. 299 *Kendal*: in Westmorland.
302 *back*: support.
304 *Irthing*: small river flowing for some distance along the boundary between Cumberland and Northumberland.

Arrayed beneath the banner tall,
That streamed o'er Acre's conquered wall;
And minstrels, as they marched in order,
Played 'Noble Lord Dacre, he dwells on the Border.'

XVIII

Behind the English bill and bow,
The mercenaries, firm and slow,
  Moved on to fight, in dark array,
By Conrad led of Wolfenstein,
Who brought the band from distant Rhine,
  And sold their blood for foreign pay.
The camp their home, their law the sword,
They knew no country, owned no lord:
They were not armed like England's sons,
But bore the levin-darting guns;
Buff coats, all frounced and 'broidered o'er,
And morsing-horns and scarfs they wore;
Each better knee was bared, to aid
The warriors in the escalade;
All as they marched, in rugged tongue,
Songs of Teutonic feuds they sung.

XIX

But louder still the clamour grew,
And louder still the minstrels blew,
When, from beneath the greenwood tree,
Rode forth Lord Howard's chivalry;
His men-at-arms, with glaive and spear,
Brought up the battle's glittering rear.
There many a youthful knight, full keen
To gain his spurs, in arms was seen;
With favour in his crest, or glove,
Memorial of his ladye-love.
So rode they forth in fair array,
Till full their lengthened lines display;
Then called a halt, and made a stand,
And cried 'St. George, for merry England!'

307 *Acre*: see end-note on lines 492–5, p. 287.
319 *levin*: lightning. 320 *frounced*: pleated.
321 *morsing-horns*: powder-flasks. 322 *better*: right.
331 *battle*: army. 337 *display*: deploy.

XX

Now every English eye, intent
On Branksome's armed towers was bent;
So near they were, that they might know
The straining harsh of each cross-bow;
On battlement and bartizan
Gleamed axe, and spear, and partisan;
Falcon and culver, on each tower,
Stood prompt their deadly hail to shower;
And flashing armour frequent broke
From eddying whirls of sable smoke,
Where upon tower and turret-head,
The seething pitch and molten lead
Reeked, like a witch's cauldron red.
While yet they gaze, the bridges fall,
The wicket opes, and from the wall
Rides forth the hoary Seneschal.

XXI

Armed he rode, all save the head,
His white beard o'er his breast-plate spread;
Unbroke by age, erect his seat,
He ruled his eager courser's bait;
Forced him, with chastened fire to prance,
And, high curvetting, slow advance;
In sign of truce, his better hand
Displayed a peeled willow wand;
His squire, attending in the rear,
Bore high a gauntlet on a spear.[n]
When they espied him riding out,
Lord Howard and Lord Dacre stout
Sped to the front of their array,
To hear what this old knight should say.

XXII

'Ye English warden lords, of you
Demands the Ladye of Buccleuch,
Why, 'gainst the truce of Border tide,
In hostile guise ye dare to ride,

344 *bartizan*: battlemented parapet.
345 *partisan*: long-handled spear like a halberd.
346 *Falcon, culver*: names of small cannon. 353 *bridges*: drawbridges.
372 *Border tide*: time during which no feud was to be prosecuted.

With Kendal bow, and Gilsland brand,
And all yon mercenary band,
Upon the bounds of fair Scotland?
My Ladye reads you swith return;
And, if but one poor straw you burn
Or do our towers so much molest
As scare one swallow from her nest,
St. Mary! but we'll light a brand
Shall warm your hearths in Cumberland.'

XXIII

A wrathful man was Dacre's lord,
But calmer Howard took the word:
'May't please thy Dame, Sir Seneschal,
To seek the castle's outward wall,
Our pursuivant-at-arms shall show
Both why we came, and when we go.'
The message sped, the noble Dame
To the wall's outward circle came;
Each chief around leaned on his spear
To see the pursuivant appear.
All in Lord Howard's livery dressed,
The lion argent decked his breast;
He led a boy of blooming hue—
O sight to meet a mother's view!
It was the heir of great Buccleuch.
Obeisance meet the herald made,
And thus his master's will he said:

XXIV

'It irks, high Dame, my noble Lords,
'Gainst ladye fair to draw their swords;
But yet they may not tamely see,
All through the Western Wardenry,
Your law-contemning kinsmen ride,
And burn and spoil the Border-side;
And ill beseems your rank and birth
To make your towers a flemens-firth.

377 *reads*: advises. 377 *swith*: quickly.
394 *lion argent*: the silver emblem of the Howards.
407 *flemens-firth*: asylum for outlaws.

We claim from thee William of Deloraine,
That he may suffer march-treason pain.
It was but last St. Cuthbert's even
He pricked to Stapleton on Leven,
Harried the lands of Richard Musgrave,
And slew his brother by dint of glaive.
Then, since a lone and widowed Dame
These restless riders may not tame,
Either receive within thy towers
Two hundred of my master's powers,
Or straight they sound their warrison,
And storm and spoil thy garrison:
And this fair boy, to London led,
Shall good King Edward's page be bred.'

XXV

He ceased—and loud the boy did cry,
And stretched his little arms on high;
Implored for aid each well-known face,
And strove to seek the Dame's embrace.
A moment changed that Ladye's cheer,
Gushed to her eye the unbidden tear;
She gazed upon the leaders round,
And dark and sad each warrior frowned;
Then, deep within her sobbing breast
She locked the struggling sigh to rest;
Unaltered and collected stood,
And thus replied in dauntless mood:

XXVI

'Say to your Lords of high emprize,
Who war on women and on boys,
That either William of Deloraine
Will cleanse him by oath[n] of march-treason stain,
Or else he will the combat take
'Gainst Musgrave, for his honour's sake.

409 *march-treason*: breach of border law.
410 *St. Cuthbert*: *c.* 635–687, sometime prior of Melrose.
411 *Leven*: Line, a Cumberland stream flowing into Solway Firth.
413 *dint of glaive*: sword-blow.
418 *warrison*: note of assault (a word-coinage).
421 *King Edward*: Edward VI (*regn.* 1547–53).

No knight in Cumberland so good,
But William may count with him kin and blood.
Knighthood he took of Douglas' sword,
When English blood swelled Ancrum's ford;
And but Lord Dacre's steed was wight,
And bare him ably in the flight,
Himself had seen him dubbed a knight.
For the young heir of Branksome's line,
God be his aid, and God be mine;
Through me no friend shall meet his doom;
Here, while I live, no foe finds room.
  Then, if thy Lords their purpose urge,
    Take our defiance loud and high;
  Our slogan is their lyke-wake dirge,
    Our moat the grave where they shall lie.'

XXVII

Proud she looked round, applause to claim—
Then lightened Thirlestane's eye of flame;
  His bugle Wat of Harden blew;
Pensils and pennons wide were flung,
To heaven the Border slogan rung,
  'St. Mary for the young Buccleuch!'
The English war-cry answered wide,
  And forward bent each southern spear;
Each Kendal archer made a stride,
  And drew the bowstring to his ear;
Each minstrel's war-note loud was blown;
But, ere a grey-goose shaft had flown,
  A horseman galloped from the rear.

XXVIII

'Ah! noble Lords!' he breathless said,
'What treason has your march betrayed?
What make you here, from aid so far,
Before you walls, around you war?
Your foemen triumph in the thought
That in the toils the lion's caught.

441 *count . . . blood*: show as good a pedigree.
443 *Ancrum*: a Scottish victory: see above p. 16, n. 17.
444 *wight*: strong. 447 *for*: as for.
453 *slogan*: battle-cry. 453 *lyke-wake*: night watch over corpse.
458 *pensil*: diminutive of pennon.

Already on dark Ruberslaw[n]
The Douglas holds his weaponschaw;
The lances, waving in his train,
Clothe the dun heath like autumn grain;
And on the Liddel's northern strand,
To bar retreat to Cumberland,
Lord Maxwell ranks his merry-men good,
Beneath the eagle and the rood;
  And Jedwood, Eske, and Teviotdale,
    Have to proud Angus come;
  And all the Merse[n] and Lauderdale
    Have risen with haughty Home.
  An exile from Northumberland,
    In Liddesdale I've wandered long;
  But still my heart was with merry England,
    And cannot brook my country's wrong;
And hard I've spurred all night, to show
The mustering of the coming foe.'

XXIX

'And let them come!' fierce Dacre cried;
'For soon yon crest, my father's pride,
That swept the shores of Judah's sea,
And waved in gales of Galilee,[n]
From Branksome's highest towers displayed,
Shall mock the rescue's lingering aid!—
Level each harquebuss on row;
Draw, merry archers, draw the bow;
Up, bill-men, to the walls, and cry,
Dacre for England, win or die!'

XXX

'Yet hear,' quoth Howard, 'calmly hear,
Nor deem my words the words of fear:
For who, in field or foray slack,
Saw the blanche lion e'er fall back?

475 *weaponschaw*: 'the military array of a county' (S).
484 *Lauderdale*: the basin of Leader water and its tributaries, in Berwickshire.
485 *Home*: title of Douglas, pronounced 'Hume'.
493 *father*: i.e., forefather.
494 *Judah's sea*: sea of Galilee.
505 *blanche lion*: the Howards' heraldic emblem.

But thus to risk our Border flower
In strife against a kingdom's power,
Ten thousand Scots 'gainst thousands three,
Certes, were desperate policy.
Nay, take the terms the Ladye made,
Ere conscious of the advancing aid:
Let Musgrave meet fierce Deloraine
In single fight, and, if he gain,
He gains for us; but if he's crossed,
'Tis but a single warrior lost:
The rest, retreating as they came,
Avoid defeat, and death, and shame.'

XXXI

Ill could the haughty Dacre brook
His brother Warden's sage rebuke;
And yet his forward step he stayed,
And slow and sullenly obeyed.
But ne'er again the Border side
Did these two lords in friendship ride;
And this slight discontent, men say,
Cost blood upon another day.

XXXII

The pursuivant-at-arms again
  Before the castle took his stand;
His trumpet called, with parleying strain,
  The leaders of the Scottish band;
And he defied, in Musgrave's right,
Stout Deloraine to single fight;
A gauntlet at their feet he laid,
And thus the terms of fight he said:
'If in the lists good Musgrave's sword
  Vanquish the Knight of Deloraine,
Your youthful chieftain, Branksome's Lord,
  Shall hostage for his clan remain:
If Deloraine foil good Musgrave,
The boy his liberty shall have.
  Howe'er it falls, the English band,
Unharming Scots, by Scots unharmed,
In peaceful march, like men unarmed,
  Shall straight retreat to Cumberland.'

510 *made*: i.e., offered. 530 *in Musgrave's right*: on Musgrave's behalf.

XXXIII

Unconscious of the near relief,
The proffer pleased each Scottish chief,
  Though much the Ladye sage gainsaid;
For though their hearts were brave and true,
From Jedwood's recent sack they knew
  How tardy was the Regent's aid:
And you may guess the noble Dame
  Durst not the secret prescience own,
Sprung from the art she might not name,
  By which the coming help was known.[n]
Closed was the compact, and agreed
That lists should be enclosed with speed,
  Beneath the castle, on a lawn:
They fixed the morrow for the strife,
On foot, with Scottish axe and knife,
  At the fourth hour from peep of dawn;
When Deloraine, from sickness freed,
Or else a champion in his stead,
Should for himself and chieftain stand
Against stout Musgrave, hand to hand.

XXXIV

I know right well, that, in their lay,
Full many minstrels sing and say,
  Such combat should be made on horse,
On foaming steed, in full career,
With brand to aid, when as the spear
  Should shiver in the course:
But he, the jovial Harper,[n] taught
Me, yet a youth, how it was fought,
  In guise which now I say;
He knew each ordinance and clause
Of Black Lord Archibald's battle-laws,
  In the old Douglas' day.

548 *sack*: Jedburgh was sacked by the Earl of Hertford (later Duke of Somerset) in 1545.

549 *Regent*: the Earl of Arran. During Mary Queen of Scots' infancy, he was regent from 1542 to 1553.

552 *art . . . name*: magic.

574 *battle laws*: statutes and ordinances regulating Border warfare drawn up in the time of Archibald Earl of Douglas (d. 1401) called the 'Black Douglas' and surnamed 'the Grim'.

He brooked not, he, that scoffing tongue
Should tax his minstrelsy with wrong,
  Or call his song untrue:
For this, when they the goblet plied,
And such rude taunt had chafed his pride,
  The Bard of Reull he slew.
On Teviot's side, in fight they stood,
And tuneful hands were stained with blood;
Where still the thorn's white branches wave,
Memorial o'er his rival's grave.

XXXV

Why should I tell the rigid doom
That dragged my master to his tomb;
  How Ousenam's maidens tore their hair,
Wept till their eyes were dead and dim,
And wrung their hands for love of him,
  Who died at Jedwood Air?
He died!—his scholars, one by one,
To the cold silent grave are gone;
And I, alas! survive alone,
To muse o'er rivalries of yore,
And grieve that I shall hear no more
The strains, with envy heard before;
For, with my minstrel brethren fled,
My jealousy of song is dead.

He paused: the listening dames again
Applaud the hoary Minstrel's strain.
With many a word of kindly cheer,
In pity half, and half sincere,
Marvelled the Duchess how so well
His legendary song could tell
Of ancient deeds, so long forgot;
Of feuds, whose memory was not;
Of Forests, now laid waste and bare;
Of towers, which harbour now the hare;
Of manners, long since changed and gone;
Of chiefs, who under their grey stone

581 see end-note on IV. 570.
588 *Ousenam*: hamlet and parish in SE. Roxburghshire.
591 *Jedwood Air*: anglicized, 'Jedburgh Eyre (assizes).'

So long had slept, that fickle Fame
Had blotted from her rolls their name,
And twined round some new minion's head
The fading wreath for which they bled—
In sooth, 'twas strange, this old man's verse
Could call them from their marble hearse.
  The Harper smiled, well-pleased; for ne'er
Was flattery lost on poet's ear:
A simple race! they waste their toil
For the vain tribute of a smile;
E'en when in age their flame expires,
Her dulcet breath can fan its fires:
Their drooping fancy wakes at praise,
And strives to trim the short-lived blaze.
  Smiled then, well pleased, the Aged Man,
And thus his tale continued ran.

Canto Fifth

I

CALL it not vain; they do not err
  Who say, that when the Poet dies,
Mute Nature mourns her worshipper
  And celebrates his obsequies:
Who say, tall cliff and cavern lone
For the departed Bard make moan;
That mountains weep in crystal rill;
That flowers in tears of balm distil;
Through his loved groves that breezes sigh
And oaks, in deeper groan, reply;
And rivers teach their rushing wave
To murmur dirges round his grave.

II

Not that, in sooth, o'er mortal urn
Those things inanimate can mourn;
But that the stream, the wood, the gale,
Is vocal with the plaintive wail
Of those who, else forgotten long,
Lived in the poet's faithful song,
And, with the poet's parting breath,
Whose memory feels a second death.
The Maid's pale shade, who wails her lot,
That love, true love, should be forgot,

From rose and hawthorn shakes the tear
Upon the gentle Minstrel's bier:
The phantom Knight, his glory fled,
Mourns o'er the field he heaped with dead;
Mounts the wild blast that sweeps amain,
And shrieks along the battle-plain:
The Chief, whose antique crownlet long
Still sparkled in the feudal song,
Now, from the mountain's misty throne,
Sees, in the thanedom once his own,
His ashes undistinguished lie,
His place, his power, his memory die:
His groans the lonely caverns fill,
His tears of rage impel the rill:
All mourn the Minstrel's harp unstrung,
Their name unknown, their praise unsung.[n]

III

Scarcely the hot assault was stayed,
The terms of truce were scarcely made,
When they could spy, from Branksome's towers,
The advancing march of martial powers.
Thick clouds of dust afar appeared,
And trampling steeds were faintly heard;
Bright spears, above the columns dun,
Glanced momentary to the sun;
And feudal banners fair displayed
The bands that moved to Branksome's aid.

IV

Vails not to tell each hardy clan,
  From the fair Middle Marches[n] came;
The Bloody Heart[n] blazed in the van,
  Announcing Douglas, dreaded name!
Vails not to tell what steeds did spurn,
Where the Seven Spears of Wedderburne
  Their men in battle-order set;
And Swinton laid the lance in rest,
That tamed of yore the sparkling crest
  Of Clarence's Plantagenet.[n]

53 *spurn*: kick up their heels.
54 *Seven Spears*: the seven sons of Sir David Home of Wedderburn, in Berwickshire, who was killed in the Scottish defeat of Flodden (1513).

Nor list I say what hundreds more,
From the rich Merse and Lammermore[n]
And Tweed's fair borders, to the war
Beneath the crest of Old Dunbar
  And Hepburn's mingled banners come,
Down the steep mountain glittering far,
  And shouting still, 'A Home! a Home!'[n]

V

Now squire and knight, from Branksome sent,
On many a courteous message went;
To every chief and lord they paid
Meet thanks for prompt and powerful aid;
And told them how a truce was made,
  And how a day of fight was ta'en
  'Twixt Musgrave and stout Deloraine;
    And how the Ladye prayed them dear,
  That all would stay the fight to see,
  And deign, in love and courtesy,
    To taste of Branksome cheer.
Nor, while they bade to feast each Scot,
Were England's noble Lords forgot.
Himself, the hoary Seneschal
Rode forth, in seemly terms to call
Those gallant foes to Branksome Hall.
Accepted Howard, than whom knight
Was never dubbed more bold in fight;
Nor, when from war and armour free,
More famed for stately courtesy:
But angry Dacre rather chose
In his pavilion to repose.

VI

Now, noble Dame, perchance you ask
  How these two hostile armies met?
Deeming it were no easy task
  To keep the truce which here was set;
Where martial spirits, all on fire,
Breathed only blood and mortal ire.—

88 *noble Dame*: the Duchess of Monmouth, to whom the minstrel sings the lay.
93 *breathed*: i.e., thought of.

By mutual inroads, mutual blows,
By habit, and by nation, foes,
  They met on Teviot's strand;
They met and sate them mingled down,
Without a threat, without a frown,
  As brothers meet in foreign land:
The hands the spear that lately grasped,
Still in the mailed gauntlet clasped,
  Were interchanged in greeting dear;
Visors were raised, and faces shown,
And many a friend, to friend made known,
  Partook of social cheer.
Some drove the jolly bowl about;
  With dice and draughts some chased the day;
And some, with many a merry shout,
In riot, revelry, and rout,
  Pursued the foot-ball play.

VII

Yet, be it known, had bugles blown,
  Or sign of war been seen,
Those bands so fair together ranged,
Those hands, so frankly interchanged,
  Had dyed with gore the green:
The merry shout by Teviot-side
Had sunk in war-cries wild and wide,
  And in the groan of death;
And whingers, now in friendship bare
The social meal to part and share,
  Had found a bloody sheath.
'Twixt truce and war, such sudden change
Was not infrequent, nor held strange,
  In the old Border-day:
But yet on Branksome's towers and town,
In peaceful merriment, sunk down
  The sun's declining ray.

VIII

The blithesome signs of wassail gay
Decayed not with the dying day:

119 *whingers*: short hangers or whinyards used as knives at meals and as swords in broils (Jamieson).
121 i.e., would have been plunged into a body.

Soon through the latticed windows tall
Of lofty Branksome's lordly hall,
Divided square by shafts of stone,
Huge flakes of ruddy lustre shone;
Nor less the gilded rafters rang
With merry harp and beakers' clang:
  And frequent, on the darkening plain,
    Loud hollo, whoop, or whistle ran,
  As bands, their stragglers to regain,
    Give the shrill watchword of their clan;
And revellers, o'er their bowls, proclaim
Douglas or Dacre's conquering name.

IX

Less frequent heard, and fainter still,
  At length the various clamours died:
And you might hear, from Branksome hill,
  No sound but Teviot's rushing tide;
Save when the changing sentinel
The challenge of his watch could tell;
And save where, through the dark profound,
The clanging axe and hammer's sound
  Rung from the nether lawn;
For many a busy hand toiled there,
Strong pales to shape, and beams to square,[n]
The lists' dread barriers to prepare
  Against the morrow's dawn.

X

Margaret from hall did soon retreat,
  Despite the Dame's reproving eye;
Nor marked she, as she left her seat,
  Full many a stifled sigh;
For many a noble warrior strove
To win the Flower of Teviot's love,
  And many a bold ally.—
With throbbing head and anxious heart,
All in her lonely bower apart,
  In broken sleep she lay:
By times from silken couch she rose;
While yet the bannered hosts repose,
  She viewed the dawning day:

165 *By times*: betimes, early.

Of all the hundreds sunk to rest,
First woke the loveliest and the best.

XI

She gazed upon the inner court,
  Which in the tower's tall shadow lay;
Where coursers' clang, and stamp, and snort
  Had rung the livelong yesterday;
Now still as death; till stalking slow—
  The jingling spurs announced his tread—
A stately warrior passed below;
  But when he raised his plumed head—
    Blessed Mary! can it be?[n]
Secure, as if in Ousenam bowers,
He walks through Branksome's hostile towers
  With fearless step and free.
She dared not sign, she dared not speak—
Oh! if one page's slumbers break,
  His blood the price must pay!
Not all the pearls Queen Mary wears,
Not Margaret's yet more precious tears,
  Shall buy his life a day.

XII

Yet was his hazard small; for well
You may bethink you of the spell
  Of that sly urchin page;
This to his lord he did impart,
And made him seem, by glamour art,
  A knight from Hermitage.[n]
Unchallenged thus, the warder's post,
The court, unchallenged, thus he crossed,
  For all the vassalage:
But O! what magic's quaint disguise
Could blind fair Margaret's azure eyes!
  She started from her seat;
While with surprise and fear she strove,
And both could scarcely master love—
  Lord Henry's at her feet.

185 *Queen Mary*: Mary Queen of Scots (1542–87).
192 *glamour*: magic. 196 *For*: in spite of.

XIII

Oft have I mused what purpose bad
That foul malicious urchin had
  To bring this meeting round;
For happy love's a heavenly sight,
And by a vile malignant sprite
  In such no joy is found;
And oft I've deemed perchance he thought
Their erring passion might have wrought
  Sorrow, and sin, and shame;
And death to Cranstoun's gallant Knight,
And to the gentle ladye bright
  Disgrace and loss of fame.
But earthly spirit could not tell
The heart of them that loved so well.
True love's the gift which God has given
To man alone beneath the heaven:
  It is not fantasy's hot fire,
    Whose wishes, soon as granted, fly;
  It liveth not in fierce desire,
    With dead desire it doth not die;
It is the secret sympathy,
The silver link, the silken tie,
Which heart to heart, and mind to mind,
In body and in soul can bind.—
Now leave we Margaret and her Knight,
To tell you of the approaching fight.

XIV

Their warning blasts the bugles blew,
  The pipe's shrill port aroused each clan;
In haste, the deadly strife to view,
  The trooping warriors eager ran:
Thick round the lists their lances stood,
Like blasted pines in Ettrick wood;
To Branksome many a look they threw,
The combatants' approach to view,
And bandied many a word of boast
About the knight each favoured most.

230 *port*: 'a martial piece of music, adapted to the bagpipes' (S).

XV

Meantime full anxious was the Dame;
For now arose disputed claim
Of who should fight for Deloraine,
'Twixt Harden and 'twixt Thirlestane:
They 'gan to reckon kin and rent,
And frowning brow on brow was bent;
  But yet not long the strife—for, lo!
Himself, the Knight of Deloraine,
Strong, as it seemed, and free from pain,
  In armour sheathed from top to toe,
Appeared and craved the combat due.
The Dame her charm successful knew,
And the fierce chiefs their claims withdrew.

XVI

When for the lists they sought the plain,
The stately Ladye's silken rein
  Did noble Howard hold;
Unarmed by her side he walked,
And much in courteous phrase, they talked
  Of feats of arms of old.
Costly his garb; his Flemish ruff
Fell o'er his doublet, shaped of buff,
  With satin slashed and lined;
Tawny his boot, and gold his spur,
His cloak was all of Poland fur,
  His hose with silver twined;
His Bilboa blade, by Marchmen felt,
Hung in a broad and studded belt;
Hence, in rude phrase, the Borderers still
Called noble Howard, Belted Will.

XVII

Behind Lord Howard and the Dame,
Fair Margaret on her palfrey came,
  Whose foot-cloth swept the ground:
White was her wimple, and her veil,
Ane her loose locks a chaplet pale
  Of whitest roses bound;

250 *charm*: see III. 291–2.
263 *hose*: not stockings, but trunk-hose—i.e., breeches reaching down to the knees.
270 *foot-cloth*: coat covering a horse almost down to the ground.

The lordly Angus, by her side,
In courtesy to cheer her tried;
Without his aid her hand in vain
Had strove to guide her broidered rein.
He deemed she shuddered at the sight
Of warriors met for mortal fight;
But cause of terror, all unguessed,
Was fluttering in her gentle breast,
When, in their chairs of crimson placed,
The Dame and she the barriers graced.

XVIII

Prize of the field, the young Buccleuch,
An English knight led forth to view;
Scarce rued the boy his present plight,
So much he longed to see the fight.
Within the lists, in knightly pride,
High Home and haughty Dacre ride;
Their leading staffs of steel they wield
As marshals of the mortal field;
While to each knight their care assigned
Like vantage of the sun and wind.[n]
Then heralds hoarse did loud proclaim,
In King and Queen and Warden's name,
  That none, while lasts the strife,
Should dare, by look, or sign, or word,
Aid to a champion to afford,
  On peril of his life;
And not a breath the silence broke,
Till thus the alternate Heralds spoke:

XIX

ENGLISH HERALD

'Here standeth Richard of Musgrave,
  Good knight and true, and freely born,
Amends from Deloraine to crave,
  For foul despiteous scathe and scorn.

274 *Angus*: Earl of Angus, chief of the Douglas family.
290 *leading staffs*: batons symbolizing authority.
305 *despiteous*: malicious.

He sayeth that William of Deloraine
 Is traitor false by Border laws;
This with his sword he will maintain,
 So help him God, and his good cause!'

XX

SCOTTISH HERALD

'Here standeth William of Deloraine,
Good knight and true, of noble strain,
Who sayeth that foul treason's stain,
 Since he bore arms, ne'er soiled his coat;
  And that, so help him God above!
  He will on Musgrave's body prove,
 He lies most foully in his throat.'

LORD DACRE

'Forward, brave champions, to the fight!
Sound trumpets!'

LORD HOME

'God defend the right!'

Then, Teviot! how thine echoes rang,[n]
When bugle-sound and trumpet-clang
 Let loose the martial foes,
And in mid list, with shield poised high,
And measured step and wary eye,
 The combatants did close.

XXI

Ill would it suit your gentle ear,
Ye lovely listeners, to hear
How to the axe the helms did sound,
And blood poured down from many a wound;
For desperate was the strife and long,
And either warrior fierce and strong.
But, were each dame a listening knight,
I well could tell how warriors fight!
For I have seen war's lightning flashing,[n]
Seen the claymore with bayonet clashing,
Seen through red blood the war-horse dashing,
And scorned, amid the reeling strife,
To yield a step for death or life.

XXII

'Tis done, 'tis done! that fatal blow
 Has stretched him on the bloody plain;
He strives to rise—brave Musgrave, no!
 Thence never shalt thou rise again!
He chokes in blood! some friendly hand
Undo the visor's barred band,
Unfix the gorget's iron clasp,
And give him room for life to gasp!
O, bootless aid! haste, holy Friar,
Haste, ere the sinner shall expire!
Of all his guilt let him be shriven,
And smooth his path from earth to heaven!

XXIII

In haste the holy Friar sped;
His naked foot was dyed with red
 As through the lists he ran;
Unmindful of the shouts on high,
That hailed the conqueror's victory,
 He raised the dying man;
Loose waved his silver beard and hair,
As o'er him he kneeled down in prayer;
And still the crucifix on high
He holds before his darkening eye;
And still he bends an anxious ear
His faltering penitence to hear;
 Still props him from the bloody sod,
Still, even when soul and body part,
Pours ghostly comfort on his heart,
 And bids him trust in God!
Unheard he prays; the death pang's o'er!
Richard of Musgrave breathes no more.

XXIV

As if exhausted in the fight,
Or musing o'er the piteous sight,
 The silent victor stands;
His beaver did he not unclasp,
Marked not the shouts, felt not the grasp
 Of gratulating hands.

When lo! strange cries of wild surprise,
Mingled with seeming terror, rise
  Among the Scottish bands;
And all, amid the thronged array,
In panic haste gave open way
To a half-naked ghastly man
Who downward from the castle ran:
He crossed the barriers at a bound,
And wild and haggard looked around,
  As dizzy, and in pain;
And all, upon the armed ground,
  Knew William of Deloraine!
Each ladye sprung from seat with speed;
Vaulted each marshal from his steed;
  'And who art thou,' they cried,
'Who hast this battle fought and won?'
His plumed helm was soon undone—
  'Cranstoun of Teviot-side!
For this fair prize I've fought and won;'
And to the Ladye led her son.

XXV

Full oft the rescued boy she kissed,
And often pressed him to her breast;
For, under all her dauntless show,
Her heart had throbbed at every blow;
Yet not Lord Cranstoun deigned she greet,
Though low he kneeled at her feet.
Me lists not tell what words were made,
What Douglas, Home, and Howard said—
  For Howard was a generous foe—
And how the clan united prayed
  The Ladye would the feud forego,
And deign to bless the nuptial hour
Of Cranstoun's Lord and Teviot's Flower.

XXVI

She looked to river, looked to hill,
  Thought on the Spirit's prophecy,
Then broke her silence stern and still—
  'Not you, but Fate, has vanquished me;

408 *prophecy*: see I. st. xvii.

Their influence kindly stars may shower
On Teviot's tide and Branksome's tower,
  For pride is quelled, and love is free.'
She took fair Margaret by the hand,
Who, breathless, trembling, scarce might stand;
  That hand to Cranstoun's lord gave she:
'As I am true to thee and thine,
Do thou be true to me and mine!
  This clasp of love our bond shall be;
For this is your betrothing day,
And all these noble lords shall stay
  To grace it with their company.'

XXVII

All as they left the listed plain,
Much of the story she did gain;
How Cranstoun fought with Deloraine,
And of his page, and of the Book
Which from the wounded knight he took;
And how he sought her castle high,
That morn, by help of gramarye;
How, in Sir William's armour dight,
Stolen by his page, while slept the knight,
He took on him the single fight.
But half his tale he left unsaid,
And lingered till he joined the maid.—
Cared not the Ladye to betray
Her mystic arts in view of day;
But well she thought, ere midnight came,
Of that strange page the pride to tame,
From his foul hands the Book to save,
And send it back to Michael's grave.—
Needs not to tell each tender word
'Twixt Margaret and 'twixt Cranstoun's lord;
Nor how she told of former woes,
And how her bosom fell and rose,
While he and Musgrave bandied blows.
Needs not these lovers' joys to tell:
One day, fair maids, you'll know them well.

429 *gramarye*: magic.

XXVIII

William of Deloraine some chance
Had wakened from his deathlike trance;
And taught that, in the listed plain,
Another, in his arms and shield,
Against fierce Musgrave axe did wield
Under the name of Deloraine.
Hence to the field unarmed he ran,
And hence his presence scared the clan,
Who held him for some fleeting wraith,
And not a man of blood and breath.
Not much this new ally he loved,
Yet, when he saw what hap had proved,
He greeted him right heartilie:
He would not waken old debate,
For he was void of rancorous hate,
Though rude, and scant of courtesy;
In raids he spilt but seldom blood,
Unless when men-at-arms withstood,
Or, as was meet, for deadly feud.
He ne'er bore grudge for stalwart blow,
Ta'en in fair fight from gallant foe:
And so 'twas seen of him, e'en now,
When on dead Musgrave he looked down;
Grief darkened on his rugged brow,
Though half disguised with a frown;
And thus, while sorrow bent his head,
His foeman's epitaph he made.

XXIX

'Now, Richard Musgrave, liest thou here!
I ween, my deadly enemy;
For, if I slew thy brother dear,
Thou slewest a sister's son to me;
And when I lay in dungeon dark
Of Naworth Castle, long months three,
Till ransomed for a thousand mark,
Dark Musgrave, it was 'long of thee.

450 *listed*: enclosed with barriers.
456 *wraith*: spectral apparition of a living person, rather than a ghost.
480 *Naworth*: Lord Howard's castle. See end-note on I. 49.
481 *mark*: Scottish coin worth 13*s*. 4*d*.

And, Musgrave, could our fight be tried,
  And thou wert now alive as I,
No mortal man should us divide,
  Till one, or both of us, did die:
Yet, rest thee God! for well I know
I ne'er shall find a nobler foe.
In all the northern counties here,
Whose word is Snaffle, spur, and spear,[n]
Thou wert the best to follow gear!
'Twas pleasure, as we looked behind,
To see how thou the chase could'st wind,
Cheer the dark blood-hound on his way,
And with the bugle rouse the fray![n]
I'd give the lands of Deloraine,
Dark Musgrave were alive again.'

XXX

So mourned he, till Lord Dacre's band
Were bowning back to Cumberland.
They raised brave Musgrave from the field,
And laid him on his bloody shield;
On levelled lances, four and four,
By turns, the noble burden bore.
Before, at times, upon the gale,
Was heard the Minstrel's plaintive wail;
Behind, four priests, in sable stole,
Sung requiem for the warrior's soul:
Around, the horsemen slowly rode;
With trailing pikes the spearmen trod;
And thus the gallant knight they bore
Through Liddesdale to Leven's shore;
Thence to Holme Coltrame's lofty nave,
And laid him in his father's grave.

THE harp's wild notes, though hushed the song,
The mimic march of death prolong;
Now seems it far, and now a-near,
Now meets, and now eludes the ear;

491 *gear*: cattle, booty.
499 *bowning back*: preparing their departure.
511 *Leven*: see IV. 411.
512 *Holme Coltrame*: family burial place of the Musgraves, in Cumberland.

Now seems some mountain side to sweep,
Now faintly dies in valley deep;
Seems now as if the Minstrel's wail,
Now the sad requiem, loads the gale;
Last, o'er the warrior's closing grave,
Rung the full choir in choral stave.

After due pause, they bade him tell,
Why he, who touched the harp so well,
Should thus, with ill-rewarded toil,
Wander a poor and thankless soil,
When the more generous Southern land
Would well requite his skilful hand.

The aged Harper, howsoe'er
His only friend, his harp, was dear,
Liked not to hear it ranked so high
Above his flowing poesy:
Less liked he still that scornful jeer
Misprized the land he loved so dear;
High was the sound, as thus again
The Bard resumed his minstrel strain.

Canto Sixth

I

BREATHES there the man, with soul so dead,
Who never to himself hath said,
  This is my own, my native land!
Whose heart hath ne'er within him burned,
As home his footsteps he hath turned,
  From wandering on a foreign strand!
If such there breathe, go, mark him well:
For him no Minstrel raptures swell;
High though his titles, proud his name,
Boundless his wealth as wish can claim;
Despite those titles, power, and pelf,
The wretch, concentred all in self,
Living, shall forfeit fair renown,
And, doubly dying, shall go down
To the vile dust, from whence he sprung,
Unwept, unhonoured and unsung.

II

O Caledonia! stern and wild,
Meet nurse for a poetic child!
Land of brown heath and shaggy wood,
Land of the mountain and the flood,
Land of my sires! what mortal hand
Can e'er untie the filial band,
That knits me to thy rugged strand!
Still as I view each well-known scene,
Think what is now, and what hath been,
Seems as, to me, of all bereft,
Sole friends thy woods and streams were left;
And thus I love them better still,
Even in extremity of ill.
By Yarrow's stream still let me stray,
Though none should guide my feeble way;
Still feel the breeze down Ettrick break,
Although it chill my withered cheek:
Still lay my head by Teviot Stone,[n]
Though there, forgotten and alone,
The Bard may draw his parting groan.

III

Not scorned like me, to Branksome Hall
The Minstrels came at festive call;
Trooping they came, from near and far,
The jovial priests of mirth and war;
Alike for feast and fight prepared,
Battle and banquet both they shared.
Of late, before each martial clan,
They blew their death-note in the van,
But now, for every merry mate,
Rose the portcullis' iron grate;
They sound the pipe, they strike the string,
They dance, they revel, and they sing,
Till the rude turrets shake and ring.

IV

Me lists not at this tide declare
  The splendour of the spousal rite,
How mustered in the chapel fair
  Both maid and matron, squire and knight;

Me lists not tell of owches rare,
Of mantles green, and braided hair,
And kirtles furred with miniver;
What plumage waved the altar round,
How spurs and ringing chainlets sound:
And hard it were for bard to speak
The changeful hue of Margaret's cheek:
That lovely hue which comes and flies
As awe and shame alternate rise!

V

Some bards have sung the Ladye high
Chapel or altar came not nigh;
Nor durst the rites of spousal grace,
So much she feared each holy place.
False slanders these—I trust right well
She wrought not by forbidden spell;[n]
For mighty words and signs have power
O'er sprites in planetary hour:
Yet scarce I praise their venturous part,
Who tamper with such dangerous art.
  But this for faithful truth I say,
    The Ladye by the altar stood;
  Of sable velvet her array,
    And on her head a crimson hood,
With pearls embroidered and entwined,
Guarded with gold, with ermine lined;
A merlin sat upon her wrist
Held by a leash of silken twist.

VI

The spousal rites were ended soon:
'Twas now the merry hour of noon,
And in the lofty arched hall
Was spread the gorgeous festival.
Steward and squire, with heedful haste,
Marshalled the rank of every guest;
Pages, with ready blade, were there
The mighty meal to carve and share:

54 *owches*: jewelled clasps or buckles.
70 *hour*: time when a given planet is in the ascendant and can exercise its influence.
78 *Guarded*: edged.
79 *merlin*: small falcon carried by ladies of rank.

O'er capon, heron-shew, and crane,
And princely peacock's[n] gilded train,
And o'er the boar-head, garnished brave,[n]
And cygnet from St. Mary's wave;
O'er ptarmigan and venison
The priest had spoke his benison.
Then rose the riot and the din,
Above, beneath, without, within!
For, from the lofty balcony,
Rung trumpet, shalm, and psaltery:
Their clanging bowls old warriors quaffed,
Loudly they spoke, and loudly laughed;
Whispered young knights, in tone more mild,
To ladies fair, and ladies smiled.
The hooded hawks, high perched on beam,
The clamour joined with whistling scream,
And flapped their wings, and shook their bells
In concert with the stag-hounds' yells,
Round go the flasks of ruddy wine,
From Bordeaux, Orleans, or the Rhine;
Their tasks the busy sewers ply,
And all is mirth and revelry.

VII

The Goblin Page, omitting still
No opportunity of ill,
Strove now, while blood ran hot and high,
To rouse debate and jealousy;
Till Conrad, Lord of Wolfenstein,
By nature fierce, and warm with wine,
And now in humour highly crossed
About some steeds his band had lost,
High words to words succeeding still,
Smote with his gauntlet stout Hunthill—[n]
A hot and hardy Rutherford,
Whom men called Dickon Draw-the-sword.
He took it on the page's say,
Hunthill had driven those steeds away,

89 *heron-shew*: young heron.
92 *St. Mary's*: the lake at the head of the Yarrow.
98 *shalm*: shawm, wind instrument with reed.
115 *Conrad*: the captain of the German mercenaries; see IV. 313.

Then Howard, Home, and Douglas rose,
The kindling discord to compose:
Stern Rutherford right little said,
But bit his glove,[n] and shook his head.—
A fortnight thence, in Inglewood,
Stout Conrad, cold, and drenched in blood,
His bosom gored with many a wound,
Was by a woodman's lyme-dog found;
Unknown the manner of his death,
Gone was his brand, both sword and sheath;
But ever from that time, 'twas said,
That Dickon wore a Cologne blade.

VIII

The dwarf, who feared his master's eye
Might his foul treachery espie,
Now sought the castle buttery,
Where many a yeoman, bold and free,
Revelled as merrily and well
As those that sat in lordly sell.
Watt Tinlinn, there, did frankly raise
The pledge to Arthur Fire-the-Braes;[n]
And he, as by his breeding bound,
To Howard's merry-men sent it round.
To quit them, on the English side,
Red Roland Forster loudly cried,
'A deep carouse to yon fair bride!'
At every pledge, from vat and pail,
Foamed forth in floods the nut-brown ale,
While shout the riders every one;
Such day of mirth ne'er cheered their clan,
Since old Buccleuch the name did gain,
When in the cleuch the buck was ta'en.[n]

IX

The wily page, with vengeful thought,
  Remembered him of Tinlinn's yew,
And swore it should be dearly bought
  That ever he the arrow drew.

132 *lyme-dog*: hunting dog normally kept on leash ('lyme').
142 *sell*: seat. 143–4 *raise . . . pledge*: drink health.
147 *quit them*: return the compliment.

First, he the yeoman did molest,
With bitter gibe and taunting jest;
Told how he fled at Solway strife,[n]
And how Hob Armstrong cheered his wife;
Then, shunning still his powerful arm,
At unawares he wrought him harm;
From trencher stole his choicest cheer,
Dashed from his lips his can of beer;
Then, to his knee sly creeping on,
With bodkin pierced him to the bone:
The venomed wound, and festering joint,
Long after rued that bodkin's point.
The startled yeoman swore and spurned,
And board and flagons overturned.
Riot and clamour wild began;
Back to the hall the Urchin ran;
Took in a darkling nook his post,
And grinned, and muttered, 'Lost! lost! lost!'

X

By this, the Dame, lest farther fray
Should mar the concord of the day,
Had bid the Minstrels tune their lay.
And first stept forth old Albert Græme,
The Minstrel of that ancient name:
Was none who struck the harp so well
Within the Land Debateable;
Well friended too, his hardy kin,
Whoever lost, were sure to win;
They sought the beeves that made their broth,
In Scotland and in England both.
In homely guise, as nature bade,
His simple song the Borderer said.

XI

ALBERT GRÆME

It was an English ladye bright,
  (The sun shines fair on Carlisle wall,)
And she would marry a Scottish knight,
  For Love will still be Lord of all.[n]

172 *spurned*: kicked. 178 *By this*: by this time.
184 *Debateable*: claimed by both kingdoms.

Blithely they saw the rising sun,
  When he shone fair on Carlisle wall;
But they were sad ere day was done,
  Though Love was still the lord of all.

Here sire gave brooch and jewel fine,
  Where the sun shines on Carlisle wall;
Her brother gave but a flask of wine,
  For ire that Love was lord of all.

For she had lands, both meadow and lea,
  Where the sun shines fair on Carlisle wall;
And he swore her death ere he would see
  A Scottish knight the lord of all!

XII

That wine she had not tasted well,
  (The sun shines fair on Carlisle wall,)
When dead in her true love's arms she fell,
  For Love was still the lord of all!

He pierced her brother to the heart,
  Where the sun shines fair on Carlisle wall:
So perish all would true love part,
  That Love may still be lord of all!

And then he took the cross divine,
  (Where the sun shines fair on Carlisle wall,)
And died for her sake in Palestine;
  So Love was still the lord of all.

Now all ye lovers that faithful prove,
  (The sun shines fair on Carlisle wall,)
Pray for their souls who died for love,
  For Love shall still be lord of all!

XIII

As ended Albert's simple lay,
  Arose a bard of loftier port;
For sonnet, rhyme, and roundelay
  Renowned in haughty Henry's court:
There rung thy harp, unrivalled long,
Fitztraver of the silver song!

215 *took . . . cross*: became a Crusader.
228 *Fitztraver*: an imaginary court poet.

The gentle Surrey loved his lyre—
 Who has not heard of Surrey's[n] fame?
His was the hero's soul of fire,
 And his the bard's immortal name,
And his was love, exalted high
By all the glow of chivalry.

XIV

They sought together climes afar,
 And oft within some olive grove,
When even came with twinkling star,
 They sung of Surrey's absent love.
His step the Italian peasant stayed,
 And deemed that spirits from on high,
Round where some hermit saint was laid,
 Were breathing heavenly melody;
So sweet did harp and voice combine
To praise the name of Geraldine.

XV

Fitztraver! O what tongue may say
 The pangs thy faithful bosom knew,
When Surrey, of the deathless lay,
 Ungrateful Tudor's sentence[n] slew?
Regardless of the tyrant's frown,
His harp called wrath and vengeance down.
He left, for Naworth's iron towers,
Windsor's green glades and courtly bowers,
And faithful to his patron's name,
With Howard still Fitztraver came;
Lord William's foremost favourite he,
And chief of all his minstrelsy.

XVI

FITZTRAVER

'Twas All-soul's eve, and Surrey's heart[n] beat high!
 He heard the midnight bell with anxious start,
Which told the mystic hour, approaching nigh,
 When wise Cornelius promised, by his art,

230 Henry Howard, Earl of Surrey, beheaded 1547 (N.S.); see end-note on line 248.

To show to him the ladye of his heart,
  Albeit betwixt them roared the ocean grim;
Yet so the sage had hight to play his part,
  That he should see her form in life and limb,
And mark, if still she loved, and still she thought of him.

XVII

Dark was the vaulted room of gramarye,
  To which the wizard led the gallant Knight,
Save that before a mirror, huge and high,
  A hallowed taper shed a glimmering light
On mystic implements of magic might:
  On cross, and character, and talisman,
And almagest, and altar, nothing bright:
  For fitful was the lustre, pale and wan,
As watchlight by the bed of some departing man.

XVIII

But soon, within that mirror huge and high,
  Was seen a self-emitted light to gleam;
And forms upon its breast the Earl 'gan spy,
  Cloudy and indistinct, as feverish dream;
Till, slow arranging, and defined, they seem
  To form a lordly and a lofty room,
Part lighted by a lamp with silver beam,
  Placed by a couch of Agra's silken loom,[n]
And part by moonshine pale, and part was hid in gloom.

XIX

Fair all the pageant: but how passing fair
  The slender form which lay on couch of Ind!
O'er her white bosom strayed her hazel hair;
  Pale her dear cheek, as if for love she pined;
All in her night-robe loose she lay reclined,
  And pensive read from tablet eburnine
Some strain that seemed her inmost soul to find:
  That favoured strain was Surrey's raptured line,
That fair and lovely form, the Ladye Geraldine.

263 *hight*: promised.
271 *character*: mystical or cabalistic letters.
271 *talisman*: magical figure cut under planetary influence.
272 *almagest*: astronomical treatise by Claudius Ptolemy.
289 *eburnine*: made of ivory.

XX

Slow rolled the clouds upon the lovely form,
  And swept the goodly vision all away—
So royal envy rolled the murky storm
  O'er my beloved Master's glorious day.
Thou jealous, ruthless tyrant! Heaven repay
  On thee, and on thy children's latest line,
The wild caprice of thy despotic sway,
  The gory bridal bed, the plundered shrine,
The murdered Surrey's blood, the tears of Geraldine!

XXI

Both Scots and Southern chiefs prolong
Applauses of Fitztraver's song;
These hated Henry's name as death,
And those still held the ancient faith.[n]
Then from his seat, with lofty air,
Rose Harold, bard of brave St. Clair;
St. Clair, who, feasting high at Home,
Had with that lord to battle come.
Harold was born where restless seas
Howl round the storm-swept Orcades;
Where erst St. Clairs held princely sway
O'er isle and islet, strait and bay;—
Still nods their palace to its fall,
Thy pride and sorrow,[n] fair Kirkwall!
Thence oft he marked fierce Pentland rave,
As if grim Odin rode her wave;
And watched the whilst, with visage pale,
And throbbing heart, the struggling sail;
For all of wonderful and wild
Had rapture for the lonely child.

XXII

And much of wild and wonderful
In these rude isles might fancy cull;

295 *envy*: i.e., of Surrey's poetry.
300 the execution of Anne Boleyn and appropriation of monastic lands by Henry VIII.
307 *St. Clair*: Sinclair, a family of Norman extraction who held lands in S. Scotland as well as in Orkney.
308 *Home*: seat of the Earl of Home.
311 *Orcades*: Orkney isles, whose inhabitants are of Norse blood.
316 *Pentland*: the firth of that name.

For thither came, in times afar,
Stern Lochlin's sons of roving war,
The Norsemen, trained to spoil and blood,
Skilled to prepare the raven's food;
Kings of the main their leaders brave,
Their barks the dragons of the wave,
And there, in many a stormy vale,
The Scald had told his wondrous tale;
And many a Runic column high
Had witnessed grim idolatry.
And thus had Harold in his youth
Learned many a Saga's rhyme uncouth—
Of that Sea-Snake,[n] tremendous curled,
Whose monstrous circle girds the world;
Of those dread Maids,[n] whose hideous yell
Maddens the battle's bloody swell;
Of Chiefs,[n] who, guided through the gloom
By the pale death-lights of the tomb,
Ransacked the graves of warriors old,
Their falchions wrenched from corpses' hold,
Waked the deaf tomb with war's alarms,
And bade the dead arise to arms!
With war and wonder all on flame,
To Roslin's bowers young Harold came,
Where, by sweet glen and greenwood tree,
He learned a milder minstrelsy;
Yet something of the Northern spell
Mixed with the softer numbers well.

XXIII

HAROLD

O listen, listen, ladies gay!
  No haughty feat of arms I tell;
Soft is the note, and sad the lay,
  That mourns the lovely Rosabelle.

325 *Lochlin*: Scandinavia (Gael.).
341 *death-lights*: fires which in Scandinavian belief burnt within dead warriors' tombs.
347 *Roslin*: seat of the St. Clairs in Midlothian.
355 *Rosabelle*: a St. Clair family name.

—'Moor, moor the barge, ye gallant crew!
  And, gentle ladye, deign to stay!
Rest thee in Castle Ravensheuch,[n]
  Nor tempt the stormy firth to-day.

The blackening wave is edged with white:
  To inch and rock the sea-mews fly;
The fishers have heard the Water-Sprite,
  Whose screams forebode that wreck is nigh.

Last night the gifted Seer did view
  A wet shroud swathed round ladye gay;
Then stay thee, Fair, in Ravensheuch:
  Why cross the gloomy firth today ?'—

—''Tis not because Lord Lindsay's heir
  To-night at Roslin leads the ball,
But that my ladye-mother there
  Sits lonely in her castle-hall.

'Tis not because the ring[n] they ride,
  And Lindsay at the ring rides well,
But that my sire the wine will chide,
  If 'tis not filled by Rosabelle.'—

O'er Roslin all that dreary night
  A wondrous blaze was seen to gleam;
'Twas broader than the watch-fire's light,
  And redder than the bright moonbeam.

It glared on Roslin's castled rock,
  It ruddied all the copse wood glen;
'Twas seen from Dryden's groves of oak,
  And seen from caverned Hawthornden.

Seemed all on fire[n] that chapel proud,
  Where Roslin's chiefs uncoffined lie,
Each Baron, for a sable shroud,
  Sheathed in his iron panoply.

Seemed all on fire within, around,
  Deep sacristy and altar's pale;
Shone every pillar foliage-bound,
  And glimmered all the dead men's mail.

361 *inch*: isle. 382 *Dryden*: ¾ mile N. of Roslin.
383 *Hawthornden*: seat of the Drummonds, on the R. Esk, 1¼ miles NE. of Roslin. There are cliffs with caves on the wooded banks.

Blazed battlement and pinnet high,
  Blazed every rose-carved[n] buttress fair—
So still they blaze when fate is nigh
  The lordly line of high St. Clair.

There are twenty of Roslin's barons bold
  Lie buried within that proud chapelle;
Each one the holy vault doth hold—
  But the sea holds lovely Rosabelle!

And each St. Clair was buried there,
  With candle, with book, and with knell;
But the sea-caves rung, and the wild winds sung,
  The dirge of lovely Rosabelle.

XXIV

So sweet was Harold's piteous lay,
  Scarce marked the guests the darkened hall,
Though, long before the sinking day,
  A wondrous shade involved them all:
It was not eddying mist or fog,
Drained by the sun from fen or bog;
  Of no eclipse had sages told;
And yet, as it came on apace,
Each one could scarce his neighbour's face,
  Could scarce his own stretched hand behold.
A secret horror checked the feast,
And chilled the soul of every guest;
Even the high Dame stood half aghast—
She knew some evil on the blast;
The elvish page fell to the ground,
And, shuddering, muttered, 'Found! found! found!'

XXV

Then sudden, through the darkened air,
  A flash of lightning came;
So broad, so bright, so red the glare,
  The castle seemed on flame.
Glanced every rafter of the hall,
Glanced every shield upon the wall;
Each trophied beam, each sculptured stone
Were instant seen, and instant gone;
Full through the guests' bedazzled band
Resistless flashed the levin-brand,

392 *pinnet*: pinnacle. 429 *levin-brand*: flash of lightning.

And filled the hall with smouldering smoke,
As on the elvish page it broke.
It broke, with thunder long and loud,
Dismayed the brave, appalled the proud,—
From sea to sea the larum rung;
On Berwick wall, and at Carlisle withal,
To arms the startled warders sprung.
When ended was the dreadful roar,
The elvish dwarf was seen no more!

XXVI

Some heard a voice in Branksome Hall,
Some saw a sight, not seen by all;
That dreadful voice was heard by some,
Cry, with loud summons, 'GYLBIN, COME!'
And on the spot where burst the brand,
Just where the page had flung him down,
Some saw an arm, and some a hand,
And some the waving of a gown.
The guests in silence prayed and shook,
And terror dimmed each lofty look.
But none of all the astonished train
Was so dismayed as Deloraine;
His blood did freeze, his brain did burn
'Twas feared his mind would ne'er return;
For he was speechless, ghastly, wan,
Like him of whom the story ran,
Who spoke the spectre-hound in Man.[n]
At length, by fits, he darkly told,
With broken hint, and shuddering cold,
That he had seen, right certainly,
A shape with amice wrapped around,
With a wrought Spanish baldric bound,
Like pilgrim from beyond the sea;
And knew—but how it mattered not—
It was the wizard, Michael Scott.

XXVII

The anxious crowd, with horror pale,
All trembling heard the wondrous tale;
No sound was made, no word was spoke,
Till noble Angus silence broke;
And he a solemn sacred plight

Did to St. Bride of Douglas make,
That he a pilgrimage would take
To Melrose Abbey, for the sake
Of Michael's restless sprite.
Then each, to ease his troubled breast,
To some blessed saint his prayers addressed:
Some to St. Modan made their vows,
Some to St. Mary of the Lowes,[n]
Some to the Holy Rood of Lisle,[n]
Some to our Ladye of the Isle;
Each did his patron witness make,
That he such pilgrimage would take,
And monks should sing, and bells should toll,
All for the weal of Michael's soul.
While vows were ta'en, and prayers were prayed,
'Tis said the noble dame, dismayed,
Renounced, for aye, dark magic's aid.

XXVIII

Nought of the bridal will I tell,
Which after in short space befell;
Nor how brave sons and daughters fair
Blessed Teviot's Flower, and Cranstoun's heir:
After such dreadful scene, 'twere vain
To wake the note of mirth again.
More meet it were to mark the day
Of penitence, and prayer divine,
When pilgrim-chiefs, in sad array,
Sought Melrose' holy shrine.

XXIX

With naked foot, and sackcloth vest,
And arms enfolded on his breast,
Did every pilgrim go;
The standers-by might hear uneath,
Footstep, or voice, or high-drawn breath,
Through all the lengthened row:

469 *St. Bride*: 'a favourite saint of the house of Douglas and of the Earl of Angus in particular' (S).
475 *St. Modan*: Scottish abbot of the 7th century.
495 *shrine*: Melrose abbey.
499 *uneath*: with difficulty.

No lordly look, nor martial stride;
Gone was their glory, sunk their pride,
  Forgotten their renown;
Silent and slow, like ghosts they glide
To the high altar's hallowed side,
  And there they kneeled them down:
Above the suppliant chieftains wave
The banners of departed brave;
Beneath the lettered stones were laid
The ashes of their fathers dead;
From many a garnished niche around,
Stern saints and tortured martyrs frowned

XXX

And slow up the dim aisle afar,
With sable cowl and scapular,
And snow-white stoles, in order due,
The holy Fathers, two and two,
  In long procession came;
Taper and host, and book they bare,
And holy banner, flourished fair
  With the Redeemer's name.
Above the prostrate pilgrim band
The mitred Abbot stretched his hand,
  And blessed them as they kneeled;
With holy cross he signed them all,
And prayed they might be sage in hall,
  And fortunate in field.
Then mass was sung, and prayers were said,
And solemn requiem for the dead;
And bells tolled out their mighty peal,
For the departed spirit's weal;
And ever in the office close
The hymn of intercession[n] rose;
And far the echoing aisles prolong
The awful burthen of the song,—
  DIES IRÆ, DIES ILLA,
  SOLVET SÆCLUM IN FAVILLA,—

512 *garnished*: decorated.
527 *field*: battlefield.
532 *office close*: interval in the prayers of the service.

While the pealing organ rung.
  Were it meet with sacred strain
  To close my lay, so light and vain,
Thus the holy Fathers sung:

XXXI

HYMN FOR THE DEAD

That day of wrath, that dreadful day,
When heaven and earth shall pass away,
What power shall be the sinner's stay?
How shall he meet that dreadful day?

When shriveling like a parched scroll,
The flaming heavens together roll;
When louder yet, and yet more dread,
Swells the high trump that wakes the dead:

Oh! on that day, that wrathful day,
When man to judgment wakes from clay,
Be THOU the trembling sinner's stay,
Though heaven and earth shall pass away!

HUSHED is the harp: the Minstrel gone.
And did he wander forth alone?
Alone, in indigence and age,
To linger out his pilgrimage?
No; close beneath proud Newark's tower,
Arose the Minstrel's lowly bower;
A simple hut; but there was seen
The little garden hedged with green,
The cheerful hearth, and lattice clean.
There sheltered wanderers, by the blaze,
Oft heard the tale of other days;
For much he loved to ope his door,
And give the aid he begged before.
So passed the winter's day; but still,
When summer smiled on sweet Bowhill,
And July's eve, with balmy breath,
Waved the blue-bells on Newark heath;

542 a paraphrase, rather than a translation, of the *Dies Irae.*
558 See below, p. 280, and note on line 27.
568 *Bowhill*: a seat of the Duke of Buccleuch: see map.

When throstles sung in Hareheadshaw,
And corn was green on Carterhaugh,
And flourished broad Blackandro's oak,
The aged Harper's soul awoke!
Then would he sing achievements high,
And circumstance of chivalry,
Till the rapt traveller would stay,
Forgetful of the closing day;
And noble youths, the strain to hear,
Forsook the hunting of the deer;
And Yarrow, as he rolled along,
Bore burden to the Minstrel's song.

571 *Hareheadshaw*: on the Yarrow, near Foulshiels; where the Battle of Philliphaugh ended.
573 *Blackandro*: a wooded hill above Newark.

The Lady of the Lake[n]

Canto First

The Chase

Harp of the North! that mouldering long hast hung
  On the witch-elm that shades Saint Fillan's spring,[n]
And down the fitful breeze thy numbers flung,
  Till envious ivy did around thee cling,
Muffling with verdant ringlet every string,—
  O minstrel Harp, still must thine accents sleep?
'Mid rustling leaves and fountains murmuring,
  Still must thy sweeter sounds their silence keep,
Nor bid a warrior smile, nor teach a maid to weep?

Not thus, in ancient days of Caledon,
  Was thy voice mute amid the festal crowd,
When lay of hopeless love, or glory won,
  Aroused the fearful, or subdued the proud.
At each according pause was heard aloud
  Thine ardent symphony sublime and high!
Fair dames and crested chiefs attention bowed;
  For still the burden of thy minstrelsy
Was Knighthood's dauntless deed, and Beauty's matchless eye.

O wake once more! how rude soe'er the hand
  That ventures o'er thy magic maze to stray;
O wake once more! though scarce my skill command
  Some feeble echoing of thine earlier lay:
Though harsh and faint, and soon to die away,
  And all unworthy of thy nobler strain,
Yet if one heart throb higher at its sway,
  The wizard note has not been touched in vain.
Then silent be no more! Enchantress wake again!

I

The stag at eve had drunk his fill,
Where danced the moon on Monan's rill,

2 *witch-elm*: i.e., wych or 'drooping' elm.
10 *Caledon* (ia): Scotland, esp. its northern part.
14 *according pause*: interval in the lay marked by chords on the harp.
29 *Monan*: 9th-century saint.

And deep his midnight lair had made
In lone Glenartney's[n] hazel shade;
But, when the sun his beacon red
Had kindled on Benvoirlich's head,
The deep-mouthed blood-hound's heavy bay
Resounded up the rocky way,
And faint, from farther distance borne,
Were heard the clanging hoof and horn.

II

As Chief, who hears his warder call,
'To arms! the foemen storm the wall,'
The antlered monarch of the waste
Sprung from his heathery couch in haste.
But, ere his fleet career he took,
The dew-drops from his flanks he shook;
Like crested leader proud and high,
Tossed his beamed frontlet to the sky;
A moment gazed adown the dale,
A moment snuffed the tainted gale,
A moment listened to the cry,
That thickened as the chase drew nigh;
Then, as the headmost foes appeared,
With one brave bound the copse he cleared,
And, stretching forward free and far,
Sought the wild heaths of Uam-Var.

III

Yelled on the view the opening pack;
Rock, glen, and cavern, paid them back;
To many a mingled sound at once
The awakened mountain gave response.
A hundred dogs bayed deep and strong,
Clattered a hundred steeds along,
Their peal the merry horns rung out,
A hundred voices joined the shout;
With hark and whoop and wild halloo,
No rest Benvoirlich's echoes knew.

33 *Benvoirlich*: 3,224 ft., at the head of the Garry, NW. of Glenartney and between it and Loch Earn.
45 *beamed*: furnished with horns; the 'beam' is the main trunk of the horn.
53 *Uam-Var*: Uaighmor, mountain NE. of Callender in Menteith.
54 *opening*: bursting into cry.

Far from the tumult fled the roe,
Close in her covert cowered the doe;
The falcon, from her cairn on high,
Cast on the rout a wondering eye,
Till far beyond her piercing ken
The hurricane had swept the glen.
Faint and more faint, its failing din
Returned from cavern, cliff, and linn,
And silence settled, wide and still,
On the lone wood and mighty hill.

IV

Less loud the sounds of silvan war
Disturbed the heights of Uam-Var,
And roused the cavern, where, 'tis told,
A giant made his den of old;
For ere that steep ascent was won,
High in his pathway hung the sun,
And many a gallant, stayed perforce,
Was fain to breathe his faltering horse,
And of the trackers of the deer,
Scarce half the lessening pack was near;
So shrewdly on the mountain side
Had the bold burst their mettle tried.

V

The noble stag was pausing now
Upon the mountain's southern brow,
Where broad extended, far beneath,
The varied realms of fair Menteith.
With anxious eye he wandered o'er
Mountain and meadow, moss and moor,
And pondered refuge from his toil
By far Lochard or Aberfoyle.
But nearer was the copse-wood grey,
That waved and wept on Loch Achray,

81 *breathe*: rest. 84 *shrewdly*: keenly.
89 *Menteith*: part of Perthshire watered by R. Teith.
93 *Lochard*: small lake E. of Loch Lomond and S. of Loch Katrine, from which the Forth flows.
93 *Aberfoyle*: village SE. of Loch Ard.
95 *Loch Achray*: between Loch Katrine and Loch Vennachar.

And mingled with the pine-trees blue
On the bold cliffs of Benvenue.
Fresh vigour with the hope returned,
With flying foot the heath he spurned,
Held westward with unwearied race,
And left behind the panting chase.

VI

'Twere long to tell what steeds gave o'er,
As swept the hunt through Cambusmore:
What reins were tightened in despair,
When rose Benledi's ridge in air;
Who flagged upon Bochastle's heath,
Who shunned to stem the flooded Teith—
For twice that day, from shore to shore,
The gallant stag swam stoutly o'er.
Few were the stragglers, following far,
That reached the lake of Vennachar;
And when the Brigg of Turk was won,
The headmost horseman rode alone.

VII

Alone, but with unbated zeal,
That horseman plied the scourge and steel;
For jaded now, and spent with toil,
Embossed with foam, and dark with soil,
While every gasp with sobs he drew,
The labouring stag strained full in view.
Two dogs of black Saint Hubert's breed,
Unmatched for courage, breath, and speed,
Fast on his flying traces came,
And all but won that desperate game;

97 *Benvenue*: 2,393 ft., to SW. of Loch Achray.

103 *Cambusmore*: two miles ESE. of Callander on the left bank of Keltie Water, a tributary of the Teith.

105 *Benledi*: 2,875 ft. 4½ miles W. by N. of Callander, between Loch Lubnaig and Loch Achray.

106 *Bochastle's heath*: between Callander and Loch Vennachar, near junction of rivers Leny and Teith.

111 *Lake of Vennachar*: an expansion of the S. head-stream of the Teith, it comes to within 2¼ m. of Callander.

112 *Brigg of Turk:* bridge over a stream flowing from Glenfinlas to join the Teith between Loch Achray and Loch Vennachar.

117 *embossed*: technical term in hunting. 120 *Hubert*: patron saint of hunting.

For, scarce a spear's length from his haunch,
Vindictive toiled the bloodhounds staunch;
Nor nearer might the dogs attain,
Nor farther might the quarry strain.
Thus up the margin of the lake,
Between the precipice and brake,
O'er stock and rock their race they take.

VIII

The Hunter marked that mountain high,
The lone lake's western boundary,
And deemed the stag must turn to bay,
Where that huge rampart barred the way;
Already glorying in the prize,
Measured his antlers with his eyes;
For the death-wound and death halloo,
Mustered his breath, his whinyard drew;—
But thundering as he came prepared,
With ready arm and weapon bared,
The wily quarry shunned the shock,
And turned him from the opposing rock;
Then, dashing down a darksome glen,
Soon lost to hound and hunter's ken,
In the deep Trossachs' wildest nook[n]
His solitary refuge took.
There, while close couched, the thicket shed
Cold dews and wild-flowers on his head,
He heard the baffled dogs in vain
Rave through the hollow pass amain,
Chiding the rocks that yelled again.

IX

Close on the hounds the hunter came,
To cheer them on the vanished game;
But, stumbling in the rugged dell,
The gallant horse exhausted fell.
The impatient rider strove in vain
To rouse him with the spur and rein,
For the good steed, his labours o'er,
Stretched his stiff limbs, to rise no more;

138 *whinyard*: long knife.

Then, touched with pity and remorse,
He sorrowed o'er the expiring horse:
'I little thought, when first thy rein
I slacked upon the banks of Seine,
That Highland eagle e'er should feed
On thy fleet limbs, my matchless steed!
Woe worth the chase, woe worth the day,
That costs thy life, my gallant grey!'

X

Then through the dell his horn resounds,
From vain pursuit to call the hounds.
Back limped, with slow and crippled pace,
The sulky leaders of the chase;
Close to their master's side they pressed,
With drooping tail and humbled crest,
But still the dingle's hollow throat
Prolonged the swelling bugle-note.
The owlets started from their dream,
The eagles answered with their scream,
Round and around the sounds were cast
Till echo seemed an answering blast;
And on the hunter hied his way,
To join some comrades of the day;
Yet often paused, so strange the road,
So wondrous were the scenes it showed.

XI

The western waves of ebbing day
Rolled o'er the glen their level way;
Each purple peak, each flinty spire,
Was bathed in floods of living fire.
But not a setting beam could glow
Within the dark ravines below,
Where twined the path in shadow hid,
Round many a rocky pyramid,
Shooting abruptly from the dell
Its thunder-splintered pinnacle;
Round many an insulated mass,
The native bulwarks of the pass,

163 *Seine*: James V resided in France in 1536–7.

Huge as the tower which builders vain
Presumptuous piled on Shinar's plain.
The rocky summits, split and rent,
Formed turret, dome, or battlement,
Or seemed fantastically set
With cupola or minaret,
Wild crests as pagod ever decked,
Or mosque of Eastern architect.
Nor were these earth-born castles bare,
Nor lacked they many a banner fair;
For, from their shivered brows displayed,
Far o'er the unfathomable glade,
All twinkling with the dewdrops sheen,
The brier-rose fell in streamers green,
And creeping shrubs, of thousand dyes,
Waved in the west-wind's summer sighs.

XII

Boon nature scattered, free and wild,
Each plant or flower, the mountain's child.
Here eglantine embalmed the air,
Hawthorn and hazel mingled there;
The primrose pale, and violet flower,
Found in each cliff a narrow bower;
Fox-glove and night-shade, side by side,
Emblems of punishment and pride,[n]
Grouped their dark hues with every stain
The weather-beaten crags retain.
With boughs that quaked at every breath,
Grey birch and aspen wept beneath;
Aloft, the ash and warrior oak
Cast anchor in the rifted rock;
And higher yet, the pine-tree hung
His shattered trunk, and frequent flung,
Where seemed the cliffs to meet on high,
His boughs athwart the narrowed sky.
Highest of all, where white peaks glanced,
Where glistening streamers waved and danced,
The wanderer's eye could barely view
The summer heaven's delicious blue;

196 *tower*: i.e., of Babel, intended to reach Heaven: see Genesis 11:1–9.
208 *sheen*, adj.: beautiful, shining.

So wondrous wild, the whole might seem
The scenery of a fairy dream.

XIII

Onward, amid the copse 'gan peep
A narrow inlet still and deep,
Affording scarce such breadth of brim
As served the wild duck's brood to swim;
Lost for a space, through thickets veering,
But broader when again appearing,
Tall rocks and tufted knolls their face
Could on the dark-blue mirror trace;
And farther as the hunter strayed,
Still broader sweep its channels made.
The shaggy mounds no longer stood,
Emerging from entangled wood,
But, wave-encircled, seemed to float,
Like castle girdled with its moat;
Yet broader floods extending still
Divide them from their parent hill,
Till each, retiring, claims to be
An islet in an inland sea.

XIV

And now, to issue from the glen,
No pathway meets the wanderer's ken,
Unless he climb, with footing nice,
A far projecting precipice.
The broom's tough roots his ladder[n] made,
The hazel saplings lent their aid;
And thus an airy point he won,
Where, gleaming with the setting sun,
One burnished sheet of living gold,
Loch Katrine lay beneath him rolled;
In all her length far winding lay,
With promontory, creek, and bay,
And islands that, empurpled bright,
Floated amid the livelier light,
And mountains, that like giants stand,
To sentinel enchanted land.

255 *ken*: reach of sight. 263 *Loch Katrine*: see map, p. 293.

High on the south, huge Benvenue
Down to the lake in masses threw
Crags, knolls, and mounds, confusedly hurled,
The fragments of an earlier world;
A wildering forest feathered o'er
His ruined sides and summit hoar,
While on the north, through middle air,
Ben-an heaved high his forehead bare.

XV

From the steep promontory gazed
The stranger, raptured and amazed.
And, 'What a scene were here,' he cried,
'For princely pomp, or churchman's pride!
On this bold brow, a lordly tower;
In that soft vale, a lady's bower;
On yonder meadow, far away,
The turrets of a cloister grey;
How blithely might the bugle-horn
Chide, on the lake, the lingering morn!
How sweet, at eve, the lover's lute
Chime, when the groves were still and mute!
And, when the midnight moon should lave
Her forehead in the silver wave,
How solemn on the ear would come
The holy matins' distant hum,
While the deep peal's commanding tone
Should wake, in yonder islet lone,
A sainted hermit from his cell,
To drop a bead with every knell—
And bugle, lute, and bell, and all,
Should each bewildered stranger call
To friendly feast, and lighted hall.

XVI

'Blithe were it then to wander here!
But now,—beshrew yon nimble deer,—
Like that same hermit's thin and spare,
The copse must give my evening fare;

277 *Ben-an*: hill to N. of the Trossachs (1,851 ft.).
299 *bewildered*: having lost his way (the literal meaning).

Some mossy bank my couch must be,
Some rustling oak my canopy.
Yet pass we that; the war and chase
Give little choice of resting-place;—
A summer night, in greenwood spent,
Were but to-morrow's merriment:
But hosts may in these wilds abound,
Such as are better missed than found;
To meet with Highland plunderers here
Were worse than loss of steed or deer.—
I am alone;—my bugle-strain
May call some straggler of the train;
Or, fall the worst that may betide,
Ere now this falchion has been tried.'

XVII

But scarce again his horn he wound,
When lo! forth starting at the sound,
From underneath an aged oak,
That slanted from the islet rock,
A damsel guider of its way,
A little skiff shot to the bay,
That round the promontory steep
Led its deep line in graceful sweep,
Eddying, in almost viewless wave,
The weeping willow-twig to lave,
And kiss, with whispering sound and slow,
The beach of pebbles bright as snow.
The boat had touched this silver strand,
Just as the Hunter left his stand,
And stood concealed amid the brake,
To view this Lady of the Lake.
The maiden paused, as if again
She thought to catch the distant strain.
With head up-raised, and look intent,
And eye and ear attentive bent,
And locks flung back, and lips apart,
Like monument of Grecian art,
In listening mood, she seemed to stand,
The guardian Naiad of the strand.

333 *brake*: thicket.

XVIII

And ne'er did Grecian chisel trace
A Nymph, a Naiad, or a Grace
Of finer form, or lovelier face!
What though the sun, with ardent frown,
Had slightly tinged her cheek with brown;
The sportive toil, which, short and light,
Had dyed her glowing hue so bright,
Served too in hastier swell to show
Short glimpses of a breast of snow:
What though no rule of courtly grace
To measured mood had trained her pace;
A foot more light, a step more true,
Ne'er from the heath-flower dashed the dew;
E'en the slight harebell raised its head,
Elastic from her airy tread:
What though upon her speech there hung
The accents of the mountain tongue;
Those silver sounds, so soft, so dear,
The listener held his breath to hear!

XIX

A Chieftain's daughter seemed the maid;
Her satin snood, her silken plaid,
Her golden brooch, such birth betrayed.
And seldom was a snood amid
Such wild luxuriant ringlets hid,
Whose glossy black to shame might bring
The plumage of the raven's wing;
And seldom o'er a breast so fair,
Mantled a plaid with modest care,
And never brooch the folds combined
Above a heart more good and kind.
Her kindness and her worth to spy,
You need but gaze on Ellen's eye;
Not Katrine, in her mirror blue,
Gives back the shaggy banks more true,
Than every free-born glance confessed
The guileless movements of her breast;

359 *accents*: she spoke Highland-English, presumably Gaelic too.
363 *snood*: hair-band worn by young unmarried women, the symbol of virginity. See end-note to III. 114 below, p. 296.

Whether joy danced in her dark eye,
Or woe or pity claimed a sigh,
Or filial love was glowing there,
Or meek devotion poured a prayer,
Or tale of injury called forth
The indignant spirit of the North.
One only passion unrevealed,
With maiden pride the maid concealed,
Yet not less purely felt the flame;—
O need I tell that passion's name?

XX

Impatient of the silent horn,
Now on the gale her voice was borne:—
'Father!' she cried; the rocks around
Loved to prolong the gentle sound.
A while she paused, no answer came;
'Malcolm, was thine the blast?' the name
Less resolutely uttered fell;
The echoes could not catch the swell.
'A stranger I,' the Huntsman said,
Advancing from the hazel shade.
The maid, alarmed, with hasty oar,
Pushed her light shallop from the shore,
And when a space was gained between,
Closer she drew her bosom's screen;
(So forth the startled swan would swing,
So turn to prune his ruffled wing.)
Then safe, though fluttered and amazed,
She paused, and on the stranger gazed.
Not his the form, nor his the eye,
That youthful maidens wont to fly.

XXI

On his bold visage middle age
Had slightly pressed its signet sage,
Yet had not quenched the open truth
And fiery vehemence of youth;
Forward and frolic glee was there,
The will to do, the soul to dare,
The sparkling glance, soon blown to fire,
Of hasty love, or headlong ire.

His limbs were cast in manly mould,
For hardy sports or contest bold;
And though in peaceful garb arrayed,
And weaponless, except his blade,
His stately mien as well implied
A high-born heart, a martial pride,
As if a Baron's crest he wore,
And sheathed in armour trode the shore.
Slighting the petty need he showed,
He told of his benighted road;
His ready speech flowed fair and free,
In phrase of gentlest courtesy;
Yet seemed that tone, and gesture bland,
Less used to sue than to command.

XXII

A while the maid the stranger eyed,
And, reassured, at length replied,
That Highland halls were open still
To wildered wanderers of the hill.
'Nor think you unexpected come
To yon lone isle, our desert home;
Before the heath had lost the dew,
This morn, a couch was pulled for you;
On yonder mountain's purple head
Have ptarmigan and heath-cock bled,
And our broad nets have swept the mere,
To furnish forth your evening cheer.'
'Now, by the rood, my lovely maid,
Your courtesy has erred,' he said;
'No right have I to claim, misplaced,
The welcome of expected guest.
A wanderer, here by fortune tost,
My way, my friends, my courser lost,
I ne'er before, believe me, fair,
Have ever drawn your mountain air,
Till on this lake's romantic strand
I found a fay in fairy land!'

XXIII

'I well believe,' the maid replied,
As her light skiff approached the side,

'I well believe that ne'er before
Your foot has trod Loch Katrine's shore;
But yet, as far as yesternight,
Old Allan-Bane foretold your plight,—
A grey-haired sire, whose eye intent
Was on the visioned future bent.
He saw your steed, a dappled grey,
Lie dead beneath the birchen way;
Painted exact your form and mien,
Your hunting suit of Lincoln green,
That tasselled horn so gaily gilt,
That falchion's crooked blade and hilt,
That cap with heron plumage trim,
And yon two hounds so dark and grim.
He bade that all should ready be
To grace a guest of fair degree;
But light I held his prophecy,
And deemed it was my father's horn
Whose echoes o'er the lake were borne.'

XXIV

The stranger smiled: 'Since to your home
A destined errant-knight I come,
Announced by prophet sooth and old,
Doomed, doubtless, for achievement bold,
I'll lightly front each high emprise
For one kind glance of those bright eyes.
Permit me, first, the task to guide
Your fairy frigate o'er the tide.'[n]
The maid, with smile suppressed and sly,
The toil unwonted saw him try;
For seldom sure, if e'er before,
His noble hand had grasped an oar:
Yet with main strength his strokes he drew,
And o'er the lake the shallop flew;
With heads erect and whimpering cry,
The hounds behind their passage ply.

460 *visioned*: Allan-Bane is gifted with 'second sight', the power of foreseeing the future. 462 *birchen*: overhung with birch trees.
466 *falchion*: broad curved convex-edged sword. 477 *doomed*: destined.
478 *front:* confront. 478 *emprise*: enterprise.
481 *frigate*: a word for a large ship, humorously applied to the shallop.

Nor frequent does the bright oar break
The darkening mirror of the lake,
Until the rocky isle they reach,
And moor their shallop on the beach.

XXV

The stranger viewed the shore around;
'Twas all so close with copsewood bound,
Nor track nor pathway might declare
That human foot frequented there,
Until the mountain-maiden showed
A clambering unsuspected road,
That winded through the tangled screen,
And opened on a narrow green,
Where weeping birch and willow round
With their long fibres swept the ground.
Here, for retreat in dangerous hour,
Some chief had framed a rustic bower.[n]

XXVI

It was a lodge of ample size,
But strange of structure and device;
Of such materials, as around
The workman's hand had readiest found.
Lopped of their boughs, their hoar trunks bared,
And by the hatchet rudely squared
To give the walls their destined height
The sturdy oak and ash unite;
While moss and clay and leaves combined
To fence each crevice from the wind.
The lighter pine-trees, over-head,
Their slender length for rafters spread,
And withered heath and rushes dry
Supplied a russet canopy.
Due westward, fronting to the green,
A rural portico was seen,
Aloft on native pillars borne,
Of mountain fir, with bark unshorn,
Where Ellen's hand had taught to twine
The ivy and Idaean vine,

525 *Idaean Vine:* Latin *Vitis Idæa*, the red whortleberry or cowberry.

The clematis, the favoured flower
Which boasts the name of virgin-bower,
And every hardy plant could bear
Loch Katrine's keen and searching air.
An instant in this porch she stayed,
And gaily to the stranger said,
'On heaven and on thy lady call,
And enter the enchanted hall!'—

XXVII

'My hope, my heaven, my trust must be,
My gentle guide, in following thee.'
He crossed the threshold—and a clang
Of angry steel that instant rang.
To his bold brow his spirit rushed,
But soon for vain alarm he blushed
When on the floor he saw displayed,
Cause of the din, a naked blade
Dropped from the sheath, that careless flung,
Upon a stag's huge antlers swung;
For all around, the walls to grace,
Hung trophies of the fight or chase:
A target there, a bugle here,
A battle-axe, a hunting-spear,
And broadswords, bows, and arrows store,
With the tusked trophies of the boar.
Here grins the wolf as when he died,
And there the wild-cat's brindled hide
The frontlet of the elk adorns,
Or mantles o'er the bison's horns;
Pennons and flags defaced and stained,
That blackening streaks of blood retained,
And deer-skins, dappled, dun, and white,
With otter's fur and seal's unite,
In rude and uncouth tapestry all,
To garnish forth the silvan hall.

XXVIII

The wondering stranger round him gazed,
And next the fallen weapon raised:

549–53 Except for the wild cat, the animals mentioned are today extinct in Scotland.

Few were the arms whose sinewy strength
Sufficed to stretch it forth at length;
And as the brand he poised and swayed,
'I never knew but one,' he said,
'Whose stalwart arm might brook to wield
A blade like this in battle-field.'
She sighed, then smiled and took the word:
'You see the guardian champion's sword;
As light it trembles in his hand,
As in my grasp a hazel wand;
My sire's tall form might grace the part
Of Ferragus or Ascabart;
But in the absent giant's hold
Are women now, and menials old.'

XXIX

The mistress of the mansion came,
Mature of age, a graceful dame;
Whose easy step and stately port
Had well become a princely court;
To whom, though more than kindred knew,
Young Ellen gave a mother's due.
Meet welcome to her guest she made,
And every courteous rite was paid
That hospitality could claim,
Though all unasked[n] his birth and name.
Such then the reverence to a guest,
That fellest foe might join the feast,
And from his deadliest foeman's door
Unquestioned turn, the banquet o'er.
At length his rank the stranger names,
'The Knight of Snowdoun, James Fitz-James;
Lord of a barren heritage,
Which his brave sires, from age to age,
By their good swords had held with toil;
His sire had fallen in such turmoil,

573 *Ferragus*: giant in Ariosto, *Orlando Furioso*, and in the Auchinleck MS. *Romance of Charlemagne*. He was a pagan, forty feet high, whom Orlando slew in single combat.

573 *Ascabart*: a dwarfish giant, only thirty feet high, driven out of his town because he was so small, and conquered by Bevis of Hampton in the Romance of that name.

574 *hold*: stronghold.

And he, God wot, was forced to stand
Oft for his right with blade in hand.
This morning, with Lord Moray's train
He chased a stalwart stag in vain,
Outstripped his comrades, missed the deer,
Lost his good steed, and wandered here.'

XXX

Fain would the Knight in turn require
The name and state of Ellen's sire.
Well showed the elder lady's mien,
That courts and cities she had seen;
Ellen, though more her looks displayed
The simple grace of silvan maid,
In speech and gesture, form and face,
Showed she was come of gentle race.
'Twere strange, in ruder rank to find
Such looks, such manners, and such mind.
Each hint the Knight of Snowdoun gave,
Dame Margaret heard with silence grave;
Or Ellen, innocently gay,
Turned all inquiry light away—
'Weird women we! by dale and down
We dwell, afar from tower and town.
We stem the flood, we ride the blast,
On wandering knights our spells we cast;
While viewless minstrels touch the string,
'Tis thus our charmed rhymes we sing.'
She sung, and still a harp unseen
Filled up the symphony between.

XXXI

SONG

'Soldier, rest! thy warfare o'er,
  Sleep the sleep that knows not breaking;
Dream of battled fields no more,
  Days of danger, nights of waking.
In our isle's enchanted hall,
  Hands unseen thy couch are strewing,
Fairy strains of music fall,
  Every sense in slumber dewing.

598 *Moray*: a natural son of James IV and therefore James V's brother.

Soldier, rest! thy warfare o'er,
Dream of fighting fields no more:
Sleep the sleep that knows not breaking,
Morn of toil, nor night of waking.

No rude sound shall reach thine ear,
  Armour's clang, or war-steed champing,
Trump nor pibroch summon here
  Mustering clan, or squadron tramping.
Yet the lark's shrill fife may come
  At the day-break from the fallow,
And the bittern sound his drum,
  Booming from the sedgy shallow.
Ruder sounds shall none be near,
Guards nor warders challenge here,
Here's no war-steed's neigh and champing,
Shouting clans, or squadrons stamping.'

XXXII

She paused—then, blushing, led the lay
To grace the stranger of the day.
Her mellow notes awhile prolong
The cadence of the flowing song,
Till to her lips in measured frame
The minstrel verse spontaneous came:

SONG CONTINUED

'Huntsman, rest! thy chase is done;
  While our slumbrous spells assail ye,
Dream not, with the rising sun,
  Bugles here shall sound reveillé.
Sleep! the deer is in his den;
  Sleep! thy hounds are by thee lying;
Sleep! nor dream in yonder glen,
  How thy gallant steed lay dying.
Huntsman, rest! the chase is done,
Think not of the rising sun,
For at dawning to assail ye,
Here no bugles sound reveillé.'

638 *pibroch*: see II. 356, end-note below, p. 295.

XXXIII

The hall was cleared—the stranger's bed
Was there of mountain heather spread,
Where oft a hundred guests had lain,
And dreamed their forest sports again.
But vainly did the heath-flower shed
Its moorland fragrance round his head;
Not Ellen's spell had lulled to rest
The fever of his troubled breast.
In broken dreams the image rose
Of varied perils, pains, and woes:
His steed now flounders in the brake,
Now sinks his barge upon the lake;
Now leader of a broken host,
His standard falls, his honour's lost.
Then,—from my couch may heavenly might
Chase that worst phantom of the night!—
Again returned the scenes of youth,
Of confident undoubting truth;
Again his soul he interchanged
With friends whose hearts were long estranged.
They come, in dim procession led,
The cold, the faithless, and the dead;
As warm each hand, each brow as gay,
As if they parted yesterday.
And doubt distracts him at the view—
O were his senses false or true?
Dreamed he of death, or broken vow,
Or is it all a vision now?

XXXIV

At length, with Ellen in a grove
He seemed to walk, and speak of love;
She listened with a blush and sigh,
His suit was warm, his hopes were high.
He sought her yielded hand to clasp,
And a cold gauntlet met his grasp:
The phantom's sex was changed and gone,
Upon its head a helmet shone;
Slowly enlarged to giant size,
With darkened cheek and threatening eyes,

The grisly visage, stern and hoar,
To Ellen still a likeness bore.
He woke, and, panting with affright,
Recalled the vision of the night.
The hearth's decaying brands were red,
And deep and dusky lustre shed,
Half-showing, half concealing, all
The uncouth trophies of the hall.
'Mid those the stranger fixed his eye,
Where that huge falchion hung on high,
And thoughts on thoughts, a countless throng,
Rushed, chasing countless thoughts along,
Until, the giddy whirl to cure,
He rose, and sought the moonshine pure.

XXXV

The wild-rose, eglantine, and broom,
Wasted around their rich perfume;
The birch-trees wept in fragrant balm,
The aspens slept beneath the calm;
The silver light, with quivering glance,
Played on the water's still expanse:
Wild were the heart whose passion's sway
Could rage beneath the sober ray!
He felt its calm, that warrior guest,
While thus he communed with his breast:
'Why is it at each turn I trace
Some memory of that exiled race?
Can I not mountain maiden spy,
But she must bear the Douglas[n] eye?
Can I not view a Highland brand,
But it must match the Douglas hand?
Can I not frame a fevered dream,
But still the Douglas is the theme?
I'll dream no more; by manly mind
Not even in sleep is will resigned.
My midnight orisons said o'er,
I'll turn to rest, and dream no more.'
His midnight orisons be told,
A prayer with every bead of gold,
Consigned to heaven his cares and woes,
And sunk in undisturbed repose;

Until the heath-cock shrilly crew,
And morning dawned on Benvenue.

Canto Second

The Island

I

At morn the black-cock trims his jetty wing,
'Tis morning prompts the linnet's blithest lay,
All Nature's children feel the matin spring
Of life reviving with reviving day;
And while yon little bark glides down the bay,
Wafting the stranger on his way again,
Morn's genial influence roused a minstrel grey,
And sweetly o'er the lake was heard thy strain,
Mixed with the sounding harp, O white-haired Allan-Bane!

II

SONG

'Not faster yonder rowers' might
Flings from their oars the spray,
Not faster yonder rippling bright,
That tracks the shallop's course in light,
Melts in the lake away,
Than men from memory erase
The benefits of former days;
Then, stranger, go! good speed the while,
Nor think again of the lonely isle.

High place to thee in royal court,
High place in battled line,
Good hawk and hound for silvan sport,
Where Beauty sees the brave resort,
The honoured meed be thine!
True be thy sword, thy friend sincere,
Thy lady constant, kind, and dear,
And lost in love's and friendship's smile
Be memory of the lonely isle.

7 *minstrel*: 'Highland chieftains, to a late period, retained in their service the bard as a family officer' (S).

13 *tracks ... in light*: marks out the shallop's path in the medium of light. Cp. 'write in ink'.

III

But if beneath yon southern sky
  A plaided stranger roam,
Whose drooping crest and stifled sigh,
And sunken cheek and heavy eye,
  Pine for his Highland home;
Then, warrior, then be thine to show
The care that soothes a wanderer's woe;
Remember then thy hap ere while,
A stranger in the lonely isle.

Or if on life's uncertain main
  Mishap shall mar thy sail;
If faithful, wise, and brave in vain,
Woe, want, and exile thou sustain
  Beneath the fickle gale;
Waste not a sigh on fortune changed,
On thankless courts, or friends estranged,
But come where kindred worth shall smile
To greet thee in the lonely isle.'

IV

As died the sounds upon the tide,
The shallop reached the mainland side,
And ere his onward way he took,
The stranger cast a lingering look,
Where easily his eye might reach
The Harper on the islet beach,
Reclined against a blighted tree,
As wasted, grey, and worn as he.
To minstrel meditation given,
His reverend brow was raised to heaven,
As from the rising sun to claim
A sparkle of inspiring flame.
His hand, reclined upon the wire,
Seemed watching the awakening fire;
So still he sate, as those who wait
Till judgment speak the doom of fate;
So still, as if no breeze might dare
To lift one lock of hoary hair;

35 *thy . . . while*: what happened to thee formerly.
44 *kindred*: similar to thine own.

So still, as life itself were fled,
In the last sound his harp had sped.

V

Upon a rock with lichens wild,
Beside him Ellen sate and smiled.
Smiled she to see the stately drake
Lead forth his fleet upon the lake,
While her vexed spaniel, from the beach
Bayed at the prize beyond his reach?
Yet tell me, then, the maid who knows,
Why deepened on her cheek the rose?
Forgive, forgive, Fidelity!
Perchance the maiden smiled to see
Yon parting lingerer wave adieu,
And stop and turn to wave anew;
And, lovely ladies, ere your ire
Condemn the heroine of my lyre,
Show me the fair would scorn to spy,
And prize such conquest of her eye!

VI

While yet he loitered on the spot,
It seemed as Ellen marked him not;
But when he turned him to the glade,
One courteous parting sign she made;
And after, oft the knight would say,
That not when prize of festal day
Was dealt him by the brightest fair
Who e'er wore jewel in her hair,
So highly did his bosom swell,
As at that simple mute farewell.
Now with a trusty mountain-guide,
And his dark stag-hounds by his side,
He parts; the maid, unconscious still,
Watched him wind slowly round the hill;
But when his stately form was hid,
The guardian in her bosom chid:

74 *Forgive . . . Fidelity*: Ellen's interest in the stranger is treated as a violation of the faith owed to Malcolm.
87 *festal day*: i.e., tournament day.

'Thy Malcolm! vain and selfish maid!'
'Twas thus upbraiding conscience said:
'Not so had Malcolm idly hung
On the smooth phrase of southern tongue;
Not so had Malcolm strained his eye,
Another step than thine to spy.'—
'Wake, Allan-Bane,' aloud she cried,
To the old Minstrel by her side;
'Arouse thee from thy moody dream!
I'll give thy harp heroic theme,
And warm thee with a noble name;
Pour forth the glory of the Græme!'[n]
Scarce from her lip the word had rushed,
When deep the conscious maiden blushed;
For of his clan, in hall and bower,
Young Malcolm Græme was held the flower.

VII

The Minstrel waked his harp; three times
Arose the well-known martial chimes,
And thrice their high heroic pride
In melancholy murmurs died.
'Vainly thou bid'st, O noble maid,'
Clasping his withered hands, he said,
'Vainly thou bid'st me wake the strain,
Though all unwont to bid in vain.
Alas! than mine a mightier hand
Has tuned my harp, my strings has spanned!
I touch the chords of joy, but low
And mournful answer notes of woe;
And the proud march, which victors tread,
Sinks in the wailing for the dead.
O well for me, if mine alone
That dirge's deep prophetic tone!
If, as my tuneful fathers said,
This harp, which erst Saint Modan[n] swayed,
Can thus its master's fate foretell,
Then welcome be the minstrel's knell!

112 *in hall and bower*: i.e., among men and women.
130 *tuneful fathers*: the office of harper was usually hereditary.

VIII

But ah! dear lady, thus it sighed
The eve thy sainted mother died;
And such the sounds which, while I strove
To wake a lay of war or love,
Came marring all the festal mirth,
Appalling me who gave them birth,
And, disobedient to my call,
Wailed loud through Bothwell's bannered hall,
Ere Douglases, to ruin driven,
Were exiled from their native heaven.
Oh! if yet worse mishap and woe
My master's house must undergo,
Or aught but weal to Ellen fair
Brood in these accents of despair,
No future bard, sad Harp! shall fling
Triumph or rapture from thy string;
One short, one final strain shall flow,
Fraught with unutterable woe,
Then shivered shall thy fragments lie,
Thy master cast him down and die!'

IX

Soothing she answered him, 'Assuage,
Mine honoured friend, the fears of age;
All melodies to thee are known,
That harp has rung, or pipe has blown,
In Lowland vale or Highland glen,
From Tweed to Spey—what marvel, then,
At times, unbidden notes should rise,
Confusedly bound in memory's ties,
Entangling, as they rush along,
The war-march with the funeral song?
Small ground is now for boding fear;
Obscure, but safe, we rest us here.
My sire, in native virtue great,
Resigning lordship, lands, and state,
Not then to fortune more resigned,
Than yonder oak might give the wind;

141 *Bothwell's . . . hall*: the Douglas stronghold in Lanark. See end-note on I. 731, for the exile of Archibald Douglas, Earl of Angus.
159 *Tweed, Spey*: southern and northern rivers respectively.
168 *resigned*: past tense, not participle.

The graceful foliage storms may reave,
The noble stem they cannot grieve.
For me,'—she stooped, and, looking round,
Plucked a blue hare-bell from the ground,—
'For me, whose memory scarce conveys
An image of more splendid days,
This little flower, that loves the lea,
May well my simple emblem be;
It drinks heaven's dew as blithe as rose
That in the king's own garden grows;
And when I place it in my hair,
Allan, a bard is bound to swear
He ne'er saw coronet so fair.'
Then playfully the chaplet wild
She wreathed in her dark locks, and smiled.

X

Her smile, her speech, with winning sway,
Wiled the old harper's mood away.
With such a look as hermits throw,
When angels stoop to soothe their woe,
He gazed, till fond regret and pride
Thrilled to a tear, then thus replied:
'Loveliest and best! thou little know'st
The rank, the honours, thou hast lost!
O might I live to see thee grace,
In Scotland's court, thy birth-right place,
To see my favourite's step advance,
The lightest in the courtly dance,
The cause of every gallant's sigh,
And leading star of every eye,
And theme of every minstrel's art,
The Lady of the Bleeding Heart!'

XI

'Fair dreams are these,' the maiden cried,
(Light was her accent, yet she sighed)
'Yet is this mossy rock to me
Worth splendid chair and canopy;
Nor would my footsteps spring more gay
In courtly dance than blithe strathspey,

200 *Bleeding Heart*: emblem of the Douglas family.

Nor half so pleased mine ear incline
To royal minstrel's lay as thine.
And then for suitors proud and high,
To bend before my conquering eye,—
Thou, flattering bard! thyself wilt say,
That grim Sir Roderick owns its sway.
The Saxon scourge, Clan-Alpine's pride,
The terror of Loch Lomond's side,
Would, at my suit, thou knows't, delay
A Lennox foray—for a day.'

XII

The ancient bard her glee repressed:
'Ill hast thou chosen theme for jest!
For who, through all this western wild,
Named Black Sir Roderick e'er, and smiled?
In Holy-Rood a knight he slew;
I saw, when back the dirk he drew,
Courtiers give place before the stride
Of the undaunted homicide;
And since, though outlawed, hath his hand
Full sternly kept his mountain land.
Who else dared give—ah! woe the day,
That I such hated truth should say—
The Douglas, like a stricken deer,[n]
Disowned by every noble peer,
Even the rude refuge we have here?
Alas, this wild marauding Chief
Alone might hazard our relief,
And now thy maiden charms expand,
Looks for his guerdon in thy hand;
Full soon may dispensation[n] sought,
To back his suit, from Rome he brought.
Then, though an exile on the hill,
Thy father, as the Douglas, still

213 *Saxon*: Sassenach (lowlander).
213 *Clan-Alpine*: the Macgregors, who claimed descent from Alpine King of Scots *c.* A.D. 787.
216 *Lennox*: the fertile district at the southern end of Loch Lomond, including the whole county of Dunbarton and part of the counties of Stirling, Perth and Renfrew.
221 *Holy-Rood*: the royal palace in Edinburgh.

Be held in reverence and fear;
And though to Roderick thou'rt so dear,
That thou might'st guide with silken thread,
Slave of thy will, this chieftain dread,
Yet, O loved maid, thy mirth refrain!
Thy hand is on a lion's mane.'

XIII

'Minstrel,' the maid replied, and high
Her father's soul glanced from her eye,
'My debts to Roderick's house I know:
All that a mother could bestow,
To Lady Margaret's care I owe,
Since first an orphan in the wild
She sorrowed o'er her sister's child;
To her brave chieftain son, from ire
Of Scotland's king who shrouds my sire,
A deeper, holier debt is owed;
And, could I pay it with my blood,
Allan! Sir Roderick should command
My blood, my life,—but not my hand.
Rather will Ellen Douglas dwell
A votaress in Maronnan's cell;[n]
Rather through realms beyond the sea,
Seeking the world's cold charity,
Where ne'er was spoke a Scottish word,
And ne'er the name of Douglas heard,
An outcast pilgrim will she rove,
Than wed the man she cannot love.

XIV

Thou shakest, good friend, thy tresses grey,
That pleading look, what can it say
But what I own?—I grant him brave,
But wild as Bracklinn's thundering wave;
And generous—save vindictive mood,
Or jealous transport, chafe his blood:
I grant him true to friendly band,
As his claymore is to his hand;
But O! that very blade of steel
More mercy for a foe would feel:

270 *Bracklinn*: a waterfall on the River Keltie, 1½ miles NNE. of Callander.

I grant him liberal, to fling
Among his clan the wealth they bring,
When back by lake and glen they wind,
And in the Lowland leave behind,
Where once some pleasant hamlet stood,
A mass of ashes slaked with blood.
The hand that for my father fought
I honour, as his daughter ought;
But can I clasp it reeking red,
From peasants slaughtered in their shed?
No! wildly while his virtues gleam,
They make his passions darker seem,
And flash along his spirit high,
Like lightning o'er the midnight sky.
While yet a child,—and children know,
Instinctive taught, the friend and foe,—
I shuddered at his brow of gloom,
His shadowy plaid, and sable plume;
A maiden grown, I ill could bear
His haughty mien and lordly air:
But, if thou join'st a suitor's claim,
In serious mood, to Roderick's name,
I thrill with anguish! or, if e'er
A Douglas knew the word, with fear.
To change such odious theme were best;
What think'st thou of our stranger guest?'

XV

'What think I of him?—woe the while
That brought such wanderer to our isle!
Thy father's battle-brand, of yore
For Tine-man forged by fairy lore,[n]
What time he leagued, no longer foes,
His Border spears with Hotspur's bows,
Did, self-unscabbarded, foreshow
The footstep of a secret foe.
If courtly spy hath harboured here,
What may we for the Douglas fear?
What for this island, deemed of old
Clan-Alpine's last and surest hold?
If neither spy nor foe, I pray
What yet may jealous Roderick say?

Nay, wave not thy disdainful head,
Bethink thee of the discord dread
That kindled, when at Beltane game
Thou led'st the dance with Malcolm Græme;
Still, though thy sire the peace renewed,
Smoulders in Roderick's breast the feud.
Beware!—But hark, what sounds are these?
My dull ears catch no faltering breeze;
No weeping birch, nor aspens wake,
Nor breath is dimpling in the lake;
Still is the canna's hoary beard;
Yet, by my minstrel faith, I heard—
And hark again! some pipe of war
Sends the bold pibroch from afar.'

XVI

Far up the lengthened lake were spied
Four darkening specks upon the tide,
That, slow enlarging on the view,
Four manned and masted barges grew,
And, bearing downwards from Glengyle,
Steered full upon the lonely isle;
The point of Brianchoil they passed,
And, to the windward as they cast,
Against the sun they gave to shine
The bold Sir Roderick's bannered Pine.
Nearer and nearer as they bear,
Spears, pikes, and axes flash in air.
Now might you see the tartans brave,
And plaids and plumage dance and wave:
Now see the bonnets sink and rise,
As his tough oar the rower plies;
See, flashing at each sturdy stroke,
The wave ascending into smoke;
See the proud pipers on the bow,
And mark the gaudy streamers flow

319 *Beltane*: a Celtic festival celebrated on or about the first of May with dances and bonfires.
327 *canna*: cotton-grass.
335 *Glengyle*: glen at head of Loch Katrine.
337 *Brianchoil*: promontory N. of Loch Katrine.
340 *Pine*: emblem of Clan-Alpine.

From their loud chanters down, and sweep
The furrowed bosom of the deep,
As, rushing through the lake amain,
They plied the ancient Highland strain.

XVII

Ever, as on they bore, more loud
And louder rung the pibroch[n] proud.
At first the sound, by distance tame,
Mellowed along the waters came,
And, lingering long by cape and bay,
Wailed every harsher note away;
Then bursting bolder on the ear,
The clan's shrill Gathering they could hear;
Those thrilling sounds, that call the might
Of old Clan-Alpine to the fight.
Thick beat the rapid notes, as when
The mustering hundreds shake the glen,
And, hurrying at the signal dread,
The battered earth returns their tread.
Then prelude light, of livelier tone,
Expressed their merry marching on,
Ere peal of closing battle rose,
With mingled outcry, shrieks, and blows;
And mimic din of stroke and ward,
As broadsword upon target jarred;
And groaning pause, ere yet again,
Condensed, the battle yelled amain;
The rapid charge, the rallying shout,
Retreat borne headlong into rout,
And bursts of triumph, to declare
Clan-Alpine's conquest—all were there.
Nor ended thus the strain; but slow
Sunk in a moan prolonged and low,
And changed the conquering clarion swell
For wild lament o'er those that fell.

XVIII

The war-pipes ceased; but lake and hill
Were busy with their echoes still;

362 *Gathering*: mustering tune.
371 *closing*: beginning (of battle).

And, when they slept, a vocal strain
Bade their hoarse chorus wake again,
While loud a hundred clansmen raise
Their voices in their Chieftain's praise.
Each boatman, bending to his oar,
With measured sweep the burden bore,
In such wild cadence, as the breeze
Makes through December's leafless trees.
The chorus first could Allan know,
'Roderick Vich Alpine, ho! iro!'
And near, and nearer as they rowed,
Distinct the martial ditty flowed.

XIX

BOAT SONG[n]

'Hail to the Chief who in triumph advances!
  Honoured and blessed be the evergreen Pine!
Long may the tree, in his banner that glances,
  Flourish, the shelter and grace of our line!
    Heaven send it happy dew,
    Earth lend it sap anew,
Gaily to burgeon, and broadly to grow,
    While every Highland glen
    Sends our shout back again,
Roderigh Vich Alpine dhu,[n] ho! ieroe!

Ours is no sapling, chance-sown by the fountain,
  Blooming at Beltane, in winter to fade;
When the whirlwind has stripped every leaf on the
    mountain,
  The more shall Clan-Alpine exult in her shade.
    Moored in the rifted rock,
    Proof to the tempest's shock,
Firmer he roots him the ruder it blow;
    Menteith and Breadalbane, then,
    Echo his praise again,
Roderigh Vich Alpine dhu, ho! ieroe!

396 *Vich*: 'mhic', vocative of 'mac', a son (Stuart, p. 185).
396 *ho*! *iro*!: boat-song's refrain.
416 *Breadalbane*: mountainous district in NW. Perthshire between Loch Lomond and Loch Tay.

XX

Proudly our pibroch has thrilled in Glen Fruin,
And Bannochar's groans to our slogan replied;
Glen Luss and Ross-dhu, they are smoking in ruin,
And the best of Loch Lomond lie dead on her side.
Widow and Saxon maid
Long shall lament our raid,
Think of Clan-Alpine with fear and with woe;
Lennox and Leven-glen
Shake when they hear again,
Roderigh Vich Alpine dhu, ho! ieroe!

Row vassals, row, for the pride of the Highlands!
Stretch to your oars, for the evergreen Pine!
O! that the rose-bud that graces yon islands
Were wreathed in a garland around him to twine!
O that some seedling gem,
Worthy such noble stem,
Honoured and blessed in their shadow might grow!
Loud should Clan-Alpine then
Ring from her deepmost glen,
Roderigh Vich Alpine dhu, ho! ieroe!'

XXI

With all her joyful female band
Had Lady Margaret sought the strand.
Loose on the breeze their tresses flew,
And high their snowy arms they threw,
As echoing back with shrill acclaim,
And chorus wild, the Chieftain's name;
While, prompt to please, with mother's art,
The darling passion of his heart,
The Dame called Ellen to the strand,
To greet her kinsman ere he land:
'Come, loiterer, come! a Douglas thou,
And shun to wreathe a victor's brow?'

419 *Glen Fruin*: valley near the SW. of Loch Lomond.
420 *Bannochar*: Bannachra, a hamlet on Fruin Water, ENE. of Helensburgh.
421 *Glen Luss*: valley on W. shore of Loch Lomond.
421 *Ross-dhu*: 'dark headland', a small promontory on W. shore of Loch Lomond.
426 *Lennox and Leven-glen*: district at S. end of Loch Lomond; the R. Leven drains Loch Lomond into the Clyde.

Reluctantly and slow, the maid
The unwelcome summoning obeyed,
And, when a distant bugle rung,
In the mid-path aside she sprung:
'List, Allan-Bane! From mainland cast,
I hear my father's signal blast.
Be ours,' she cried, 'the skiff to guide,
And waft him from the mountain side.'
Then, like a sunbeam, swift and bright,
She darted to her shallop light,
And, eagerly while Roderick scanned,
For her dear form, his mother's band,
The islet far behind her lay,
And she had landed in the bay.

XXII

Some feelings are to mortals given,
With less of earth in them than heaven:
And if there be a human tear
From passion's dross refined and clear,
A tear so limpid and so meek,
It would not stain an angel's cheek,
'Tis that which pious fathers shed
Upon a duteous daughter's head!
And as the Douglas to his breast
His darling Ellen closely pressed,
Such holy drops her tresses steeped,
Though 'twas an hero's eye that weeped.
Nor while on Ellen's faltering tongue
Her filial welcomes crowded hung,
Marked she that fear (affection's proof)
Still held a graceful youth aloof;
No! not till Douglas named his name,
Although the youth was Malcolm Græme.

XXIII

Allan, with wistful look the while,
Marked Roderick landing on the isle;
His master piteously he eyed,
Then gazed upon the Chieftain's pride.
Then dashed, with hasty hand, away
From his dimmed eye the gathering spray;

And Douglas, as his hand he laid
On Malcolm's shoulder, kindly said,
'Canst thou, young friend, no meaning spy
In my poor follower's glistening eye?
I'll tell thee:—he recalls the day,
When in my praise he led the lay
O'er the arched gate of Bothwell proud,
While many a minstrel answered loud,
When Percy's Norman pennon,[n] won
In bloody field, before me shone,
And twice ten knights, the least a name
As mighty as yon Chief may claim,
Gracing my pomp, behind me came.
Yet trust me, Malcolm, not so proud
Was I of all that marshalled crowd,
Though the waned crescent owned my might,
And in my train trooped lord and knight,
Though Blantyre hymned her holiest lays,
And Bothwell's bards flung back my praise,
As when this old man's silent tear,
And this poor maid's affection dear,
A welcome give more kind and true,
Than aught my better fortunes knew.
Forgive, my friend, a father's boast,
O! it out-beggars all I lost!'

XXIV

Delightful praise! Like summer rose,
That brighter in the dew-drop glows,
The bashful maiden's cheek appeared,
For Douglas spoke, and Malcolm heard.
The flush of shame-faced joy to hide,
The hounds, the hawk, her cares divide;
The loved caresses of the maid
The dogs with crouch and whimper paid;
And, at her whistle, on her hand
The falcon took his favourite stand,
Closed his dark wing, relaxed his eye,
Nor, though unhooded, sought to fly.

495 *Bothwell*: the Douglas stronghold in Lanark county.
504 *crescent*: one of the emblems of the Percies of Northumberland.
506 *Blantyre*: a priory on the opposite bank of the Clyde from Bothwell Castle.

And, trust, while in such guise she stood,
Like fabled Goddess of the wood,
That if a father's partial thought
O'erweighed her worth and beauty aught,
Well might the lover's judgment fail
To balance with a juster scale;
For with each secret glance he stole,
The fond enthusiast sent his soul.

XXV

Of stature tall, and slender frame,
But firmly knit, was Malcolm Græme.
The belted plaid and tartan hose
Did ne'er more graceful limbs disclose;
His flaxen hair, of sunny hue,
Curled closely round his bonnet blue.
Trained to the chase, his eagle eye
The ptarmigan in snow could spy:
Each pass, by mountain, lake, and heath,
He knew, through Lennox and Menteith;
Vain was the bound of dark-brown doe
When Malcolm bent his sounding bow;
And scarce that doe, though winged with fear,
Outstripped in speed the mountaineer:
Right up Ben-Lomond could he press,
And not a sob his toil confess.
His form accorded with a mind
Lively and ardent, frank and kind;
A blither heart, till Ellen came,
Did never love nor sorrow tame;
It danced as lightsome in his breast
As played the feather on his crest.
Yet friends, who nearest knew the youth,
His scorn of wrong, his zeal for truth,
And bards, who saw his features bold
When kindled by the tales of old,
Said, were that youth to manhood grown,
Not long should Roderick Dhu's renown
Be foremost voiced by mountain fame,
But quail to that of Malcolm Græme.

527 *Goddess*: Diana.
541 In winter the ptarmigan's feathers become white.

XXVI

Now back they wend their watery way,
And, 'O my sire!' did Ellen say,
'Why urge thy chase so far astray?
And why so late returned? And why'—
The rest was in her speaking eye.
'My child, the chase I follow far,
'Tis mimicry of noble war;
And with that gallant pastime reft
Were all of Douglas I have left.
I met young Malcolm as I strayed,
Far eastward, in Glenfinlas' shade.
Nor strayed I safe; for, all around,
Hunters and horsemen scoured the ground.
This youth, though still a royal ward,
Risked life and land to be my guard,
And through the passes of the wood
Guided my steps, not unpursued;
And Roderick shall his welcome make,
Despite old spleen, for Douglas' sake.
Then must he seek Strath-Endrick glen,
Nor peril aught for me again.'

XXVII

Sir Roderick, who to meet them came,
Reddened at sight of Malcolm Græme,
Yet, not in action, word, or eye,
Failed aught in hospitality.
In talk and sport they whiled away
The morning of that summer day;
But at high noon a courier light
Held secret parley with the knight,
Whose moody aspect soon declared
That evil were the news he heard.
Deep thought seemed toiling in his head;
Yet was the evening banquet made,

574 *Glenfinlas*: in Scott's etymology, 'the valley of the green woman', to the west of Ben Ledi and NE. of the Trossachs. See above, Introduction, p. viii.

577 *royal ward*: under feudal law the King was guardian of any minor who held a fief under the crown.

583 *Strath-Endrick*: valley of Endrick, a small river flowing into Loch Lomond on the SE.

Ere he assembled round the flame
His mother, Douglas, and the Græme,
And Ellen too; then cast around
His eyes, then fixed them on the ground,
As studying phrase that might avail
Best to convey unpleasant tale.
Long with his dagger's hilt he played,
Then raised his haughty brow, and said:

XXVIII

'Short be my speech; nor time affords,
Nor my plain temper, glozing words.
Kinsman and father—if such name
Douglas vouchsafe to Roderick's claim;
Mine honoured mother; Ellen—why,
My cousin, turn away thine eye?
And Græme—in whom I hope to know
Full soon a noble friend or foe,
When age shall give thee thy command
And leading in thy native land:
List all!—The King's vindictive pride
Boasts to have tamed the Border-side,[n]
Where chiefs, with hound and hawk who came
To share their monarch's silvan game,
Themselves in bloody toils were snared;
And when the banquet they prepared,
And wide their loyal portals flung,
O'er their own gateway struggling hung.
Loud cries their blood from Meggat's mead,
From Yarrow braes, and banks of Tweed,
Where the lone streams of Ettrick glide,
And from the silver Teviot's side;
The dales, where martial clans did ride,
Are now one sheep-walk, waste and wide.
This tyrant of the Scottish throne,
So faithless and so ruthless known,
Now hither comes; his end the same,
The same pretext of silvan game.
What grace for Highland Chiefs, judge ye
By fate of Border chivalry.[n]

623 *Meggat*: a tributary of the Yarrow.
624–6 *Yarrow . . . Teviot*: see Map, p. 281.

Yet more; amid Glenfinlas green,
Douglas, thy stately form was seen:
This by espial sure I know.—
Your counsel in the strait I show.'

XXIX

Ellen and Margaret fearfully
Sought comfort in each other's eye,
Then turned their ghastly look, each one,
This to her sire, that to her son.
The hasty colour went and came
In the bold cheek of Malcolm Græme;
But from his glance it well appeared,
'Twas but for Ellen that he feared;
While, sorrowful, but undismayed,
The Douglas thus his counsel said:—
'Brave Roderick, though the tempest roar,
It may but thunder and pass o'er;
Nor will I here remain an hour,
To draw the lightning on thy bower;
For well thou know'st, at this grey head
The royal bolt were fiercest sped.
For thee, who, at thy King's command,
Canst aid him with a gallant band,
Submission, homage, humbled pride,
Shall turn the Monarch's wrath aside.
Poor remnants of the Bleeding Heart,
Ellen and I will seek, apart,
The refuge of some forest cell;
There, like the hunted quarry, dwell,
Till on the mountain and the moor,
The stern pursuit be passed and o'er.'

XXX

'No, by mine honour,' Roderick said,
'So help me heaven, and my good blade!
No, never! Blasted be yon Pine,
My fathers' ancient crest and mine,
If from its shade in danger part
The lineage of the Bleeding Heart!

637 *espial*: spies' reports.
638 'I request your advice in the difficulties which I reveal.'
654 *bolt*: thunderbolt.

Hear my blunt speech: grant me this maid
To wife, thy counsel to mine aid;
To Douglas, leagued with Roderick Dhu,
Will friends and allies flock enow;
Like cause of doubt, distrust, and grief,
Will bind to us each Western Chief.
When the loud pipes my bridal tell,
The Links of Forth shall hear the knell,
The guards shall start in Stirling's porch;
And, when I light the nuptial torch,
A thousand villages in flames
Shall scare the slumbers of King James!
Nay, Ellen, blench not thus away,
And, mother, cease these signs, I pray;
I meant not all my heat might say.
Small need of inroad, or of fight,
When the sage Douglas may unite
Each mountain clan in friendly band,
To guard the passes of their land,
Till the foiled king, from pathless glen,
Shall bootless turn him home again.'

XXXI

There are who have, at midnight hour,
In slumber scaled a dizzy tower,
And, on the verge that beetled o'er
The ocean-tide's incessant roar,
Dreamed calmly out their dangerous dream,
Till wakened by the morning beam;
When, dazzled by the eastern glow,
Such startler cast his glance below,
And saw unmeasured depth around,
And heard unintermitted sound,
And thought the battled fence so frail,
It waved like cobweb in the gale;—
Amid his senses' giddy wheel,
Did he not desperate impulse feel,

678 *Links*: the windings of a river; the rich land among these windings (Jamieson).
679 *Stirling* (castle): a favourite royal residence.
685 'What I have said is not meant literally, but is merely the expression of my overwrought emotions.'
699 *startler*: one who is startled. 702 *battled*: battlemented.

Headlong to plunge himself below,
And meet the worst his fears foreshow?
Thus, Ellen, dizzy and astound,
As sudden ruin yawned around,
By crossing terrors wildly tossed,
Still for the Douglas fearing most,
Could scarce the desperate thought withstand,
To buy his safety with her hand.

XXXII

Such purpose dread could Malcolm spy
In Ellen's quivering lip and eye,
And eager rose to speak; but ere
His tongue could hurry forth his fear,
Had Douglas marked the hectic strife,
Where death seemed combating with life;
For to her cheek, in feverish flood,
One instant rushed the throbbing blood,
Then ebbing back, with sudden sway,
Left its domain as wan as clay.
'Roderick, enough! enough!' he cried,
'My daughter cannot be thy bride;
Not that the blush to wooer dear,
Nor paleness that of maiden fear.
It may not be; forgive her, Chief,
Nor hazard aught for our relief.
Against his sovereign, Douglas ne'er
Will level a rebellious spear.
'Twas I that taught his youthful hand
To rein a steed and wield a brand;
I see him yet, the princely boy!
Not Ellen more my pride and joy;
I love him still, despite my wrongs,
By hasty wrath, and slanderous tongues.
O seek the grace you well may find,
Without a cause to mine combined.'

XXXIII

Twice through the hall the Chieftain strode;
The waving of his tartans broad,

708 *astound*: in violent confusion.
739 'If your cause is not combined with mine'.

And darkened brow, where wounded pride
With ire and disappointment vied,
Seemed, by the torch's gloomy light,
Like the ill Demon of the night,
Stooping his pinions' shadowy sway
Upon the nighted pilgrim's way:
But, unrequited Love! thy dart
Plunged deepest its envenomed smart,
And Roderick, with thine anguish stung,
At length the hand of Douglas wrung,
While eyes, that mocked at tears before,
With bitter drops were running o'er.
The death-pangs of long-cherished hope
Scarce in that ample breast had scope,
But, struggling with his spirit proud,
Convulsive heaved its chequered shroud,
While every sob—so mute were all—
Was heard distinctly through the hall.
The son's despair, the mother's look,
Ill might the gentle Ellen brook;
She rose, and to her side there came,
To aid her parting steps, the Græme.

XXXIV

Then Roderick from the Douglas broke
As flashes flame through sable smoke,
Kindling its wreaths, long, dark, and low,
To one broad blaze of ruddy glow,
So the deep anguish of despair
Burst, in fierce jealousy, to air.
With stalwart grasp his hand he laid
On Malcolm's breast and belted plaid:
'Back, beardless boy!' he sternly said,
'Back, minion! hold'st thou thus at naught
The lesson I so lately taught?
This roof, the Douglas, and that maid,
Thank thou for punishment delayed.'
Eager as greyhound on his game,
Fiercely with Roderick grappled Græme.
'Perish my name, if aught afford
Its Chieftain safety save his sword!'

757 *chequered*: tartan. His plaid is the shroud of his hope.

Thus as they strove, their desperate hand
Griped to the dagger or the brand,
And death had been—but Douglas rose,
And thrust between the struggling foes
His giant strength:—'Chieftains, forego!
I hold the first who strikes, my foe.
Madmen, forbear your frantic jar!
What! is the Douglas fallen so far,
His daughter's hand is doomed the spoil
Of such dishonourable broil?'
Sullen and slowly they unclasp,
As struck with shame, their desperate grasp,
And each upon his rival glared,
With foot advanced, and blade half bared.

XXXV

Ere yet the brands aloft were flung,
Margaret on Roderick's mantle hung,
And Malcolm heard his Ellen's scream,
As faltered through terrific dream.
Then Roderick plunged in sheath his sword,
And veiled his wrath in scornful word.
'Rest safe till morning; pity 'twere
Such cheek should feel the midnight air!
Then mayst thou to James Stuart tell
Roderick will keep the lake and fell,
Nor lackey, with his freeborn clan,
The pageant pomp of earthly man.
More would he of Clan-Alpine know,
Thou canst our strength and passes show.—
Malise, what ho!'—his henchman[n] came;
'Give our safe-conduct to the Græme.'
Young Malcolm answered, calm and bold,
'Fear nothing for thy favourite hold;
The spot an angel deigned to grace
Is blessed, though robbers haunt the place.
Thy churlish courtesy for those
Reserve, who fear to be thy foes.

782 *Griped to*: reached towards. 783 *had been*: would have been.
786 *I . . . foe*: taken verbatim from John Home's tragedy *Douglas* (1756). Scott apologised for his plagiarism in the second edition (1810, p. 433).
789 *doomed the spoil*: adjudged as the prize.
798 *faltered*: uttered incoherently. 812 *hold*: stronghold.

As safe to me the mountain way
At midnight as in blaze of day,
Though with his boldest at his back
Even Roderick Dhu beset the track.
Brave Douglas,—lovely Ellen,—nay,
Nought here of parting will I say.
Earth does not hold a lonesome glen
So secret, but we meet again.—
Chieftain! we too shall find an hour.'
He said, and left the silvan bower.

XXXVI

Old Allan followed to the strand
(Such was the Douglas's command)
And anxious told, how, on the morn,
The stern Sir Roderick deep had sworn
The Fiery Cross should circle o'er
Dale, glen, and valley, down, and moor.
Much were the peril to the Græme,
From those who to the signal came;
Far up the lake 'twere safest land,
Himself would row him to the strand.
He gave his counsel to the wind,
While Malcolm did, unheeding, bind
Round dirk and pouch and broadsword rolled,
His ample plaid in tightened fold,
And stripped his limbs to such array
As best might suit the watery way—

XXXVII

Then[n] spoke abrupt: 'Farewell to thee,
Pattern of old fidelity!'
The Minstrel's hand he kindly pressed,—
'O! could I point a place of rest!
My sovereign holds in ward my land,
My uncle leads my vassal band;
To tame his foes, his friends to aid,
Poor Malcolm has but heart and blade.
Yet, if there be one faithful Græme
Who loves the Chieftain of his name,

831 *Fiery Cross*: method of summoning the clan. See below, p. 296.
847 *in ward*: see above, II. 577.

Not long shall honoured Douglas dwell,
Like hunted stag, in mountain cell;
Nor, ere yon pride—swollen robber dare—
I may not give the rest to air!
Tell Roderick Dhu, I owed him nought,
Not the poor service of a boat,
To waft me to yon mountain-side.'
Then plunged he in the flashing tide.
Bold o'er the flood his head he bore,
And stoutly steered him from the shore;
And Allan strained his anxious eye,
Far 'mid the lake his form to spy,
Darkening across each puny wave,
To which the moon her silver gave.
Fast as the cormorant could skim,
The swimmer plied each active limb;
Then landing in the moonlight dell,
Loud shouted, of his weal to tell.
The Minstrel heard the far halloo,
And joyful from the shore withdrew.

Canto Third

The Gathering

I

TIME rolls his ceaseless course. The race of yore,
  Who danced our infancy upon their knee,
And told our marvelling boyhood legends store,
  Of their strange ventures happed by land or sea,
How are they blotted from the things that be!
  How few, all weak and withered of their force,
Wait on the verge of dark eternity,
  Like stranded wrecks, the tide returning hoarse
To sweep them from our sight! Time rolls his ceaseless course.

Yet live there still who can remember well,
  How, when a mountain chief his bugle blew,
Both field and forest, dingle, cliff, and dell,
  And solitary heath, the signal knew;

8 *tide*: object of 'wait' in line 7.

And fast the faithful clan around him drew,
  What time the warning note was keenly wound,
What time aloft their kindred banner flew,
  While clamorous war-pipes yelled the gathering sound,
And while the Fiery Cross[n] glanced, like a meteor, round.

II

The summer dawn's reflected hue
To purple changed Loch Katrine blue;
Mildly and soft the western breeze
Just kissed the Lake, just stirred the trees,
And the pleased lake, like maiden coy,
Trembled but dimpled not for joy;
The mountain-shadows on her breast
Were neither broken nor at rest;
In bright uncertainty they lie,
Like future joys to Fancy's eye.
The water-lily to the light
Her chalice reared of silver bright;
The doe awoke, and to the lawn,
Begemmed with dew-drops, led her fawn;
The grey mist left the mountain side,
The torrent showed its glistening pride;
Invisible in flecked sky,
The lark sent down her revelry;
The blackbird and the speckled thrush
Good-morrow gave from brake and bush;
In answer cooed the cushat dove
Her notes of peace, and rest, and love.

III

No thought of peace, no thought of rest,
Assuaged the storm in Roderick's breast.
With sheathed broadsword in his hand,
Abrupt he paced the islet strand,
And eyed the rising sun, and laid
His hand on his impatient blade.
Beneath a rock, his vassals' care
Was prompt the ritual to prepare,
With deep and deathful meaning fraught;
For such Antiquity had taught

16 *kindred*: i.e., of their clan.

Was preface meet, ere yet abroad
The Cross of Fire should take its road.
The shrinking band stood oft aghast
At the impatient glance he cast;—
Such glance the mountain eagle threw,
As, from the cliffs of Benvenue,
She spread her dark sails on the wind,
And, high in middle heaven, reclined,
With her broad shadow on the lake,
Silenced the warblers of the brake.

IV

A heap of withered boughs was piled,
Of juniper and rowan wild,
Mingled with shivers from the oak,
Rent by the lightning's recent stroke.
Brian, the Hermit,[n] by it stood,
Barefooted, in his frock and hood.
His grizzled beard and matted hair
Obscured a visage of despair;
His naked arms and legs, seamed o'er,
The scars of frantic penance bore.
That monk, of savage form and face,
The impending danger of his race
Had drawn from deepest solitude,
Far in Benharrow's bosom rude.
Not his the mien of Christian priest,
But Druid's, from the grave released,
Whose hardened heart and eye might brook
On human sacrifice to look;
And much, 'twas said, of heathen lore
Mixed in the charms he muttered o'er.
The hallowed creed gave only worse
And deadlier emphasis of curse;
No peasant sought that Hermit's prayer,
His cave the pilgrim shunned with care,
The eager huntsman knew his bound,
And in mid chase called off his hound;
Or if, in lonely glen or strath,
The desert-dweller met his path,

62 *rowan*: mountain ash, supposed to have magical properties.
74 *Benharrow*: mountain E. of Loch Lomond. 81 *hallowed creed*: Christianity.

He prayed, and signed the cross between,
While terror took devotion's mien.

V

Of Brian's birth[n] strange tales were told.
His mother watched a midnight fold,
Built deep within a dreary glen,
Where scattered lay the bones of men,
In some forgotten battle slain,
And bleached by drifting wind and rain.
It might have tamed a warrior's heart,
To view such mockery of his art!
The knot-grass fettered there the hand
Which once could burst an iron band;
Beneath the broad and ample bone
That bucklered heart to fear unknown,
A feeble and a timorous guest,
The field-fare framed her lowly nest;
There the slow blind-worm left his slime
On the fleet limbs that mocked at time;
And there, too, lay the leader's skull,
Still wreathed with chaplet, flushed and full,
For heath-bell with her purple bloom
Supplied the bonnet and the plume.
All night, in this sad glen, the maid
Sate, shrouded in her mantle's shade:
—She said no shepherd sought her side,
No hunter's hand her snood[n] untied;
Yet ne'er again to braid her hair
The virgin snood did Alice wear;
Gone was her maiden glee and sport,
Her maiden girdle all too short,
Nor sought she, from that fatal night,
Or holy church or blessed rite,
But locked her secret in her breast,
And died in travail, unconfessed.

VI

Alone, among his young compeers,
Was Brian from his infant years;
A moody and heart-broken boy,
Estranged from sympathy and joy,

Bearing each taunt which careless tongue
On his mysterious lineage flung.
Whole nights he spent by moonlight pale,
To wood and stream his hap to wail,
Till, frantic, he as truth received
What of his birth the crowd believed,
And sought, in mist and meteor fire,
To meet and know his Phantom Sire!
In vain, to soothe his wayward fate,
The cloister oped her pitying gate;
In vain, the learning of the age
Unclasped the sable-lettered page;
Even in its treasures he could find
Food for the fever of his mind.
Eager he read whatever tells
Of magic, cabala, and spells,
And every dark pursuit allied
To curious and presumptuous pride;
Till, with fired brain and nerves o'erstrung,
And heart with mystic horrors wrung,
Desperate he sought Benharrow's den,
And hid him from the haunts of men.

VII

The desert gave him visions wild,
Such as might suit the Spectre's child.
Where with black cliffs the torrents toil,
He watched the wheeling eddies boil,
Till, from their foam, his dazzled eyes
Beheld the river demon[n] rise;
The mountain mist took form and limb,
Of noontide hag,[n] or goblin grim;[n]
The midnight wind came wild and dread,
Swelled with the voices of the dead;
Far on the future battle-heath
His eye beheld the ranks of death:
Thus the lone Seer, from mankind hurled,
Shaped forth a disembodied world.
One lingering sympathy of mind
Still bound him to the mortal kind;

142 *cabala*: secret doctrine, esoteric knowledge.

The only parent he could claim
Of ancient Alpine's lineage came.
Late had he heard, in prophet's dream,
The fatal Ben-Shie's boding scream;
Sounds, too, had come in midnight blast,
Of charging steeds, careering fast
Along Benharrow's shingly side,
Where mortal horseman ne'er might ride;
The thunderbolt had split the pine;
All augured ill to Alpine's line.
He girt his loins, and came to show
The signals of impending woe,
And now stood prompt to bless or ban,
As bade the Chieftain of his clan.

VIII

'Twas all prepared; and from the rock,
A goat, the patriarch of the flock,
Before the kindling pile was laid,
And pierced by Roderick's ready blade.
Patient the sickening victim eyed
The life-blood ebb in crimson tide,
Down his clogged beard and shaggy limb,
Till darkness glazed his eyeballs dim.
The grisly priest, with murmuring prayer,
A slender crosslet formed with care,
A cubit's length in measure due;
The shaft and limbs were rods of yew,
Whose parents in Inch-Cailliach wave
Their shadows o'er Clan-Alpine's grave,
And, answering Lomond's breezes deep,
Soothe many a chieftain's endless sleep.
The Cross, thus formed, he held on high,
With wasted hand, and haggard eye,
And strange and mingled feelings woke,
While his anathema he spoke:

IX

'Woe to the clansman, who shall view
This symbol of sepulchral yew,

168 *Ben-Shie*: banshee (Irish), 'spirit whose wail portends death in a house'.
191 *Inch-Cailliach*: isle of nuns (or of 'old women') at the lower end of Loch Lomond.

Forgetful that its branches grew
Where weep the heavens their holiest dew
    On Alpine's dwelling low!
Deserter of his Chieftain's trust,
He ne'er shall mingle with their dust,[n]
But, from his sires and kindred thrust,
Each clansman's execration just
    Shall doom him wrath and woe.'
He paused;—the word the vassals took,
With forward step and fiery look,
On high their naked brands they shook,
Their clattering targets wildly strook;
    And first in murmur low,
Then, like the billow in his course,
That far to seaward finds his source,
And flings to shore his mustered force,
Burst, with loud roar, their answer hoarse,
    'Woe to the traitor, woe!'
Ben-an's grey scalp the accents knew,
The joyous wolf from covert drew,
The exulting eagle screamed afar,—
They knew the voice of Alpine's war.

X

The shout was hushed on lake and fell,
The monk resumed his muttered spell:
Dismal and low its accents came,
The while he scathed the Cross with flame;
And the few words that reached the air,
Although the holiest name was there,
Had more of blasphemy than prayer.
But when he shook above the crowd
Its kindled points, he spoke aloud:

'Woe to the wretch who fails to rear
At this dread sign the ready spear!
For, as the flames this symbol sear,
His home, the refuge of his fear,
    A kindred fate shall know;
Far o'er its roof the volumed flame
Clan-Alpine's vengeance shall proclaim,

203 *dwelling low*: burial place. 237 *volumed*: vast and billowing.

While maids and matrons on his name
Shall call down wretchedness and shame,
And infamy and woe.'
Then rose the cry of females, shrill
As goshawk's whistle on the hill,
Denouncing misery and ill,
Mingled with childhood's babbling trill
Of curses stammered slow;
Answering, with imprecation dread,
'Sunk be his home in embers red!
And cursed be the meanest shed
That e'er shall hide the houseless head,
We doom to want and woe!'
A sharp and shrieking echo gave,
Coir-Uriskin, thy goblin cave!
And the grey pass where birches wave
On Beala-nam-bo.

XI

Then deeper paused the priest anew,
And hard his labouring breath he drew,
While, with set teeth and clenched hand,
And eyes that glowed like fiery brand,
He meditated curse more dread,
And deadlier, on the clansman's head,
Who, summoned to his Chieftain's aid,
The signal saw and disobeyed.
The crosslet's points of sparkling wood,
He quenched among the bubbling blood,
And, as again the sign he reared,
Hollow and hoarse his voice was heard:
'When flits this Cross from man to man,
Vich-Alpine's summons to his clan,
Burst be the ear that fails to heed!
Palsied the foot that shuns to speed!
May ravens tear the careless eyes,
Wolves make the coward heart their prize!
As sinks that blood-stream in the earth,
So may his heart's blood drench his hearth!

253 *Coir-Uriskin*: see end-note on l. 622, below.
255 *Beala-nam-bo*: 'Pass of the cattle', a glade on Ben Venue near the shore of Loch Katrine.

As dies in hissing gore the spark,
Quench thou his light, Destruction dark!
And be the grace to him denied,
Bought by this sign to all beside!'
He ceased; no echo gave again
The murmur of the deep Amen.

XII

Then Roderick, with impatient look,
From Brian's hand the symbol took:
'Speed, Malise, speed!' he said, and gave
The crosslet to his henchman brave.
'The muster-place be Lanrick mead—
Instant the time; speed, Malise, speed!'
Like heath-bird, when the hawks pursue,
A barge across Loch Katrine flew;
High stood the henchman on the prow;
So rapidly the barge-men row,
The bubbles, where they launched the boat,
Were all unbroken and afloat,
Dancing in foam and ripple still,
When it had neared the mainland hill;
And from the silver beach's side
Still was the prow three fathom wide,
When lightly bounded to the land
The messenger of blood and brand.

XIII

Speed, Malise, speed! the dun deer's hide[n]
On fleeter foot was never tied.
Speed, Malise, speed! such cause of haste
Thine active sinews never braced.
Bend 'gainst the steepy hill thy breast,
Burst down like torrent from its crest;
With short and springing footstep pass
The trembling bog and false morass;
Across the brook like roebuck bound,
And thread the brake like questing hound;
The crag is high, the scaur is deep,
Yet shrink not from the desperate leap:

286 *Lanrick mead*: at NW. end of Loch Vennachar.
311 *scaur*: bare cliff-face.

Parched are thy burning lips and brow,
Yet by the fountain pause not now;
Herald of battle, fate, and fear,
Stretch onward in thy fleet career!
The wounded hind thou track'st not now,
Pursuest not maid through greenwood bough,
Nor pliest thou now thy flying pace,
With rivals in the mountain race;
But danger, death, and warrior deed,
Are in thy course; speed, Malise, speed!

XIV

Fast as the fatal symbol flies,
In arms the huts and hamlets rise;
From winding glen, from upland brown
They poured each hardy tenant down.
Nor slacked the messenger his pace;
He showed the sign, he named the place,
And pressing forward like the wind,
Left clamour and surprise behind.
The fisherman forsook the strand,
The swarthy smith took dirk and brand;
With changed cheer, the mower blithe
Left in the half-cut swath the scythe;
The herds without a keeper strayed,
The plough was in mid-furrow stayed,
The falconer tossed his hawk away,
The hunter left the stag at bay;
Prompt at the signal of alarms,
Each son of Alpine rushed to arms;
So swept the tumult and affray
Along the margin of Achray.
Alas, thou lovely lake! that e'er
Thy banks should echo sounds of fear!
The rocks, the bosky thickets, sleep
So stilly on thy bosom deep,
The lark's blithe carol, from the cloud,
Seems for the scene too gaily loud.

XV

Speed, Malise, speed! the lake is past,
Duncraggan's huts appear at last,

349 *Duncraggan*: between Lochs Achray and Vennachar, near the Brig o' Turk.

And peep, like moss-grown rocks, half seen,
Half hidden in the copse so green;
There mayest thou rest, thy labour done,
Their Lord shall speed the signal on.
As stoops the hawk upon his prey,
The henchman shot him down the way.
—What woeful accents load the gale?
The funeral yell, the female wail!
A gallant hunter's sport is o'er,
A valiant warrior fights no more.
Who, in the battle or the chase,
At Roderick's side shall fill his place!—
Within the hall, where torches' ray
Supplies the excluded beams of day,
Lies Duncan on his lowly bier,
And o'er him streams his widow's tear.
His stripling son stands mournful by,
His youngest weeps, but knows not why;
The village maids and matrons round
The dismal coronach resound.

XVI

CORONACH

'He is gone on the mountain,
He is lost to the forest,
Like a summer-dried fountain,
When our need was the sorest.
The font, reappearing,
From the rain-drops shall borrow,
But to us comes no cheering,
To Duncan no morrow!

The hand of the reaper
Takes the ears that are hoary,
But the voice of the weeper
Wails manhood in glory.
The autumn winds rushing
Waft the leaves that are searest,
But our flower was in flushing,
When blighting was nearest.

Fleet foot on the corrie,
  Sage counsel in cumber,
Red hand in the foray,
  How sound is thy slumber!
Like the dew on the mountain,
  Like the foam on the river,
Like the bubble on the fountain,
  Thou art gone, and for ever!'

XVII

See Stumah, who, the bier beside,
His master's corpse with wonder eyed,
Poor Stumah! whom his least halloo
Could send like lightning o'er the dew,
Bristles his crest, and points his ears,
As if some stranger step he hears.
'Tis not a mourner's muffled tread
Who comes to sorrow o'er the dead,
But headlong haste, or deadly fear,
Urge the precipitate career.
All stand aghast:—unheeding all,
The henchman bursts into the hall;
Before the dead man's bier he stood;
Held forth the Cross besmeared with blood;
'The muster-place is Lanrick mead;
Speed forth the signal! clansmen, speed!'

XVIII

Angus, the heir of Duncan's line,
Sprung forth and seized the fatal sign.
In haste the stripling to his side
His father's dirk and broadsword tied;
But when he saw his mother's eye
Watch him in speechless agony,
Back to her opened arms he flew,
Pressed on her lips a fond adieu—
'Alas!' she sobbed,—'and yet, be gone,
And speed thee forth, like Duncan's son!'

386 *corrie*: circular hollow in mountainside 'where game usually lies' (S), i.e., Duncan was swift in the chase.
387 *cumber*: difficulty.
394 *Stumah*: 'faithful' (dog's name).

One look he cast upon the bier,
Dashed from his eye the gathering tear,
Breathed deep to clear his labouring breast,
And tossed aloft his bonnet crest,
Then, like the high-bred colt when, freed,
First he essays his fire and speed,
He vanished, and o'er moor and moss
Sped forward with the Fiery Cross.
Suspended was the widow's tear,
While yet his footsteps she could hear;
And when she marked the henchman's eye
Wet with unwonted sympathy,
'Kinsman,' she said, 'his race is run,
That should have sped thine errand on;
The oak has fallen,—the sapling bough
Is all Duncraggan's shelter now.
Yet trust I well, his duty done,
The orphan's God will guard my son
And you, in many a danger true,
At Duncan's hest your blades that drew,
To arms, and guard that orphan's head!
Let babes and women wail the dead.'
Then weapon-clang, and martial call,
Resounded through the funeral hall,
While from the walls the attendant band
Snatched sword and targe, with hurried hand;
And short and flitting energy
Glanced from the mourner's sunken eye,
As if the sounds to warrior dear
Might rouse her Duncan from his bier.
But faded soon that borrowed force;
Grief claimed his right, and tears their course.

XIX

Benledi saw the Cross of Fire,
It glanced like lightning up Strath-Ire;
O'er dale and hill the summons flew,
Nor rest nor pause young Angus knew;
The tear that gathered in his eye
He left the mountain breeze to dry;

453 *Strath-Ire*: valley N. of Loch Lubnaig.

Until, where Teith's young waters roll,
Betwixt him and a wooded knoll,
That graced the sable strath with green,
The chapel of St Bride was seen.
Swoln was the stream, remote the bridge,
But Angus paused not on the edge;
Though the dark waves danced dizzily,
Though reeled his sympathetic eye,
He dashed amid the torrent's roar:
His right hand high the crosslet bore,
His left the pole-axe grasped, to guide
And stay his footing in the tide.
He stumbled twice—the foam splashed high,
With hoarser swell the stream raced by;
And had he fallen,—for ever there
Farewell Duncraggan's orphan heir!
But still, as if in parting life,
Firmer he grasped the Cross of strife,
Until the opposing bank he gained,
And up the chapel pathway strained.

XX

A blithesome rout, that morning tide,
Had sought the chapel of St Bride.
Her troth Tombea's Mary gave
To Norman, heir of Armandave.
And, issuing from the Gothic arch,
The bridal now resumed their march.
In rude, but glad procession, came
Bonneted sire and coif-clad dame;
And plaided youth, with jest and jeer,
Which snooded maiden would not hear;
And children, that, unwitting why,
Lent the gay shout their shrilly cry;
And minstrels, that in measures vied
Before the young and bonny bride,
Whose downcast eye and cheek disclose
The tear and blush of morning rose.
With virgin step, and bashful hand,
She held the kerchief's snowy band;

458 *young waters*: near the source, esp. the river Leny.
461 *St. Bride*: Irish saint of 5th century.
480–1 *Tombea, Armandave*: homesteads in Strathire.

The gallant bridegroom by her side
Beheld his prize with victor's pride,
And the glad mother in her ear
Was closely whispering word of cheer.

XXI

Who meets them at the churchyard gate?
The messenger of fear and fate!
Haste in his hurried accent lies,
And grief is swimming in his eyes.
All dripping from the recent flood,
Panting and travel-soiled he stood,
The fatal sign of fire and sword
Held forth, and spoke the appointed word:
'The muster-place is Lanrick mead;
Speed forth the signal! Norman-speed!'
And must he change so soon the hand,
Just linked to his by holy band,
For the fell Cross of blood and brand?
And must the day, so blithe that rose,
And promised rapture in the close,
Before its setting hour, divide
The bridegroom from the plighted bride?
O fatal doom! it must! it must!
Clan-Alpine's cause, her Chieftain's trust,
Her summons dread, brook no delay;
Stretch to the race; away! away!

XXII

Yet slow he laid his plaid aside,
And, lingering, eyed his lovely bride,
Until he saw the starting tear
Speak woe he might not stop to cheer;
Then, trusting not a second look,
In haste he sped him up the brook,
Nor backward glanced, till on the heath
Where Lubnaig's lake supplies the Teith.
What in the racer's bosom stirred?
The sickening pang of hope deferred,
And memory, with a torturing train
Of all his morning visions vain.
Mingled with love's impatience, came
The manly thirst for martial fame;

The stormy joy of mountaineers,
Ere yet they rush upon the spears;
And zeal for Clan and Chieftain burning,
And hope, from well-fought field returning,
With war's red honours on his crest,
To clasp his Mary to his breast.
Stung by such thoughts, o'er bank and brae,
Like fire from flint he glanced away,
While high resolve, and feeling strong,
Burst into voluntary song.

XXIII

SONG[n]

'The heath this night must be my bed,
The bracken curtain for my head,
My lullaby the warder's tread,
    Far, far from love and thee, Mary;
To-morrow eve, more stilly laid,
My couch may be my bloody plaid,
My vesper song, thy wail, sweet maid!
    It will not waken me, Mary!

I may not, dare not, fancy now
The grief that clouds thy lovely brow,
I dare not think upon thy vow,
    And all it promised me, Mary.
No fond regret must Norman know;
When bursts Clan-Alpine on the foe,
His heart must be like bended bow,
    His foot like arrow free, Mary.

A time will come with feeling fraught,
For, if I fall in battle fought,
Thy hapless lover's dying thought
    Shall be a thought on thee, Mary.
And if returned from conquered foes,
How blithely will the evening close,
How sweet the linnet sing repose,
    To my young bride and me, Mary!'

547 *warder*: camp sentinel.

XXIV

Not faster o'er thy heathery braes,
Balquidder, speeds the midnight blaze,
Rushing, in conflagration strong,
Thy deep ravines and dells along,
Wrapping thy cliffs in purple glow,
And reddening the dark lakes below;
Nor faster speeds it, nor so far,
As o'er thy heaths the voice of war.
The signal roused to martial coil
The sullen margin of Loch Voil,
Waked still Loch Doine, and to the source
Alarmed, Balvaig, thy swampy course;
Thence southward turned its rapid road
Adown Strath-Gartney's valley broad,
Till rose in arms each man might claim
A portion in Clan-Alpine's name,
From the grey sire, whose trembling hand
Could hardly buckle on his brand,
To the raw boy, whose shaft and bow
Were yet scarce terror to the crow.
Each valley, each sequestered glen,
Mustered its little horde of men,
That met as torrents from the height
In Highland dales their streams unite,
Still gathering, as they pour along,
A voice more loud, a tide more strong,
Till at the rendezvous they stood
By hundreds prompt for blows and blood;
Each trained to arms since life began,
Owning no tie but to his clan,
No oath, but by his Chieftain's hand,
No law, but Roderick Dhu's command.

XXV

That summer morn had Roderick Dhu
Surveyed the skirts of Benvenue,

570 *Balquidder*: the 'Braes of Balquhidder' form the N. side of a valley, N. of Strathire.

570 *midnight blaze*: the moorland heather is often fired so that the sheep may have fresh grazing.

577 *coil*: bustle, confusion.

578–9 *Loch Voil, Loch Doine*: two lakes in Balquhidder which communicate by means of the R. Balvaig.

582 *Strath-Gartney*: N. of Loch Katrine.

And sent his scouts o'er hill and heath
To view the frontiers of Menteith.
All backward came with news of truce;
Still lay each martial Græme and Bruce,
In Rednock courts no horsemen wait,
No banner waved on Cardross gate,
On Duchray's towers no beacon shone,
Nor scared the herons from Loch Con;
All seemed at peace.—Now, wot ye why
The Chieftain, with such anxious eye,
Ere to the muster he repair,
The western frontier scanned with care?—
In Benvenue's most darksome cleft,
A fair, though cruel, pledge was left;
For Douglas, to his promise true,
That morning from the isle withdrew,
And in a deep sequestered dell
Had sought a low and lonely cell.
By many a bard, in Celtic tongue,
Has Coir-nan-Uriskin[n] been sung;
A softer name the Saxons gave,
And called the grot the Goblin-cave.

XXVI

It was a wild and strange retreat,
As e'er was trod by outlaw's feet.
The dell, upon the mountain's crest,
Yawned like a gash on warrior's breast;
Its trench had stayed full many a rock,
Hurled by primeval earthquake shock
From Benvenue's grey summit wild,
And here, in random ruin piled,
They frowned incumbent o'er the spot,
And formed the rugged silvan grot.
The oak and birch, with mingled shade,
At noontide there a twilight made,
Unless when short and sudden shone
Some straggling beam on cliff or stone,

607–9 *Rednock, Cardross, Duchray*: fortified castles in Forth valley, on the borders of the Highlands, S. of Roderick's territory.
610 *Loch Con*: $1\frac{1}{2}$ m. south of the upper waters of Loch Katrine.

With such a glimpse as prophet's eye
Gains on thy depth, Futurity.
No murmur waked the solemn still,
Save tinkling of a fountain rill;
But when the wind chafed with the lake,
A sullen sound would upward break,
With dashing hollow voice, that spoke
The incessant war of wave and rock.
Suspended cliffs, with hideous sway,
Seemed nodding o'er the cavern grey.
From such a den the wolf had sprung,
In such the wild-cat leaves her young;
Yet Douglas and his daughter fair
Sought for a space their safety there.
Grey Superstition's whisper dread
Debarred the spot to vulgar tread;
For there, she said, did fays resort,
And satyrs hold their silvan court,
By moonlight tread their mystic maze,
And blast the rash beholder's gaze.

XXVII

Now eve, with western shadows long,
Floated on Katrine bright and strong,
When Roderick, with a chosen few,
Repassed the heights of Benvenue.
Above the Goblin-cave they go,
Through the wild pass of Beal-nam-bo:
The prompt retainers speed before,
To launch the shallop from the shore,
For 'cross Loch Katrine lies his way
To view the passes of Achray,
And place his clansmen in array.
Yet lags the chief in musing mind,
Unwonted sight, his men behind.
A single page, to bear his sword,
Alone attended on his lord;
The rest their way through thickets break,
And soon await him by the lake.

664 *Beal-nam-bo*: see above, l. 255.

It was a fair and gallant sight,
To view them from the neighbouring height,
By the low-levelled sunbeam's light!
For strength and stature, from the clan
Each warrior was a chosen man,
As even afar might well be seen,
By their proud step and martial mien.
Their feathers dance, their tartans float,
Their targets gleam, as by the boat
A wild and warlike group they stand,
That well became such mountain-strand.

XXVIII

Their Chief, with step reluctant, still
Was lingering on the craggy hill,
Hard by where turned apart the road
To Douglas's obscure abode.
It was but with that dawning morn,
That Roderick Dhu had proudly sworn
To drown his love in war's wild roar,
Nor think of Ellen Douglas more;
But he who stems a stream with sand,
And fetters flame with flaxen band,
Has yet a harder task to prove,
By firm resolve to conquer love!
Eve finds the Chief, like restless ghost,
Still hovering near his treasure lost;
For though his haughty heart deny
A parting meeting to his eye,
Still fondly strains his anxious ear,
The accents of her voice to hear,
And inly did he curse the breeze
That waked to sound the rustling trees.
But hark! what mingles in the strain?
It is the harp of Allan-Bane,
That wakes its measure slow and high,
Attuned to sacred minstrelsy.
What melting voice attends the strings?
'Tis Ellen, or an angel, sings.

686 *mountain-strand*: i.e., shore of Loch Katrine.

XXIX

HYMN TO THE VIRGIN

'Ave Maria! maiden mild!
  Listen to a maiden's prayer!
Thou canst hear though from the wild,
  Thou canst save amid despair.
Safe may we sleep beneath thy care,
  Though banished, outcast, and reviled—
Maiden! hear a maiden's prayer;
  Mother, hear a suppliant child!
            Ave Maria!

Ave Maria! undefiled!
  The flinty couch we now must share
Shall seem with down of eider piled,
  If thy protection hover there.
The murky cavern's heavy air
  Shall breathe of balm if thou hast smiled;
Then, Maiden! hear a maiden's prayer,
  Mother, list a suppliant child!
            Ave Maria!

Ave Maria! stainless styled!
  Foul demons of the earth and air,
From this their wonted haunt exiled,
  Shall flee before thy presence fair.
We bow us to our lot of care,
  Beneath thy guidance reconciled;
Hear for a maid a maiden's prayer,
  And for a father hear a child!
            Ave Maria!'

XXX

Died on the harp the closing hymn—
Unmoved in attitude and limb,
As listening still, Clan-Alpine's lord
Stood leaning on his heavy sword,
Until the page, with humble sign,
Twice pointed to the sun's decline.
Then while his plaid he round him cast,
'It is the last time, 'tis the last,'

715 *wild*: desert.

He muttered thrice,—'the last time e'er
That angel voice shall Roderick hear!'
It was a goading thought—his stride
Hied hastier down the mountain-side;
Sullen he flung him in the boat,
And instant 'cross the lake it shot.
They landed in that silvery bay,
And eastward held their hasty way,
Till, with the latest beams of light,
The band arrived on Lanrick height,
Where mustered, in the vale below,
Clan-Alpine's men in martial show.

XXXI

A various scene the clansmen made;
Some sate, some stood, some slowly strayed;
But most, with mantles folded round,
Were couched to rest upon the ground,
Scarce to be known by curious eye,
From the deep heather where they lie,
So well was matched the tartan screen
With heath-bell dark and brackens green;
Unless where, here and there, a blade,
Or lance's point, a glimmer made,
Like glow-worm twinkling through the shade.
But when, advancing through the gloom,
They saw the Chieftain's eagle plume,
Their shout of welcome, shrill and wide,
Shook the steep mountain's steady side.
Thrice it arose, and lake and fell
Three times returned the martial yell;
It died upon Bochastle's plain,
And Silence claimed her evening reign.

Canto Fourth

The Prophecy

I

'The rose is fairest when 'tis budding new,
  And hope is brightest when it dawns from fears;
The rose is sweetest washed with morning dew,
  And love is loveliest when embalmed in tears.

777 *Bochastle's plain*: see map, p. 293.

O wilding rose, whom fancy thus endears,
  I bid your blossoms in my bonnet wave,
Emblem of hope and love through future years!'
  Thus spoke young Norman, heir of Armandave,
What time the sun arose on Vennachar's broad wave.

II

Such fond conceit, half said, half sung,
Love prompted to the bridegroom's tongue.
All while he stripped the wild-rose spray,
His axe and bow beside him lay,
For on a pass 'twixt lake and wood,
A wakeful sentinel he stood.
Hark! on the rock a footstep rung,
And instant to his arms he sprung.
'Stand, or thou diest!—What, Malise? soon
Art thou returned from Braes of Doune.
By thy keen step and glance I know,
Thou bring'st us tidings of the foe.'
(For while the Fiery Cross hied on,
On distant scout had Malise gone.)
'Where sleeps the Chief?' the henchman said.
'Apart, in yonder misty glade;
To his lone couch I'll be your guide;'
Then called a slumberer by his side,
And stirred him with his slackened bow—
'Up, up, Glentarkin! rouse thee, ho!
We seek the Chieftain; on the track,
Keep eagle watch till I come back.'

II

Together up the pass they sped:
'What of the foemen?' Norman said.—
'Varying reports from near and far;
This certain, that a band of war
Has for two days been ready boune,
At prompt command, to march from Doune;
King James the while, with princely powers,
Holds revelry in Stirling towers.

19 *Braes of Doune*: hills on the N. bank of the Teith between the village of Doune and Callander.

29 *Glentarkin*: this man is addressed by the name of his croft or other residence.

36 *boune*: bound. 38 *powers*: chiefs, rather than 'armed force'.

Soon will this dark and gathering cloud
Speak on our glens in thunder loud.
Inured to bide such bitter bout,
The warrior's plaid may bear it out;
But, Norman, how wilt thou provide
A shelter for thy bonny bride?'—
'What! know ye not that Roderick's care
To the lone isle hath caused repair
Each maid and matron of the clan,
And every child and aged man
Unfit for arms; and given his charge,
Nor skiff nor shallop, boat nor barge,
Upon these lakes shall float at large,
But all beside the islet moor,
That such dear pledge may rest secure?'—

IV

''Tis well advised; the Chieftain's plan
Bespeaks the father of his clan.
But wherefore sleeps Sir Roderick Dhu
Apart from all his followers true?'—
'It is, because last evening-tide
Brian an augury hath tried,
Of that dread kind which must not be
Unless in dread extremity,
The Taghairm[n] called; by which, afar,
Our sires foresaw the events of war.
Duncraggan's milk-white bull they slew'.—

MALISE

'Ah! well the gallant brute I knew!
The choicest of the prey we had,
When swept our merry-men Gallangad.
His hide was snow his horns were dark,
His red eye glowed like fiery spark;
So fierce, so tameless, and so fleet,
Sore did he cumber our retreat,
And kept our stoutest kerns in awe,
Even at the pass of Beal'maha

42 *bout*: this word for a 'turn' or 'trial of strength' seems to merge with the Scots pronunciation of 'bolt' (thunderbolt).
68 *Gallangad*: stream and glen in Dumbarton, S. of Loch Lomond.
74 *Beal'maha*: pass of E. Loch Lomond.

But steep and flinty was the road,
And sharp the hurrying pikemen's goad,
And when we came to Dennan's Row,
A child might scatheless stroke his brow.'[n]

V

NORMAN

'That bull was slain: his reeking hide
They stretched the cataract beside,
Whose waters their wild tumult toss
Adown the black and craggy boss
Of that huge cliff, whose ample verge
Tradition calls the Hero's Targe.
Couched on a shelve beneath its brink,
Close where the thundering torrents sink,
Rocking beneath their headlong sway,
And drizzled by the ceaseless spray,
Midst groan of rock, and roar of stream,
The wizard waits prophetic dream.
Nor distant rests the Chief;—but hush!
See, gliding slow through mist and bush,
The hermit gains yon rock, and stands
To gaze upon our slumbering bands.
Seems he not, Malise, like a ghost,
That hovers o'er a slaughtered host?
Or raven on the blasted oak,
That, watching while the deer is broke,
His morsel claims with sullen croak?'

MALISE

'Peace! peace! to other than to me,
Thy words were evil augury;
But still I hold Sir Roderick's blade
Clan-Alpine's omen and her aid,
Not aught that, gleaned from heaven or hell,
Yon fiend-begotten monk can tell.
The Chieftain joins him, see; and now,
Together they descend the brow.'

77 *Dennan's Row*: Rowardennan, at foot of Ben Lomond.
84 *Hero's Targe*: name of a rock in a ravine in Glenfinlas.
85 *shelve*: perhaps not 'shelf', but a coinage from the verb 'shelve', to slope.
98 *broke*: (of slain animal), quartered.

VI

And, as they came, with Alpine's Lord
The Hermit Monk held solemn word:
'Roderick! it is a fearful strife,
For man endowed with mortal life,
Whose shroud of sentient clay can still
Feel feverish pang and fainting chill,
Whose eye can stare in stony trance,
Whose hair can rouse like warrior's lance,—
'Tis hard for such to view unfurled
The curtain of the future world.
Yet—witness every quaking limb,
My sunken pulse, my eyeballs dim,
My soul with harrowing anguish torn—
This for my Chieftain have I borne!
The shapes that sought my fearful couch,
An human tongue may ne'er avouch;
No mortal man, save he who, bred
Between the living and the dead,
Is gifted beyond nature's law,
Had e'er survived to say he saw.
At length the fateful answer came,
In characters of living flame!
Not spoke in word, nor blazed in scroll,
But borne and branded on my soul—
WHICH SPILLS THE FOREMOST FOEMAN'S LIFE,
THAT PARTY CONQUERS IN THE STRIFE!'[n]

VII

'Thanks, Brian, for thy zeal and care!
Good is thine augury, and fair.
Clan-Alpine ne'er in battle stood,
But first our broadswords tasted blood.
A surer victim still I know,
Self-offered to the auspicious blow:
A spy has sought my land this morn,—
No eve shall witness his return!
My followers guard each pass's mouth,
To east, to westward, and to south;

115 *rouse*: stand on end.
130 *blazed in scroll*: emblazoned in parchment.
132 *spill*: destroy.

Red Murdoch, bribed to be his guide,
Has charge to lead his steps aside,
Till, in deep path or dingle brown,
He light on those shall bring him down.
—But see who comes his news to show!
Malise! what tidings of the foe?'

VIII

'At Doune, o'er many a spear and glaive
Two Barons proud their banners wave.
I saw the Moray's silver star,
And marked the sable pale of Mar.'[n]—
'By Alpine's soul, high tidings those!
I love to hear of worthy foes.
When move they on?' 'To-morrow's noon
Will see them here for battle boune.'—
'Then shall it see a meeting stern!
But, for the place—say, couldst thou learn
Nought of the friendly clans of Earn?
Strengthened by them, we well might bide
The battle on Benledi's side.
Thou couldst not? Well! Clan-Alpine's men
Shall man the Trossachs' shaggy glen;
Within Loch Katrine's gorge we'll fight,
All in our maids' and matrons' sight,
Each for his hearth and household fire,
Father for child, and son for sire,—
Lover for maid beloved!—But why—
Is it the breeze affects mine eye?
Or dost thou come, ill omened tear!
A messenger of doubt or fear?
No! sooner may the Saxon lance
Unfix Benledi from his stance,
Than doubt or terror can pierce through
The unyielding heart of Roderick Dhu!
'Tis stubborn as his trusty targe.—
Each to his post—all know their charge.'
The pibroch sounds, the bands advance,
The broadswords gleam, the banners dance,
Obedient to the Chieftain's glance.—

160 *Earn*: i.e., the upper valley of the Earn, which rises in Loch Earn near Balquhidder and flows across Perthshire into the Firth of Tay.

I turn me from the martial roar,
And seek Coir-Uriskin once more.

IX

Where is the Douglas?—he is gone;
And Ellen sits on the grey stone
Fast by the cave, and makes her moan;
While vainly Allan's words of cheer
Are poured on her unheeding ear:
'He will return—Dear lady, trust!—
With joy return; he will—he must.
Well was it time to seek afar
Some refuge from impending war,
When e'en Clan-Alpine's rugged swarm
Are cowed by the approaching storm.
I saw their boats with many a light
Floating the live-long yesternight,
Shifting like flashes darted forth
By the red streamers of the north;
I marked at morn how close they ride,
Thick moored by the lone islet's side,
Like wild ducks couching in the fen,
When stoops the hawk upon the glen.
Since this rude race dare not abide
The peril on the mainland side,
Shall not thy noble father's care
Some safe retreat for thee prepare?'

X

ELLEN

'No, Allan, no! Pretext so kind
My wakeful terrors could not blind.
When in such tender tone, yet grave,
Douglas a parting blessing gave,
The tear that glistened in his eye
Drowned not his purpose fixed and high.
My soul, though feminine and weak,
Can image his; e'en as the lake,
Itself disturbed by slightest stroke,
Reflects the invulnerable rock.

198 *red . . . north*: Aurora Borealis.

He hears report of battle rife,
He deems himself the cause of strife.
I saw him redden, when the theme
Turned, Allan, on thine idle dream
Of Malcolm Græme in fetters bound,
Which I, thou saidst, about him wound.
Think'st thou he trowed thine omen aught?
Oh no! 'twas apprehensive thought
For the kind youth,—for Roderick too—
(Let me be just) that friend so true;
In danger both, and in our cause!
Minstrel, the Douglas dare not pause.
Why else that solemn warning given.
"If not on earth, we meet in heaven!"
Why else, to Cambus-kenneth's fane,
If eve return him not again,
Am I to hie, and make me known?
Alas! he goes to Scotland's throne,
Buys his friend's safety with his own;
He goes to do—what I had done,
Had Douglas' daughter been his son!'

XI

ALLAN

'Nay, lovely Ellen!—dearest, nay!
If aught should his return delay,
He only named yon holy fane
As fitting place to meet again.
Be sure he's safe; and for the Græme,—
Heaven's blessing on his gallant name!
My visioned sight may yet prove true,
Nor bode of ill to him or you.
When did my gifted dream beguile?
Think of the stranger at the isle,
And think upon the harpings slow,
That presaged this approaching woe!
Sooth was my prophecy of fear;
Believe it when it augurs cheer.
Would we had left this dismal spot!
Ill luck still haunts a fairy grot.

231 *Cambus-kenneth*: abbey on left bank of the Forth, ¾ mile E. of Stirling.

Of such a wondrous tale I know—
Dear lady, change that look of woe,
My harp was wont thy grief to cheer.'

ELLEN

'Well, be it as thou wilt; I hear,
But cannot stop the bursting tear.'

The Minstrel tried his simple art,
But distant far was Ellen's heart:

XII

BALLAD

ALICE BRAND[n]

Merry it is in the good greenwood,
  When the mavis and merle are singing,
When the deer sweeps by, and the hounds are in cry,
  And the hunter's horn is ringing.

'O Alice Brand, my native land
  Is lost for love of you;
And we must hold by wood and wold,
  As outlaws wont to do.

O Alice, 'twas all for thy locks so bright,
  And 'twas all for thine eyes so blue,
That on the night of our luckless flight
  Thy brother bold I slew.

Now must I teach to hew the beech
  The hand that held the glaive,
For leaves to spread our lowly bed,
  And stakes to fence our cave.

And for vest of pall, thy fingers small,
  That wont on harp to stray,
A cloak must shear from the slaughtered deer,
  To keep the cold away.'—

'O Richard! if my brother died,
  'Twas but a fatal chance;
For darkling was the battle tried,
  And fortune sped the lance.

277 *pall*: warm cloth, probably of red or purple colour.

If pall and vair no more I wear,
  Nor thou the crimson sheen,
As warm, we'll say, is the russet grey,
  As gay the forest-green.

And, Richard, if our lot be hard,
  And lost thy native land,
Still Alice has her own Richard,
  And he his Alice Brand.'—

XIII

'Tis merry, 'tis merry, in good greenwood,
  So blithe Lady Alice is singing;
On the beech's pride, and oak's brown side,
  Lord Richard's axe is ringing.

Up spoke the moody Elfin King,
  Who woned within the hill;
Like wind in the porch of a ruined church,
  His voice was ghostly shrill.

'Why sounds yon stroke on beech and oak,
  Our moonlight circle's screen?
Or who comes here to chase the deer,
  Beloved of our Elfin Queen?
Or who may dare on wold to wear
  The fairies' fatal green?

Up, Urgan, up! to yon mortal hie,
  For thou wert christened man;[n]
For cross or sign thou wilt not fly,
  For muttered word or ban.

Lay on him the curse of the withered heart,
  The curse of the sleepless eye;
Till he wish and pray that his life would part,
  Nor yet find leave to die.'—

285 *vair*: a variegated fur.
298 *woned*: dwelt.
302 *circle*: rings supposedly made by fairies' feet.
306 *fatal green*: the fairies were thought to object to mortals wearing their own colour.
307 *Urgan*: name borrowed from that of a gigantic knight in the romance of *Sir Tristrem* which Scott edited.

XIV

'Tis merry, 'tis merry, in good greenwood,
  Though the birds have stilled their singing;
The evening blaze doth Alice raise,
  And Richard is fagots bringing.

Up Urgan starts, that hideous dwarf,
  Before Lord Richard stands,
And, as he crossed and blessed himself,
'I fear not sign,' quoth the grisly elf,
  'That is made with bloody hands.'

But out then spoke she, Alice Brand,
  That woman, void of fear—
'And if there's blood upon his hand,
  'Tis but the blood of deer.'—

'Now loud thou liest, thou bold of mood!
  It cleaves unto his hand,
The stain of thine own kindly blood,
  The blood of Ethert Brand.'

Then forward stepped she, Alice Brand,
  And made the holy sign—
'And if there's blood on Richard's hand,
  A spotless hand is mine.

And I conjure thee, Demon elf,
  By Him whom Demons fear,
To show us whence thou art thyself,
  And what thine errand here?'—

XV

''Tis merry, 'tis merry, in Fairy-land,
  When fairy birds are singing,
When the court doth ride by their monarch's side,
  With bit and bridle ringing:

And gaily shines the Fairy-land—
  But all is glistening show,
Like the idle gleam that December's beam
  Can dart on ice and snow.

330 *kindly*: of kin.

And fading, like that varied gleam,
  Is our inconstant shape,
Who now like knight and lady seem,
  And now like dwarf and ape.

It was between the night and day,
  When the Fairy King has power,
That I sunk down in a sinful fray,
And, 'twixt life and death, was snatched away
  To the joyless Elfin bower.

But wist I of a woman bold,
  Who thrice my brow durst sign,
I might regain my mortal mould,
  As fair a form as thine.'

She crossed him once, she crossed him twice,
  That lady was so brave;
The fouler grew his goblin hue,
  The darker grew the cave.

She crossed him thrice, that lady bold;
  He rose beneath her hand
The fairest knight on Scottish mould,
  Her brother, Ethert Brand!

Merry it is in good greenwood,
  When the mavis and merle are singing,
But merrier were they in Dunfermline grey,
  When all the bells were ringing.

XVI

Just as the minstrel sounds were stayed,
A stranger climbed the steepy glade:
His martial step, his stately mien,
His hunting suit of Lincoln green,
His eagle glance remembrance claims—
'Tis Snowdoun's Knight, 'tis James Fitz-James.
Ellen beheld as in a dream,
Then, starting, scarce suppressed a scream:
'O stranger! in such hour of fear,
What evil hap has brought thee here?'—
'An evil hap how can it be,
That bids me look again on thee?

371 *Dunfermline grey*: the Grey Friars' abbey in Dunfermline, Fife.

By promise bound, my former guide
Met me betimes this morning tide,
And marshalled, over bank and bourne,
The happy path of my return.'—
'The happy path!—what! said he nought
Of war, of battle to be fought,
Of guarded pass?'—'No, by my faith!
Nor saw I aught could augur scathe.'—
'O haste thee, Allan, to the kern,—
Yonder his tartans I discern;
Learn thou his purpose, and conjure
That he will guide the stranger sure!—
What prompted thee, unhappy man?
The meanest serf in Roderick's clan
Had not been bribed by love or fear,
Unknown to him to guide thee here.'—

XVII

'Sweet Ellen, dear my life must be,
Since it is worthy care from thee;
Yet life I hold but idle breath,
When love or honour's weighed with death.
Then let me profit by my chance,
And speak my purpose bold at once.
I come to bear thee from a wild,
Where ne'er before such blossom smiled;
By this soft hand to lead thee far
From frantic scenes of feud and war.
Near Bochastle my horses wait;
They bear us soon to Stirling gate.
I'll place thee in a lovely bower,
I'll guard thee like a tender flower'—
'O! hush, Sir Knight! 'twere female art,
To say I do not read thy heart;
Too much, before, my selfish ear
Was idly soothed my praise to hear.
That fatal bait hath lured thee back,
In deathful hour, o'er dangerous track;
And how, O how, can I atone
The wreck my vanity brought on!

387 *bourne*: either stream ('burn'), or boundary.
420 *deathful*: fatal.

One-way remains—I'll tell him all—
Yes! struggling bosom, forth it shall!
Thou, whose light folly bears the blame,
Buy thine own pardon with thy shame!
But first—my father is a man
Outlawed and exiled, under ban;
The price of blood is on his head;
With me 'twere infamy to wed.
Still wouldst thou speak? then hear the truth!
Fitz-James, there is a noble youth,
If yet he is! exposed for me
And mine to dread extremity—
Thou hast the secret of my heart;
Forgive, be generous, and depart!'

XVIII

Fitz-James knew every wily train
A lady's fickle heart to gain;
But here he knew and felt them vain.
There shot no glance from Ellen's eye,
To give her steadfast speech the lie;
In maiden confidence she stood,
Though mantled in her cheek the blood,
And told her love with such a sigh
Of deep and hopeless agony,
As death had sealed her Malcolm's doom,
And she sat sorrowing on his tomb.
Hope vanished from Fitz-James's eye,
But not with hope fled sympathy.
He proffered to attend her side,
As brother would a sister guide.—
'O! little know'st thou Roderick's heart!
Safer for both we go apart.
O haste thee, and from Allan learn,
If thou may'st trust yon wily kern.'
With hand upon his forehead laid,
The conflict of his mind to shade,
A parting step or two he made;
Then, as some thought had crossed his brain,
He paused, and turned, and came again.

433 *If yet he is*: if he still lives.
437 *train*: snare.

XIX

'Hear, lady, yet, a parting word!
It chanced in fight that my poor sword
Preserved the life of Scotland's lord.
This ring the grateful Monarch gave,
And bade, when I had boon to crave,
To bring it back, and boldly claim
The recompense that I would name.
Ellen, I am no courtly lord,
But one who lives by lance and sword,
Whose castle is his helm and shield,
His lordship the embattled field.
What from a prince can I demand,
Who neither reck of state nor land?
Ellen, thy hand—the ring is thine;
Each guard and usher knows the sign.
Seek thou the King without delay;
This signet shall secure thy way;
And claim thy suit, whate'er it be,
As ransom of his pledge to me.'
He placed the golden circlet on,
Paused, kissed her hand, and then was gone.
The aged Minstrel stood aghast,
So hastily Fitz-James shot past.
He joined his guide, and wending down
The ridges of the mountain brown,
Across the stream they took their way,
That joins Loch Katrine to Achray.

XX

All in the Trossachs' glen was still,
Noontide was sleeping on the hill:
Sudden his guide whooped loud and high—
'Murdoch! was that a signal cry?'
He stammered forth, 'I shout to scare
Yon raven from his dainty fare.'
He looked, he knew the raven's prey—
His own brave steed:—'Ah! gallant grey!
For thee,—for me perchance—'twere well
We ne'er had seen the Trossachs' dell.
Murdoch, move first—but silently;
Whistle or whoop, and thou shalt die!'

Jealous and sullen, on they fared,
Each silent, each upon his guard.

XXI

Now wound the path its dizzy ledge
Around a precipice's edge,
When lo! a wasted female form,
Blighted by wrath of sun and storm,
In tattered weeds and wild array,
Stood on a cliff beside the way,
And glancing round her restless eye,
Upon the wood, the rock, the sky,
Seemed nought to mark, yet all to spy.
Her brow was wreathed with gaudy broom;
With gesture wild she waved a plume
Of feathers, which the eagles fling
To crag and cliff from dusky wing;
Such spoils her desperate step had sought,
Where scarce was footing for the goat.
The tartan plaid she first descried,
And shrieked till all the rocks replied;
As loud she laughed when near they drew,
For then the Lowland garb she knew;
And then her hands she wildly wrung,
And then she wept, and then she sung.
She sung!—the voice, in better time,
Perchance to harp or lute might chime;
And now, though strained and roughened, still
Rung wildly sweet to dale and hill.

XXII

SONG

'They bid me sleep, they bid me pray,
  They say my brain is warped and wrung;
I cannot sleep on Highland brae,
  I cannot pray in Highland tongue.
But were I now where Allan glides,
Or heard my native Devan's tides,
So sweetly would I rest, and pray
That Heaven would close my wintry day!

531–2 *Allan, Devan*: rivers which flow from the Perthshire hills to join the Forth near Stirling.

'Twas thus my hair they bade me braid,
  They made me to the church repair;
It was my bridal morn, they said,
  And my true love would meet me there.
But woe betide the cruel guile,
That drowned in blood the morning smile!
And woe betide the fairy dream!
I only waked to sob and scream.'—

XXIII

'Who is this maid? what means her lay?
She hovers o'er the hollow way,
And flutters wide her mantle grey,
As the lone heron spreads his wing,
By twilight, o'er a haunted spring.'
''Tis Blanche of Devan,' Murdoch said,
'A crazed and captive Lowland maid,
Ta'en on the morn she was a bride,
When Roderick forayed Devan-side.
The gay bridegroom resistance made,
And felt our Chief's unconquered blade;
I marvel she is now at large,
But oft she 'scapes from Maudlin's charge.—
Hence, brain-sick fool!' He raised his bow:—
'Now if thou strik'st her but one blow,
I'll pitch thee from the cliff as far
As ever peasant pitched a bar!'
'Thanks, champion, thanks!' the maniac cried,
And pressed her to Fitz-James's side.
'See the grey pennons I prepare
To seek my true-love through the air!
I will not lend that savage groom,
To break his fall, one downy plume!
No! deep amid disjointed stones,
The wolves shall batten on his bones,
And then shall his detested plaid,
By bush and brier in mid-air staid,
Wave forth a banner fair and free,
Meet signal for their revelry.'—

559 *pitched a bar*: tossed the caber (a roughly-trimmed pine-trunk, pitched in Highland Sport).

XXIV

'Hush thee, poor maiden, and be still!'—
'O! thou look'st kindly, and I will.
Mine eye has dried and wasted been,
But still it loves the Lincoln green;
And though mine ear is all unstrung,
Still, still it loves the Lowland tongue.

For O my sweet William was forester true,
He stole poor Blanche's heart away!
His coat it was all of the greenwood hue,
And so blithely he trilled the Lowland lay![n]

'It was not that I meant to tell . . .
But thou art wise and guessest well.'
Then, in a low and broken tone,
And hurried note, the song went on.
Still on the Clansman, fearfully,
She fixed her apprehensive eye;
Then turned it on the Knight, and then
Her look glanced wildly o'er the glen.

XXV

'The toils are pitched, and the stakes are set,
Ever sing merrily, merrily;
The bows they bend, and the knives they whet,
Hunters live so cheerily.

It was a stag, a stag of ten,
Bearing its branches sturdily;
He came stately down the glen,
Ever sing hardily, hardily.

It was there he met with a wounded doe,
She was bleeding deathfully;
She warned him of the toils below,
O, so faithfully, faithfully!

He had an eye, and he could heed,
Ever sing warily, warily;
He had a foot, and he could speed—
Hunters watch so narrowly.'

590–605 This song is a figurative warning of Fitz-James's dangers.
590 *toils*: snares. 594 *of ten*: with ten points (branches).

XXVI

Fitz-James's mind was passion-tossed,
When Ellen's hints and fears were lost;
But Murdoch's shout suspicion wrought,
And Blanche's song conviction brought.
Not like a stag that spies the snare,
But lion of the hunt aware,
He waved at once his blade on high,
'Disclose thy treachery, or die!'
Forth at full speed the Clansman flew,
But in his race his bow he drew.
The shaft just grazed Fitz-James's crest,
And thrilled in Blanche's faded breast.
Murdoch of Alpine! prove thy speed,
For ne'er had Alpine's son such need!
With heart of fire, and foot of wind,
The fierce avenger is behind!
Fate judges of the rapid strife—
The forfeit death—the prize is life!
Thy kindred ambush lies before,
Close couched upon the heathery moor;
Them couldst thou reach!—it may not be—
Thine ambushed kin thou ne'er shalt see,
The fiery Saxon gains on thee!
—Resistless speeds the deadly thrust,
As lightning strikes the pine to dust;
With foot and hand Fitz-James must strain,
Ere he can win his blade again.
Bent o'er the fallen, with falcon eye,
He grimly smiled to see him die;
Then slower wended back his way,
Where the poor maiden bleeding lay.

XXVII

She sat beneath the birchen-tree,
Her elbow resting on her knee;
She had withdrawn the fatal shaft,
And gazed on it, and feebly laughed;
Her wreath of broom and feathers grey,
Daggled with blood, beside her lay.

642 *daggled*: wet.

The Knight to stanch the life-stream tried;
'Stranger, it is in vain!' she cried.
'This hour of death has given me more
Of reason's power than years before;
For, as these ebbing veins decay,
My frenzied visions fade away.
A helpless injured wretch I die,
And something tells me in thine eye,
That thou wert mine avenger born.—
Seest thou this tress?—O! still I've worn
This little tress of yellow hair,
Through danger, frenzy, and despair!
It once was bright and clear as thine,
But blood and tears have dimmed its shine.
I will not tell thee when 'twas shred,
Nor from what guiltless victim's head—
My brain would turn!—but it shall wave
Like plumage on thy helmet brave,
Till sun and wind shall bleach the stain,
And thou wilt bring it me again.—
I waver still. O God! more bright
Let reason beam her parting light!
O! by thy knighthood's honoured sign,
And for thy life preserved by mine,
When thou shalt see a darksome man,
Who boasts him Chief of Alpine's Clan,
With tartans broad and shadowy plume,
And hand of blood, and brow of gloom,
Be thy heart bold, thy weapon strong,
And wreak poor Blanche of Devan's wrong!—
They watch for thee by pass and fell . . .
Avoid the path . . . O God! . . . farewell.'

XXVIII

A kindly heart had brave Fitz-James;
Fast poured his eyes at pity's claims;
And now, with mingled grief and ire,
He saw the murdered maid expire.
'God, in my need, be my relief,
As I wreak this on yonder Chief!'
A lock from Blanche's tresses fair
He blended with her bridegroom's hair;

The mingled braid in blood he dyed,
And placed it on his bonnet-side:
'By Him whose word is truth! I swear,
No other favour will I wear,
Till this sad token I imbrue
In the best blood of Roderick Dhu!
But hark! what means yon faint halloo?
The chase is up; but they shall know,
The stag at bay's a dangerous foe.'
Barred from the known but guarded way,
Through copse and cliffs Fitz-James must stray,
And oft must change his desperate track,
By stream and precipice turned back.
Heartless, fatigued, and faint, at length,
From lack of food and loss of strength,
He couched him in a thicket hoar,
And thought his toils and perils o'er:
'Of all my rash adventures past,
This frantic feat must prove the last!
Who e'er so mad but might have guessed,
That all this Highland hornet's nest
Would muster up in swarms so soon
As e'er they heard of bands at Doune?
Like bloodhounds now they search me out,—
Hark, to the whistle and the shout!—
If farther through the wilds I go,
I only fall upon the foe:
I'll couch me here till evening grey,
Then darkling try my dangerous way.'

XXIX

The shades of eve come slowly down,
The woods are wrapt in deeper brown,
The owl awakens from her dell,
The fox is heard upon the fell;
Enough remains of glimmering light
To guide the wanderer's steps aright,
Yet not enough from far to show
His figure to the watchful foe.

690 *up*: i.e., 'on'; 'is beginning'.

With cautious step, and ear awake,
He climbs the crag and threads the brake;
And not the summer solstice there
Tempered the midnight mountain air,
But every breeze that swept the wold
Benumbed his drenched limbs with cold.
In dread, in danger, and alone,
Famished and chilled, through ways unknown,
Tangled and steep, he journeyed on;
Till, as a rock's huge point he turned,
A watch-fire close before him burned.

XXX

Beside its embers red and clear
Basked in his plaid a mountaineer;
And up he sprung with sword in hand,—
'Thy name and purpose! Saxon, stand!'—
'A stranger.'—'What dost thou require?'—
'Rest and a guide, and food and fire.
My life's beset, my path is lost,
The gale has chilled my limbs with frost.'—
'Art thou a friend to Roderick?'—'No.'—
'Thou darest not call thyself a foe?'—
'I dare! to him and all the band
He brings to aid his murderous hand.'—
'Bold words! but, though the beast of game
The privilege of chase may claim,
Though space and law the stag we lend,
Ere hound we slip, or bow we bend,
Who ever recked, where, how, or when,
The prowling fox was trapped or slain?
Thus treacherous scouts,—yet sure they lie
Who say thou camest a secret spy!'—
'They do, by heaven! Come Roderick Dhu,
And of his clan the boldest two,
And let me but till morning rest,
I write the falsehood on their crest.'—
'If by the blaze I mark aright,
Thou bear'st the belt and spur of Knight.'—

743–5 *but . . . lend*: a stag was allowed a start before the hounds were unleashed, but predators were hunted at sight.

'Then by these tokens mayest thou know
Each proud oppressor's mortal foe.'—
'Enough, enough; sit down and share
A soldier's couch, a soldier's fare.'

XXXI

He gave him of his Highland cheer,
The hardened flesh [n] of mountain deer;
Dry fuel on the fire he laid,
And bade the Saxon share his plaid.
He tended him like welcome guest,
Then thus his farther speech addressed:
'Stranger, I am to Roderick Dhu
A clansman born, a kinsman true;
Each word against his honour spoke,
Demands of me avenging stroke;
Yet more,—upon thy fate, 'tis said,
A mighty augury is laid.
It rests with me to wind my horn,—
Thou art with numbers overborne;
It rests with me, here, brand to brand,
Worn as thou art, to bid thee stand:
But, not for clan, nor kindred's cause,
Will I depart from honour's laws;
To assail a wearied man were shame,
And stranger is a holy name;
Guidance and rest, and food and fire,
In vain he never must require.
Then rest thee here till dawn of day;
Myself will guide thee on the way,
O'er stock and stone, through watch and ward,
Till past Clan-Alpine's outmost guard,
As far as Coilantogle's ford;
From thence thy warrant is thy sword.'
'I take thy courtesy, by Heaven,
As freely as 'tis nobly given!'—
'Well, rest thee; for the bittern's cry
Sings us the lake's wild lullaby.'
With that he shook the gathered heath,
And spread his plaid upon the wreath;

787 *Coilantogle*: on stream at E. end of Loch Vennachar.
794 *wreath*: bed of heather.

And the brave foemen, side by side,
Lay peaceful down, like brothers tried,
And slept until the dawning beam
Purpled the mountain and the stream.

Canto Fifth

The Combat

I

Fair as the earliest beam of eastern light,
  When first, by the bewildered pilgrim spied,
It smiles upon the dreary brow of night,
  And silvers o'er the torrent's foaming tide,
And lights the fearful path on mountain side—
  Fair as that beam, although the fairest far,
Giving to horror grace, to danger pride,
  Shine martial Faith, and Courtesy's bright star,
Through all the wreckful storms that cloud the brow of War.

II

That early beam, so fair and sheen,
Was twinkling through the hazel screen,
When, rousing at its glimmer red,
The warriors left their lowly bed,
Looked out upon the dappled sky,
Muttered their soldier matins by,
And then awaked their fire, to steal,
As short and rude, their soldier meal.
That o'er, the Gael around him threw
His graceful plaid of varied hue,
And, true to promise, led the way,
By thicket green and mountain grey.
A wildering path!—they winded now
Along the precipice's brow,
Commanding the rich scenes beneath,
The windings of the Forth and Teith,
And all the vales beneath that lie,
Till Stirling's turrets melt in sky;
Then, sunk in copse, their farthest glance
Gained not the length of horseman's lance.

10 *sheen*: beautiful, with sense of 'shining'.
17 *as short*: i.e., as their prayers.
27 *till*: to the point (rather than time) when.

'Twas oft so steep, the foot was fain
Assistance from the hand to gain;
So tangled oft, that, bursting through,
Each hawthorn shed her showers of dew,—
That diamond dew, so pure and clear,
It rivals all but Beauty's tear.

III

At length they came where, stern and steep,
The hill sinks down upon the deep.
Here Vennachar in silver flows,
There, ridge on ridge, Benledi rose;
Ever the hollow path twined on,
Beneath steep bank and threatening stone;
An hundred men might hold the post
With hardihood against a host.
The rugged mountain's scanty cloak
Was dwarfish shrubs of birch and oak,
With shingles bare, and cliffs between,
And patches bright of bracken green,
And heather black, that waved so high,
It held the copse in rivalry.
But where the lake slept deep and still,
Dank osiers fringed the swamp and hill;
And oft both path and hill were torn,
Where wintry torrents down had borne,
And heaped upon the cumbered land
Its wreck of gravel, rocks, and sand.
So toilsome was the road to trace,
The guide, abating of his pace,
Led slowly through the pass's jaws,
And asked Fitz-James, by what strange cause
He sought these wilds, traversed by few,
Without a pass from Roderick Dhu.

IV

'Brave Gael, my pass in danger tried,
Hangs in my belt, and by my side;
Yet, sooth to tell,' the Saxon said,
'I dreamed not now to claim its aid.

37 *deep*: i.e., lake (not sea).

When here, but three days since, I came,
Bewildered in pursuit of game,
All seemed as peaceful and as still
As the mist slumbering on yon hill;
Thy dangerous Chief was then afar,
Nor soon expected back from war.
Thus said, at least, my mountain-guide,
Though deep, perchance, the villain lied.'—
'Yet why a second venture try?'—
'A warrior thou, and ask me why?
Moves our free course by such fixed cause
As gives the poor mechanic laws?
Enough, I sought to drive away
The lazy hours of peaceful day;
Slight cause will then suffice to guide
A Knight's free footsteps far and wide—
A falcon flown, a greyhound strayed,
The merry glance of mountain maid:
Or, if a path be dangerous known,
The danger's self is lure alone.'—

V

'Thy secret keep, I urge thee not;
Yet, ere again ye sought this spot,
Say, heard ye nought of Lowland war,
Against Clan-Alpine, raised by Mar?'—
'No, by my word;—of bands prepared
To guard King James's sports I heard;
Nor doubt I aught, but, when they hear
This muster of the mountaineer,
Their pennons will abroad be flung,
Which else in Doune had peaceful hung.'—
'Free be they flung!—for we were loth
Their silken folds should feast the moth.
Free be they flung!—as free shall wave
Clan-Alpine's pine in banner brave.
But, Stranger, peaceful since you came,
Bewildered in the mountain game,

89 *Mar*: probably John 5th Lord Erskine (d. ?1555) and father of the first of the Earls of Mar to belong to the Erskine family.

94 *flung*: i.e., unfurled.

95 *Doune*: 'castle situated at the confluence of the Ardoch and the Teith' (L), S. of the Braes of Doune.

Whence the bold boast by which you show
Vich-Alpine's vowed and mortal foe?'—
'Warrior, but yester-morn, I knew
Nought of thy Chieftain, Roderick Dhu,
Save as an outlawed desperate man,
The chief of a rebellious clan,
Who, in the Regent's court and sight,
With ruffian dagger stabbed a knight:
Yet this alone might from his part
Sever each true and loyal heart.'

VI

Wrathful at such arraignment foul,
Dark lowered the clansman's sable scowl.
A space he paused, then sternly said,
'And heard'st thou why he drew his blade?
Heard'st thou that shameful word and blow
Brought Roderick's vengeance on his foe?
What recked the Chieftain if he stood
On Highland heath, or Holy-Rood?
He rights such wrong where it is given,
If it were in the court of Heaven.'—
'Still was it outrage;—yet, 'tis true,
Not then claimed sovereignty his due;
While Albany, with feeble hand,
Held borrowed truncheon of command,
The young King, mewed in Stirling tower,
Was stranger to respect and power.
But then, thy Chieftain's robber life!—
Winning mean prey by causeless strife,
Wrenching from ruined Lowland swain
His herds and harvest reared in vain—
Methinks a soul like thine should scorn
The spoils from such foul foray borne.'

VII

The Gael beheld him grim the while,
And answered with disdainful smile,
'Saxon, from yonder mountain high,
I marked thee send delighted eye,

108 *Regent*: John Stewart, younger brother of James III, Regent of Scotland 1515–23.

Far to the south and east, where lay,
Extended in succession gay,
Deep waving fields and pastures green,
With gentle slopes and groves between:
These fertile plains, that softened vale,
Were once the birthright of the Gael;
The stranger came with iron hand,
And from our fathers reft the land.
Where dwell we now? See, rudely swell
Crag over crag, and fell o'er fell.
Ask we this savage hill we tread,
For fattened steer or household bread;
Ask we for flocks these shingles dry,
And well the mountain might reply—
"To you, as to your sires of yore,
Belong the target and claymore!
I give you shelter in my breast,
Your own good blades must win the rest."
Pent in this fortress of the North,
Think'st thou we will not sally forth
To spoil the spoiler as we may,
And from the robber rend the prey?
Ay, by my soul! While on yon plain
The Saxon rears one shock of grain,
While of ten thousand herds there strays
But one along yon river's maze,
The Gael, of plain and river heir,
Shall with strong hand redeem his share.
Where live the mountain Chiefs who hold
That plundering Lowland field and fold
Is aught but retribution true?
Seek other cause 'gainst Roderick Dhu.'[n]

VIII

Answered Fitz-James, 'And, if I sought,
Think'st thou no other could be brought?
What deem ye of my path waylaid?
My life given o'er to ambuscade?'—
'As of a meed to rashness due:
Hadst thou sent warning fair and true—
I seek my hound, or falcon strayed,
I seek, good faith, a Highland maid—

Free hadst thou been to come and go;
But secret path marks secret foe.
Nor yet, for this, even as a spy,
Hadst thou unheard been doomed to die,
Save to fulfil an augury.'—
'Well, let it pass; nor will I now
Fresh cause of enmity avow,
To chafe thy mood and cloud thy brow.
Enough, I am by promise tied
To match me with this man of pride:
Twice have I sought Clan-Alpine's glen
In peace; but when I come again,
I come with banner, brand, and bow,
As leader seeks his mortal foe.
For love-lorn swain, in lady's bower,
Ne'er panted for the appointed hour,
As I, until before me stand
This rebel Chieftain and his band!'

IX

'Have, then, thy wish!' He whistled shrill,
And he was answered from the hill;
Wild as the scream of the curlew,
From crag to crag the signal flew.
Instant, through copse and heath, arose
Bonnets and spears and bended bows;
On right, on left, above, below,
Sprung up at once the lurking foe;
From shingles grey their lances start,
The bracken bush sends forth the dart,
The rushes and the willow-wand
Are bristling into axe and brand,
And every tuft of broom gives life
To plaided warrior armed for strife.
That whistle garrisoned the glen
At once with full five hundred men,
As if the yawning hill to heaven
A subterranean host had given.
Watching their leader's beck and will,
All silent there they stood, and still.
Like the loose crags, whose threatening mass
Lay tottering o'er the hollow pass,

As if an infant's touch could urge
Their headlong passage down the verge,
With step and weapon forward flung,
Upon the mountain-side they hung.
The Mountaineer cast glance of pride
Along Benledi's living side,
Then fixed his eye and sable brow
Full on Fitz-James—'How say'st thou now?
These are Clan-Alpine's warriors true;
And, Saxon,—I am Roderick Dhu!'

X

Fitz-James was brave. Though to his heart
The life-blood thrilled with sudden start,
He manned himself with dauntless air,
Returned the Chief his haughty stare,
His back against a rock he bore,
And firmly placed his foot before:
'Come one, come all! this rock shall fly
From its firm base as soon as I.'
Sir Roderick marked, and in his eyes
Respect was mingled with surprise,
And the stern joy which warriors feel
In foemen worthy of their steel.
Short space he stood—then waved his hand:
Down sunk the disappearing band;
Each warrior vanished where he stood,
In broom or bracken, heath or wood;
Sunk brand and spear and bended bow,
In osiers pale and copses low;
It seemed as if their mother Earth
Had swallowed up her warlike birth.
The wind's last breath had tossed in air
Pennon, and plaid, and plumage fair—
The next but swept a lone hill-side,
Where heath and fern were waving wide;
The sun's last glance was glinted back,
From spear and glaive, from targe and jack—
The next, all unreflected, shone
On bracken green and cold grey stone.

253 *jack*: short coat of mail or leather plated with iron.

XI

Fitz-James looked round—yet scarce believed
The witness that his sight received;
Such apparition well might seem
Delusion of a dreadful dream.
Sir Roderick in suspense he eyed,
And to his look the Chief replied,
'Fear nought—nay, that I need not say—
But—doubt not aught from mine array.
Thou art my guest; I pledged my word
As far as Coilantogle ford:
Nor would I call a clansman's brand
For aid against one valiant hand,
Though on our strife lay every vale
Rent by the Saxon from the Gael.
So move we on; I only meant
To show the reed on which you leant,
Deeming this path you might pursue
Without a pass from Roderick Dhu.'
They moved. I said Fitz-James was brave
As ever knight that belted glaive,
Yet dare not say that now his blood
Kept on its wont and tempered flood,
As, following Roderick's stride, he drew
That seeming lonesome pathway through,
Which yet, by fearful proof, was rife
With lances, that, to take his life,
Waited but signal from a guide
So late dishonoured and defied.
Ever, by stealth, his eye sought round
The vanished guardians of the ground,
And still, from copse and heather deep,
Fancy saw spear and broadsword peep,
And in the plover's shrilly strain,
The signal-whistle heard again.
Nor breathed he free till far behind
The pass was left; for then they wind
Along a wide and level green,
Where neither tree nor tuft was seen,
Nor rush nor bush of broom was near,
To hide a bonnet or a spear.

XII

The Chief in silence strode before,
And reached that torrent's sounding shore,
Which, daughter of three mighty lakes,
From Vennachar in silver breaks,
Sweeps through the plain, and ceaseless mines
On Bochastle the mouldering lines,
Where Rome, the Empress of the world,
Of yore her eagle wings unfurled.
And here his course the Chieftain stayed,
Threw down his target and his plaid,
And to the Lowland warrior said:
'Bold Saxon! to his promise just,
Vich-Alpine has discharged his trust.
This murderous Chief, this ruthless man,
This head of a rebellious clan,
Hath led thee safe, through watch and ward,
Far past Clan-Alpine's outmost guard.
Now man to man, and steel to steel,
A Chieftain's vengeance thou shalt feel.
See here, all vantageless I stand,
Armed like thyself with single brand:
For this is Coilantogle ford,
And thou must keep thee with thy sword.'

XIII

The Saxon paused: 'I ne'er delayed,
When foeman bade me draw my blade;
Nay, more, brave Chief, I vowed thy death;
Yet sure thy fair and generous faith,
And my deep debt for life preserved,
A better meed have well deserved:
Can nought but blood our feud atone?
Are there no means?'—'No, Stranger, none!
And hear, to fire thy flagging zeal—
The Saxon cause rests on thy steel;
For thus spoke Fate, by prophet bred
Between the living and the dead:

298 *three . . . lakes*: Katrine, Achray, Vennachar.
301 *Bochastle*: 'Upon a small eminence called the *Dun* of Bochastle and indeed on the plain itself, are some intrenchments, which have been thought Roman' (S).

"Who spills the foremost foeman's life
His party conquers in the strife."'
'Then, by my word,' the Saxon said,
'The riddle is already read.
Seek yonder brake beneath the cliff—
There lies Red Murdoch, stark and stiff.
Thus Fate has solved her prophecy,
Then yield to Fate, and not to me.
To James, at Stirling, let us go,
When, if thou wilt be still his foe,
Or if the King shall not agree
To grant thee grace and favour free,
I plight mine honour, oath, and word,
That, to thy native strengths restored,
With each advantage shalt thou stand,
That aids thee now, to guard thy land.'

XIV

Dark lightning flashed from Roderick's eye—
'Soars thy presumption, then, so high,
Because a wretched kern ye slew,
Homage to name to Roderick Dhu?
He yields not, he, to man nor Fate!
Thou add'st but fuel to my hate:
My clansman's blood demands revenge.
Not yet prepared?—By heaven, I change
My thought, and hold thy valour light
As that of some vain carpet knight,
Who ill deserved my courteous care,
And whose best boast is but to wear
A braid of his fair lady's hair.'—
'I thank thee, Roderick, for the word!
It nerves my heart, it steels my sword;
For I have sworn this braid to stain
In the best blood that warms thy vein.
Now, truce, farewell! and, ruth, be gone!
Yet think not that by thee alone,
Proud Chief! can courtesy be shown;
Though not from copse, or heath, or cairn,
Start at my whistle clansmen stern,

344 *strengths*: strongholds.
356 *carpet knight*: stay-at-home soldier, ladies' man.

Of this small horn one feeble blast
Would fearful odds against thee cast.
But fear not, doubt not—which thou wilt—
We try this quarrel hilt to hilt.'—
Then each at once his falchion drew,
Each on the ground his scabbard threw,
Each looked to sun, and stream, and plain,
As what he ne'er might see again;
Then foot, and point, and eye opposed,
In dubious strife they darkly closed.

XV

Ill fared it then with Roderick Dhu,
That on the field his targe[n] he threw,
Whose brazen studs and tough bull-hide
Had death so often dashed aside;
For, trained abroad his arms to wield,
Fitz-James's blade was sword and shield.
He practised every pass and ward,
To thrust, to strike, to feint, to guard;
While less expert, though stronger far,
The Gael maintained unequal war.
Three times in closing strife they stood,
And thrice the Saxon blade drank blood;
No stinted draught, no scanty tide,
The gushing flood the tartans dyed.
Fierce Roderick felt the fatal drain,
And showered his blows like wintry rain;
And, as firm rock, or castle-roof,
Against the winter shower is proof,
The foe, invulnerable still,
Foiled his wild rage by steady skill;
Till, at advantage ta'en, his brand
Forced Roderick's weapon from his hand,
And backward borne upon the lea,
Brought the proud Chieftain to his knee.

XVI

'Now, yield thee, or by Him who made
The world, thy heart's blood dyes my blade!'—

383 *trained abroad*: in France, where rapiers alone were used, without target or buckler.

'Thy threats, thy mercy, I defy!
Let recreant yield, who fears to die.'
Like adder darting from his coil,
Like wolf that dashes through the toil,
Like mountain-cat who guards her young,
Full at Fitz-James's throat he sprung;
Received, but recked not of a wound,
And locked his arms his foeman round.
Now, gallant Saxon, hold thine own!
No maiden's hand is round thee thrown!
That desperate grasp thy frame might feel
Through bars of brass and triple steel!—
They tug, they strain! down, down they go,
The Gael above, Fitz-James below.
The Chieftain's gripe his throat compressed,
His knee was planted in his breast;
His clotted locks he backward threw,
Across his brow his hand he drew,
From blood and mist to clear his sight,
Then gleamed aloft his dagger bright!
But hate and fury ill supplied
The stream of life's exhausted tide,
And all too late the advantage came,
To turn the odds of deadly game;
For, while the dagger gleamed on high,
Reeled soul and sense, reeled brain and eye.
Down came the blow—but in the heath;
The erring blade found bloodless sheath.
The struggling foe may now unclasp
The fainting Chief's relaxing grasp;
Unwounded from the dreadful close,
But breathless all, Fitz-James arose.

XVII

He faltered thanks to Heaven for life,
Redeemed, unhoped, from desperate strife;
Next on his foe his look he cast,
Whose every gasp appeared his last;
In Roderick's gore he dipped the braid—
'Poor Blanche! thy wrongs are dearly paid:
Yet with thy foe must die, or live,
The praise that Faith and Valour give.'[n]

With that he blew a bugle-note,
Undid the collar from his throat,
Unbonneted, and by the wave
Sat down his brow and hands to lave.
Then faint afar are heard the feet
Of rushing steeds in gallop fleet;
The sounds increase, and now are seen
Four mounted squires in Lincoln green;
Two who bear lance, and two who lead,
By loosened rein, a saddled steed;
Each onward held his headlong course,
And by Fitz-James reined up his horse,
With wonder viewed the bloody spot—
—'Exclaim not, gallants! question not.
You, Herbert and Luffness, alight,
And bind the wounds of yonder knight;
Let the grey palfrey bear his weight,
We destined for a fairer freight,
And bring him on to Stirling straight;
I will before at better speed,
To seek fresh horse and fitting weed.
The sun rides high; I must be boune,
To see the archer-game at noon;
But lightly Bayard clears the lea.—
De Vaux and Herries, follow me.

XVIII

'Stand, Bayard, stand!' The steed obeyed,
With arching neck and bended head,
And glancing eye and quivering ear,
As if he loved his lord to hear.
No foot Fitz-James in stirrup stayed,
No grasp upon the saddle laid,
But wreathed his left hand in the mane,
And lightly bounded from the plain,
Turned on the horse his armed heel,
And stirred his courage with the steel.

465 *weed*: clothing. 466 *boune*: ready.

468 *Bayard*: horse's name, originally from the bay-coloured steed given by Charlemagne to Rinaldo in medieval romance.

469 *De Vaux*, *Herries*: members of these Anglo-Norman families settled in Scotland in the 12th century.

Bounded the fiery steed in air,
The rider sat erect and fair,
Then like a bolt from steel crossbow
Forth launched, along the plain they go.
They dashed that rapid torrent through,
And up Carhonie's hill they flew;
Still at the gallop pricked the Knight,
His merry-men followed as they might.
Along thy banks, swift Teith! they ride,
And in the race they mock thy tide;
Torry and Lendrick now are past,
And Deanstown lies behind them cast;
They rise, the bannered towers of Doune,
They sink in distant woodland soon;
Blair-Drummond[n] sees the hoofs strike fire,
They sweep like breeze through Ochtertyre;
They mark just glance and disappear
The lofty brow of ancient Kier;
They bathe their coursers' sweltering sides,
Dark Forth! amid thy sluggish tides,
And on the opposing shore take ground,
With plash, with scramble, and with bound.
Right-hand they leave thy cliffs, Craig-Forth![n]
And soon the bulwark of the North,
Grey Stirling, with her towers and town,
Upon their fleet career looked down.

XIX

As up the flinty path they strained
Sudden his steed the leader reined;
A signal to his squire he flung,
Who instant to his stirrup sprung:
'Seest thou, De Vaux, yon woodsman grey,
Who town-ward holds the rocky way,
Of stature tall and poor array?
Mark'st thou the firm, yet active stride,
With which he scales the mountain-side?

485 *Carhonie*: Gartchonzie at the E. end of Loch Vennachar.
490 *Torry*: 2½ miles NW. of Lanrick.
490 *Lendrick*: Lanrick, 2½ miles NNW. of Doune Castle.
491 *Deanstown*: 1 mile NNW. of Doune Castle.
492 *Doune*: see above, p. 231.
503 *bulwark of the North*: defending the road that leads to the Highlands.

Know'st thou from whence he comes, or whom?'—
'No, by my word; a burly groom
He seems, who in the field or chase
A baron's train would nobly grace.'—
'Out, out, De Vaux! can fear supply,
And jealousy, no sharper eye?
Afar, ere to the hill he drew,
That stately form and step I knew;
Like form in Scotland is not seen,
Treads not such step on Scottish green.
'Tis James of Douglas, by Saint Serle!
The uncle of the banished Earl.
Away, away to court, to show
The near approach of dreaded foe:
The King must stand upon his guard;
Douglas and he must meet prepared.'
Then right-hand wheeled their steeds, and straight
They won the castle's postern gate.

XX

The Douglas, who had bent his way
From Cambus-Kenneth's abbey grey,
Now, as he climbed the rocky shelf,
Held sad communion with himself:
'Yes! all is true my fears could frame;
A prisoner lies the noble Græme,
And fiery Roderick soon will feel
The vengeance of the royal steel.
I, only I, can ward their fate—
God grant the ransom come not late!
The Abbess hath her promise given
My child shall be the bride of Heaven;—
Be pardoned one repining tear!
For He who gave her knows how dear,
How excellent—but that is by,
And now my business is to die.

525 *James*: 'an imaginary person, a supposed uncle of the Earl of Angus' see p. 294, end-note on II. 229.
525 *St. Serle*: probably St. Serlo, d. 1104, a Norman who was appointed abbot of Gloucester in 1074.
541 *ward*: i.e., 'ward off'.
544 *bride of Heaven*: nun.

Ye towers! within whose circuit dread
A Douglas by his sovereign bled;
And thou, O sad and fatal mound!
That oft hast heard the death-axe sound,
As on the noblest of the land
Fell the stern headsman's bloody hand—
The dungeon, block, and nameless tomb
Prepare—for Douglas seeks his doom!
But hark! what blithe and jolly peal
Makes the Franciscan steeple reel?
And see! upon the crowded street,
In motley groups what masquers meet!
Banner and pageant, pipe and drum,
And merry morrice-dancers come.
I guess, by all this quaint array,
The burghers hold their sports to-day.
James will be there; he loves such show,
Where the good yeoman bends his bow,
And the tough wrestler foils his foe,
As well as where, in proud career,
The high-born tilter shivers spear.
I'll follow to the Castle-park,
And play my prize; King James shall mark
If age has tamed these sinews stark,
Whose force so oft, in happier days,
His boyish wonder loved to praise.'

XXI

The Castle gates were open flung,
The quivering drawbridge rocked and rung,
And echoed loud the flinty street
Beneath the coursers' clattering feet,
As slowly down the steep descent
Fair Scotland's King and nobles went,
While all along the crowded way
Was jubilee and loud huzza.
And ever James was bending low
To his white jennet's saddle-bow,

550 *A Douglas*: William, Earl of Douglas, was stabbed by James II in Stirling Castle in 1452.
558 *steeple*: a Franciscan church was built on the castle rock in 1492.
571 *play*: gain by taking part in the sport.

Doffing his cap to city dame,
Who smiled and blushed for pride and shame.
And well the simperer might be vain—
He chose the fairest of the train.
Gravely he greets each city sire,
Commends each pageant's quaint attire,
Gives to the dancers thanks aloud,
And smiles and nods upon the crowd,
Who rend the heavens with their acclaims,
'Long live the Commons' King, King James!'
Behind the King thronged peer and knight,
And noble dame and damsel bright,
Whose fiery steeds ill brooked the stay
Of the steep street and crowded way.—
But in the train you might discern
Dark lowering brow and visage stern;
There nobles mourned their pride restrained,
And the mean burgher's joys disdained;
And chiefs who, hostage for their clan,
Were each from home a banished man,
There thought upon their own grey tower,
Their waving woods, their feudal power,
And deemed themselves a shameful part
Of pageant which they cursed in heart.

XXII

Now, in the Castle-park, drew out
Their chequered bands the joyous rout.
Their morricers, with bell at heel
And blade in hand, their mazes wheel;
But chief, beside the butts, there stand
Bold Robin Hood and all his band[n]—
Friar Tuck with quarterstaff and cowl,
Old Scathelocke with his surly scowl,
Maid Marion fair as ivory bone,
Scarlet and Mutch and Little John;
Their bugles challenge all that will,
In archery to prove their skill.
The Douglas bent a bow of might—
His first shaft centered in the white,

610 *chequered*: dressed in parti-coloured clothes.
622 *white*: the centre or 'bull's eye' of the target was painted white.

And when in turn he shot again,
His second split the first in twain.
From the King's hand must Douglas take
A silver dart, the archer's stake;
Fondly he watched, with watery eye,
Some answering glance of sympathy—
No kind emotion made reply!
Indifferent as to archer wight,
The Monarch gave the arrow bright.[n]

XXIII

Now, clear the ring! for, hand to hand,
The manly wrestlers take their stand.
Two o'er the rest superior rose,
And proud demanded mightier foes,
Nor called in vain; for Douglas came.
—For life is Hugh of Larbert lame;
Scarce better John of Alloa's fare,
Whom senseless home his comrades bear.
Prize of the wrestling match, the King
To Douglas gave a golden ring,[n]
While coldly glanced his eye of blue,
As frozen drop of wintry dew.
Douglas would speak, but in his breast
His struggling soul his words suppressed;
Indignant then he turned him where
Their arms the brawny yeomen bare,
To hurl the massive bar in air.
When each his utmost strength had shown,
The Douglas rent an earth-fast stone
From its deep bed, then heaved it high,
And sent the fragment through the sky
A rood beyond the farthest mark—
And still in Stirling's royal park,
The grey-haired sires, who know the past,
To strangers point the Douglas-cast,
And moralize on the decay
Of Scottish strength in modern day.

637 *Larbert*: village in East Stirling, $2\frac{3}{4}$ miles NW. of Falkirk.
638 *Alloa*: town in Clackmannan, on the North bank of the tidal Forth.
638 *fare*: lot.

XXIV

The vale with loud applauses rang,
The Ladies' Rock[n] sent back the clang.
The King, with look unmoved, bestowed
A purse well-filled with pieces broad.
Indignant smiled the Douglas proud,
And threw the gold among the crowd,
Who now, with anxious wonder scan,
And sharper glance, the dark grey man;
Till whispers rose among the throng,
That heart so free, and hand so strong,
Must to the Douglas blood belong:
The old men marked, and shook the head,
To see his hair with silver spread;
And winked aside, and told each son
Of feats upon the English done,
Ere Douglas of the stalwart hand
Was exiled from his native land.
The women praised his stately form,
Though wrecked by many a winter's storm;
The youth with awe and wonder saw
His strength surpassing Nature's law.
Thus judged, as is their wont, the crowd,
Till murmur rose to clamours loud.
But not a glance from that proud ring
Of peers who circled round the King,
With Douglas held communion kind,
Or called the banished man to mind;
No, not from those who, at the chase,
Once held his side the honoured place,
Begirt his board, and, in the field,
Found safety underneath his shield;
For he, whom royal eyes disown,
When was his form to courtiers known?

XXV

The Monarch saw the gambols flag
And bade let loose a gallant stag,

666 *dark grey*: according to a once popular theory 'Douglas' is derived from Gaelic 'dubh glas', black-grey.
683 *circled*: stood in a circle.

Whose pride, the holiday to crown,
Two favourite greyhounds should pull down,
That venison free, and Bordeaux wine,
Might serve the archery to dine.
But Lufra—whom from Douglas' side
Nor bribe nor threat could e'er divide,
The fleetest hound in all the North—
Brave Lufra saw, and darted forth.
She left the royal hounds mid-way,
And dashing on the antlered prey,
Sunk her sharp muzzle in his flank,
And deep the flowing life-blood drank.
The King's stout huntsman saw the sport
By strange intruder broken short,
Came up, and with his leash unbound,
In anger struck the noble hound.—
The Douglas had endured, that morn,
The King's cold look, the nobles' scorn,
And last, and worst to spirit proud,
Had borne the pity of the crowd;
But Lufra had been fondly bred,
To share his board, to watch his bed,
And oft would Ellen Lufra's neck
In maiden glee with garlands deck;
They were such playmates, that with name
Of Lufra, Ellen's image came.
His stifled wrath is brimming high,
In darkened brow and flashing eye;
As waves before the bark divide,
The crowd gave way before his stride;
Needs but a buffet and no more,
The groom lies senseless in his gore.
Such blow no other hand could deal,
Though gauntleted in glove of steel.

XXVI

Then clamoured loud the royal train,
And brandished swords and staves amain.
But stern the Baron's warning—'Back!
Back, on your lives, ye menial pack!

697 *archery*: the archers.

Beware the Douglas. Yes! behold,
King James! the Douglas, doomed of old,
And vainly sought for near and far,
A victim to atone the war,
A willing victim, now attends,
Nor craves thy grace but for his friends.'—
'Thus is my clemency repaid?
Presumptuous Lord!' the Monarch said;
'Of thy mis-proud ambitious clan,
Thou, James of Bothwell, wert the man,
The only man, in whom a foe
My woman-mercy would not know:
But shall a Monarch's presence brook
Injurious blow, and haughty look?—
What ho! the Captain of our Guard!
Give the offender fitting ward.—
Break off the sports!'—for tumult rose,
And yeomen 'gan to bend their bows.
'Break off the sports!' he said, and frowned,
'And bid our horsemen clear the ground.'

XXVII

Then uproar wild and misarray
Marred the fair form of festal day.
The horsemen pricked among the crowd,
Repelled by threats and insult loud;
To earth are borne the old and weak,
The timorous fly, the women shriek;
With flint, with shaft, with staff, with bar,
The hardier urge tumultuous war.
At once round Douglas darkly sweep
The royal spears in circle deep,
And slowly scale the pathway steep;
While on the rear in thunder pour
The rabble with disordered roar.
With grief the noble Douglas saw
The Commons rise against the law,
And to the leading soldier said,
'Sir John of Hyndford![n] 'twas my blade
That knighthood on thy shoulder laid;

740 *mis-proud*: arrogant.
768 *Hyndford*: then a village 2½ miles SE. of Lanark town.

For that good deed, permit me then
A word with these misguided men.—

XXVIII

'Hear, gentle friends! ere yet for me,
Ye break the bands of fealty.
My life, my honour, and my cause,
I tender free to Scotland's laws.
Are these so weak as must require
The aid of your misguided ire?
Or, if I suffer causeless wrong,
Is then my selfish rage so strong,
My sense of public weal so low,
That, for mean vengeance on a foe,
Those cords of love I should unbind,
Which knit my country and my kind?
Oh no! Believe, in yonder tower
It will not soothe my captive hour
To know those spears our foes should dread,
For me in kindred gore are red;
To know, in fruitless brawl begun,
For me, that mother wails her son;
For me, that widow's mate expires;
For me, that orphans weep their sires;
That patriots mourn insulted laws,
And curse the Douglas for the cause.
O let your patience ward such ill,
And keep your right to love me still!'

XXIX

The crowd's wild fury sunk again
In tears, as tempests melt in rain.
With lifted hands and eyes, they prayed
For blessings on his generous head,
Who for his country felt alone,
And prized her blood beyond his own.
Old men, upon the verge of life,
Blessed him who stayed the civil strife;
And mothers held their babes on high,
The self-devoted Chief to spy,
Triumphant over wrongs and ire,
To whom the prattlers owed a sire:

Even the rough soldier's heart was moved;
As if behind some bier beloved,
With trailing arms and drooping head,
The Douglas up the hill he led,
And at the Castle's battled verge,
With sighs resigned his honoured charge.

XXX

The offended Monarch rode apart,
With bitter thought and swelling heart,
And would not now vouchsafe again
Through Stirling streets to lead his train.
'O Lennox, who would wish to rule
This changeling crowd, this common fool?
Hear'st thou,' he said, 'the loud acclaim,
With which they shout the Douglas name?
With like acclaim, the vulgar throat
Strained for King James their morning note;
With like acclaim they hailed the day
When first I broke the Douglas' sway;
And like acclaim would Douglas greet,
If he could hurl me from my seat.
Who o'er the herd would wish to reign,
Fantastic, fickle, fierce, and vain?
Vain as the leaf upon the stream,
And fickle as a changeful dream;
Fantastic as a woman's mood,
And fierce as Frenzy's fevered blood.
Thou many-headed monster-thing,
O who would wish to be thy king?[n]

XXXI

'But soft! what messenger of speed
Spurs hitherward his panting steed?
I guess his cognizance afar—
What from our cousin, John of Mar?'—
'He prays, my liege, your sports keep bound
Within the safe and guarded ground:
For some foul purpose yet unknown—
Most sure for evil to the throne—

810 *trailing arms*: here, spears balanced in one hand in horizontal position.
812 *battled verge*: battlemented gateway. 819 *changeling*: i.e., changeful.

The outlawed Chieftain, Roderick Dhu,
Has summoned his rebellious crew;
'Tis said, in James of Bothwell's aid
These loose banditti stand arrayed.
The Earl of Mar, this morn, from Doune,
To break their muster marched, and soon
Your grace will hear of battle fought;
But earnestly the Earl besought,
Till for such danger he provide,
With scanty train you will not ride.'—

XXXII

'Thou warn'st me I have done amiss;
I should have earlier looked to this:
I lost it in this bustling day.
Retrace with speed thy former way;
Spare not for spoiling of thy steed,
The best of mine shall be thy meed.
Say to our faithful Lord of Mar,
We do forbid the intended war:
Roderick, this morn, in single fight,
Was made our prisoner by a knight;
And Douglas hath himself and cause
Submitted to our kingdom's laws.
The tidings of their leaders lost
Will soon dissolve the mountain host,
Nor would we that the vulgar feel,
For their Chief's crimes, avenging steel.
Bear Mar our message, Braco: fly!'
He turned his steed,—'My liege, I hie,
Yet, ere I cross this lily lawn,
I fear the broadswords will be drawn.'
The turf the flying courser spurned,
And to his towers the King returned.

XXXIII

Ill with King James's mood, that day,
Suited gay feast and minstrel lay;
Soon were dismissed the courtly throng,
And soon cut short the festal song.

870 *Braco*: son of the Earl of Mar, Braco being his father's second title.

Nor less upon the saddened town
The evening sunk in sorrow down.
The burghers spoke of civil jar,
Of rumoured feuds and mountain war,
Of Moray, Mar, and Roderick Dhu,
All up in arms—the Douglas too,
They mourned him pent within the hold
'Where stout Earl William was of old,'
And there his word the speaker stayed,
And finger on his lip he laid,
Or pointed to his dagger blade.
But jaded horsemen, from the west,
At evening to the Castle pressed;
And busy talkers said they bore
Tidings of fight on Katrine's shore;
At noon the deadly fray begun,
And lasted till the set of sun.
Thus giddy rumour shook the town,
Till closed the Night her pennons brown.

Canto Sixth

The Guard-Room

I

THE sun, awakening, through the smoky air
  Of the dark city casts a sullen glance,
Rousing each caitiff to his task of care,
  Of sinful man the sad inheritance;
Summoning revellers from the lagging dance,
  Scaring the prowling robber to his den;
Gilding on battled tower the warder's lance,
  And warning student pale to leave his pen,
And yield his drowsy eyes to the kind nurse of men.

What various scenes, and, O! what scenes of woe,
  Are witnessed by that red and struggling beam!
The fevered patient, from his pallet low,
  Through crowded hospital beholds its stream;
The ruined maiden trembles at its gleam,
  The debtor wakes to thought of gyve and jail,
The love-lorn wretch starts from tormenting dream;

887 *Earl William*: see p. 244n. 4 *inheritance*: see Genesis 3:19.
9 *nurse of men*: sleep, from *2 Henry IV*, III. i. 5.

The wakeful mother, by the glimmering pale,
Trims her sick infant's couch, and soothes his feeble wail.

II

At dawn the towers of Stirling rang
With soldier-step and weapon-clang.
While drums, with rolling note, foretell
Relief to weary sentinel.
Through narrow loop and casement barred,
The sunbeams sought the Court of Guard,
And, struggling with the smoky air,
Deadened the torches' yellow glare.
In comfortless alliance shone
The lights through arch of blackened stone,
And showed wild shapes in garb of war,
Faces deformed with beard and scar,
All haggard from the midnight watch,
And fevered with the stern debauch;
For the oak table's massive board,
Flooded with wine, with fragments stored,
And beakers drained, and cups o'erthrown,
Showed in what sport the night had flown.
Some, weary, snored on floor and bench;
Some laboured still their thirst to quench;
Some, chilled with watching, spread their hands
O'er the huge chimney's dying brands,
While round them, or beside them flung,
At every step their harness rung.

III

These drew not for their fields the sword,
Like tenants of a feudal lord,
Nor owned the patriarchal claim
Of Chieftain in their leader's name;
Adventurers they, from far who roved,
To live by battle which they loved.
There the Italian's clouded face,
The swarthy Spaniard's there you trace;
The mountain-loving Switzer there
More freely breathed in mountain-air;

24 *Court of Guard*: sentinels' quarters.

The Fleming there despised the soil,
That paid so ill the labourer's toil;
Their rolls showed French and German name;
And merry England's exiles came,
To share, with ill concealed disdain,
Of Scotland's pay the scanty gain.
All brave in arms, well trained to wield
The heavy halberd, brand, and shield;
In camps licentious, wild, and bold;
In pillage fierce and uncontrolled;
And now, by holytide and feast,
From rules of discipline released.[n]

IV

They held debate of bloody fray,
Fought 'twixt Loch Katrine and Achray.
Fierce was their speech, and, 'mid their words,
Their hands oft grappled to their swords;
Nor sunk their tone to spare the ear
Of wounded comrades groaning near,
Whose mangled limbs and bodies gored
Bore token of the mountain sword,
Though, neighbouring to the Court of Guard,
Their prayers and feverish wails were heard—
Sad burden to the ruffian joke,
And savage oath by fury spoke!
At length up-started John of Brent,
A yeoman from the banks of Trent;
A stranger to respect or fear,
In peace a chaser of the deer—
In host a hardy mutineer,
But still the boldest of the crew
When deed of danger was to do.
He grieved that day their games cut short,
And marred the dicer's brawling sport
And shouted loud, 'Renew the bowl!
And, while a merry catch I troll,
Let each the buxom chorus bear
Like brethren of the brand and spear:

88 *buxom*: lively.

V

SOLDIER'S SONG

Our vicar still preaches that Peter and Poule
Laid a swinging long curse on the bonny brown bowl,
That there's wrath and despair in the jolly black-jack,
And the seven deadly sins in a flagon of sack;
Yet whoop, Barnaby! off with thy liquor,
Drink upsees out, and a fig for the vicar!

Our vicar he calls it damnation to sip
The ripe ruddy dew of a woman's dear lip,
Says, that Beelzebub lurks in her kerchief so sly,
And Apollyon shoots darts from her merry black eye;
Yet whoop, Jack! kiss Gillian the quicker,
Till she bloom like a rose, and a fig for the vicar!

Our vicar thus preaches—and why should he not?
For the dues of his cure are the placket and pot;
And 'tis right of his office poor laymen to lurch,
Who infringe the domains of our good Mother Church.
Yet whoop, bully-boys! off with your liquor,
Sweet Marjorie's the word, and a fig for the vicar!'

VI

The warder's challenge, heard without,
Stayed in mid-roar the merry shout.
A soldier to the portal went—
'Here is old Bertram, sirs, of Ghent;
And, beat for jubilee the drum!
A maid and minstrel with him come.'
Bertram, a Fleming, grey and scarred,
Was entering now the Court of Guard,
A harper with him, and in plaid
All muffled close, a mountain maid,
Who backward shrunk to 'scape the view
Of the loose scene and boisterous crew.
'What news?' they roared.—'I only know,
From noon till eve we fought with foe,

90 *Poule*: Paul.
92 *black-jack*: tarred leather bottle for wine or beer.
95 *upsees*: 'Bacchanalian interjection borrowed from the Dutch' (S).
104 *lurch*: cheat.

As wild and as untameable
As the rude mountains where they dwell;
On both sides store of blood is lost,
Nor much success can either boast.'—
'But whence thy captives, friend? such spoil
As theirs must needs reward thy toil.
Old dost thou wax, and wars grow sharp;
Thou now hast glee-maiden and harp!
Get thee an ape, and trudge the land,
The leader of a juggler band.'—[n]

VII

'No, comrade; no such fortune mine.
After the fight these sought our line,
That aged harper and the girl,
And, having audience of the Earl,
Mar bade I should purvey them steed,
And bring them hitherward with speed.
Forbear your mirth and rude alarm,
For none shall do them shame or harm.'
'Hear ye his boast?' cried John of Brent,
Ever to strife and jangling bent;
'Shall he strike doe beside our lodge,
And yet the jealous niggard grudge
To pay the forester his fee?
I'll have my share, howe'er it be,
Despite of Moray, Mar, or thee.'
Bertram his forward step withstood;
And, burning in his vengeful mood,
Old Allan, though unfit for strife,
Laid hand upon his dagger-knife;
But Ellen boldly stepped between,
And dropped at once the tartan screen:
So, from his morning cloud, appears
The sun of May through summer tears.
The savage soldiery, amazed,
As on descended angel gazed;
Even hardy Brent, abashed and tamed,
Stood half admiring, half ashamed.

138 *alarm*: disturbance.
144 *pay . . . fee*: give him a kiss.

VIII

Boldly she spoke—'Soldiers, attend!
My father was the soldier's friend;
Cheered him in camps, in marches led,
And with him in the battle bled.
Not from the valiant, or the strong,
Should exile's daughter suffer wrong.'
Answered De Brent, most forward still
In every feat of good or ill—
'I shame me of the part I played:
And thou an outlaw's child, poor maid!
An outlaw I by forest laws,
And merry Needwood knows the cause.
Poor Rose—if Rose be living now'—
He wiped his iron eye and brow—
'Must bear such age, I think, as thou.—
Hear ye, my mates—I go to call
The Captain of our watch to hall:
There lies my halberd on the floor;
And he that steps my halberd o'er
To do the maid injurious part,
My shaft shall quiver in his heart!
Beware loose speech, or jesting rough:
Ye all know John de Brent. Enough.'

IX

Their Captain came, a gallant young,
(Of Tullibardine's house he sprung,)
Nor wore he yet the spurs of knight;
Gay was his mien, his humour light,
And, though by courtesy controlled,
Forward his speech, his bearing bold,
The high-born maiden ill could brook
The scanning of his curious look
And dauntless eye—and yet, in sooth.
Young Lewis was a generous youth:
But Ellen's lovely face and mien,
Ill suited to the garb and scene,

170 *Needwood*: part of Staffordshire, formerly a forest.
183 *Tullibardine*: family of Murrays in county of Perth.

Might lightly bear construction strange
And give loose fancy scope to range.
'Welcome to Stirling towers, fair maid!
Come ye to seek a champion's aid,
On palfrey white, with harper hoar,
Like errant damosel of yore?
Does thy high quest a knight require,
Or may the venture suit a squire?'
Her dark eye flashed; she paused and sighed,
'O what have I to do with pride!—
Through scenes of sorrow, shame, and strife,
A suppliant for a father's life,
I crave an audience of the King.
Behold, to back my suit, a ring,
The royal pledge of grateful claims,
Given by the Monarch to Fitz-James.'

X

The signet-ring young Lewis took
With deep respect and altered look;
And said, 'This ring our duties own;
And pardon, if to worth unknown,
In semblance mean obscurely veiled,
Lady, in aught my folly failed.
Soon as the day flings wide his gates,
The King shall know what suitor waits.
Please you, meanwhile, in fitting bower
Repose you till his waking hour;
Female attendance shall obey
Your hest, for service or array.
Permit I marshall you the way.'
But, ere she followed, with the grace
And open bounty of her race,
She bade her slender purse be shared
Among the soldiers of the guard.
The rest with thanks their guerdon took;
But Brent, with shy and awkward look,
On the reluctant maiden's hold
Forced bluntly back the proffered gold—

208 *grateful claims*: claims of gratitude.
212 *This ring . . . own*: our duties include respect towards this ring.

'Forgive a haughty English heart,
And O forget its ruder part!
The vacant purse shall be my share,
Which in my barret-cap I'll bear,
Perchance, in jeopardy of war,
Where gayer crests may keep afar.'
With thanks ('twas all she could) the maid
His rugged courtesy repaid.

XI

When Ellen forth with Lewis went,
Allan made suit to John of Brent:
'My lady safe, O let your grace
Give me to see my master's face!
His minstrel I—to share his doom
Bound from the cradle to the tomb;
Tenth in descent, since first my sires
Waked for his noble house their lyres;
Nor one of all the race was known
But prized its weal above their own.
With the Chief's birth begins our care;
Our harp must soothe the infant heir,
Teach the youth tales of fight, and grace
His earliest feat of field or chase;
In peace, in war, our rank we keep,
We cheer his board, we soothe his sleep,
Nor leave him till we pour our verse,
A doleful tribute! o'er his hearse.
Then let me share his captive lot;
It is my right—deny it not!'
'Little we reck,' said John of Brent,
'We Southern men, of long descent;
Nor wot we how a name—a word—
Makes clansmen vassals to a lord:
Yet kind my noble landlord's part—
God bless the house of Beaudesert!
And, but I loved to drive the deer,
More than to guide the labouring steer,
I had not dwelt an outcast here.
Come, good old Minstrel, follow me;
Thy Lord and Chieftain shalt thou see.'

234 *barret-cap*: flat cap.

XII

Then, from a rusted iron hook,
A bunch of ponderous keys he took,
Lighted a torch, and Allan led
Through grated arch and passage dread.
Portals they passed, where, deep within,
Spoke prisoner's moan, and fetters' din;
Through rugged vaults, where, loosely stored,
Lay wheel, and axe, and headsman's sword,
And many an hideous engine grim,
For wrenching joint, and crushing limb,
By artists formed, who deemed it shame
And sin to give their work a name.
They halted at a low-browed porch,
And Brent to Allan gave the torch,
While bolt and chain he backward rolled,
And made the bar unhasp its hold.
They entered: 'twas a prison-room
Of stern security and gloom,
Yet not a dungeon; for the day
Through lofty gratings found its way,
And rude and antique garniture
Decked the sad walls and oaken floor;
Such as the rugged days of old
Deemed fit for captive noble's hold.
'Here,' said De Brent, 'thou mayst remain
Till the leech visit him again.
Strict is his charge, the warders tell,
To tend the noble prisoner well.'
Retiring then the bolt he drew,
And the lock's murmurs growled anew.
Roused at the sound, from lowly bed
A captive feebly raised his head;
The wondering Minstrel looked, and knew
Not his dear lord, but Roderick Dhu!
For, come from where Clan-Alpine fought,
They, erring, deemed the Chief he sought.

XIII

As the tall ship, whose lofty prore
Shall never stem the billows more,

277 *wheel*: the instrument of torture. 293 *hold*: prison. 306 *prore*: prow.

Deserted by her gallant band,
Amid the breakers lies astrand—
So, on his couch, lay Roderick Dhu!
And oft his fevered limbs he threw
In toss abrupt, as when her sides
Lie rocking in the advancing tides,
That shake her frame with ceaseless beat,
Yet cannot heave her from her seat—
O! how unlike her course on sea!
Or his free step on hill and lea!—
Soon as the Minstrel he could scan,
'What of thy lady?—of my clan?—
My mother?—Douglas?—tell me all!
Have they been ruined in my fall?
Ah, yes! or wherefore art thou here?
Yet speak, speak boldly, do not fear.'
(For Allan, who his mood well knew,
Was choked with grief and terror too.)—
'Who fought—who fled? Old man, be brief;
Some might—for they had lost their Chief.
Who basely live?—who bravely died?'—
'O, calm thee, Chief!' the Minstrel cried,
'Ellen is safe.'—'For that, thank Heaven!'—
'And hopes are for the Douglas given;
The Lady Margaret, too, is well;
And, for thy clan—on field or fell,
Has never harp of minstrel told,
Of combat fought so true and bold.
Thy stately Pine is yet unbent,
Though many a goodly bough is rent.'

XIV

The Chieftain reared his form on high,
And fever's fire was in his eye;
But ghastly, pale, and livid streaks
Chequered his swarthy brow and cheeks.
—'Hark, Minstrel! I have heard thee play,
With measure bold, on festal day,
In yon lone isle, . . . again where ne'er
Shall harper play, or warrior hear! . . .

309 *astrand*: beached.

That stirring air that peals on high
O'er Dermid's race our victory.
Strike it! and then (for well thou canst)
Free from thy minstrel-spirit glanced,
Fling me the picture of the fight
When met my clan the Saxon might.
I'll listen, till my fancy hears
The clang of swords, the crash of spears!
These grates, these walls, shall vanish then,
For the fair field of fighting men,
And my free spirit burst away,
As if it soared from battle fray.'
The trembling Bard with awe obeyed—
Slow on the harp his hand he laid;
But soon remembrance of the sight
He witnessed from the mountain's height,
With what old Bertram told at night,
Awakened the full power of song,
And bore him in career along—
As shallop launched on river's tide,
That slow and fearful leaves the side,
But, when it feels the middle stream,
Drives downward swift as lightning's beam.

XV

BATTLE OF BEAL' AN DUINE[n]

'The Minstrel came once more to view
The eastern ridge of Benvenue,
For, ere he parted, he would say
Farewell to lovely Loch Achray—
Where shall he find in foreign land,
So lone a lake, so sweet a strand!
  There is no breeze upon the fern,
    Nor ripple on the lake;
  Upon her eyrie nods the erne,
    The deer has sought the brake;
  The small birds will not sing aloud,
    The springing trout lies still,
  So darkly glooms yon thunder-cloud,
  That swathes, as with a purple shroud,
    Benledi's distant hill.

347 *Dermid's race*: the Campbells, constantly at feud with the Macgregors.

Is it the thunder's solemn sound
  That mutters deep and dread,
Or echoes from the groaning ground
  The warrior's measured tread?
Is it the lightning's quivering glance
  That on the thicket streams,
Or do they flash on spear and lance
  The sun's retiring beams?—
I see the dagger-crest of Mar,
I see the Moray's silver star
Wave o'er the cloud of Saxon war,
That up the lake comes winding far!
  To hero bound for battle-strife,
    Or bard of martial lay,
  'Twere worth ten years of peaceful life,
    One glance at their array!

XVI

Their light-armed archers far and near
  Surveyed the tangled ground;
Their centre ranks, with pike and spear,
  A twilight forest frowned;
Their barded horsemen, in the rear,
  The stern battalia crowned.
No cymbal clashed, no clarion rang,
  Still were the pipe and drum;
Save heavy tread and armour's clang,
  The sullen march was dumb.
There breathed no wind their crests to shake,
  Or wave their flags abroad;
Scarce the frail aspen seemed to quake,
  That shadowed o'er their road.
Their vaward scouts no tidings bring,
  Can rouse no lurking foe,
Nor spy a trace of living thing,
  Save when they stirred the roe;
The host moves like a deep-sea wave,
Where rise no rocks its pride to brave,
  High-swelling, dark, and slow.

393 *star*: see p. 297 (note on IV. 152).
404 *barded*: from Fr. *barde*, horse-armour.
405 *battalia*: battle-array. 414 *vaward*: vanguard.

The lake is passed, and now they gain
A narrow and a broken plain,
Before the Trossachs' rugged jaws;
And here the horse and spearmen pause,
While, to explore the dangerous glen,
Dive through the pass the archer-men.

XVII

At once there rose so wild a yell
Within that dark and narrow dell,
As all the fiends, from heaven that fell,
Had pealed the banner-cry of hell!
  Forth from the pass in tumult driven,
  Like chaff before the wind of heaven,
    The archery appear;
  For life! for life! their plight they ply—
  And shriek, and shout, and battle-cry,
  And plaids and bonnets waving high,
  And broadswords flashing to the sky,
    Are maddening in the rear.
  Onward they drive, in dreadful race,
    Pursuers and pursued;
  Before that tide of flight and chase,
  How shall it keep its rooted place,
    The spearmen's twilight wood?—
  "Down, down," cried Mar, "your lances down!
    Bear back both friend and foe!"
  Like reeds before the tempest's frown,
  That serried grove of lances brown
    At once lay levelled low;
  And closely shouldering side to side,
  The bristling ranks the onset bide.
  "We'll quell the savage mountaineer,
    As their Tinchel cows the game!
  They come as fleet as forest deer,
    We'll drive them back as tame."

XVIII

Bearing before them, in their course,
The relics of the archer force,

434 *plight they ply*: struggle in their dangerous occupation.
452 *Tinchel*: from Gael. *tinchioll*, a wide circle of hunters driving together a number of deer by gradually closing in on them.

Like wave with crest of sparkling foam,
Right onward did Clan-Alpine come.
  Above the tide, each broadsword bright
  Was brandishing like beam of light,
    Each targe was dark below;
  And with the ocean's mighty swing,
  When heaving to the tempest's wing,
    They hurled them on the foe.
I heard the lance's shivering crash,
As when the whirlwind rends the ash,
I heard the broadsword's deadly clang,
As if an hundred anvils rang!
But Moray wheeled his rearward rank
Of horsemen on Clan-Alpine's flank,
    "My banner-man, advance!
  I see," he cried, "their column shake.
  Now, gallants! for your ladies' sake,
    Upon them with the lance!"—
  The horsemen dashed among the rout,
    As deer break through the broom;
  Their steeds are stout, their swords are out,
    They soon make lightsome room.
  Clan-Alpine's best are backward borne!
    Where, where was Roderick then?
  One blast upon his bugle-horn
    Were worth a thousand men!
  And refluent through the pass of fear,
    The battle's tide was poured;
  Vanished the Saxon's struggling spear,
    Vanished the mountain-sword.
  As Bracklinn's chasm, so black and steep,
    Receives her roaring linn,
  As the dark caverns of the deep
    Suck the wild whirlpool in,
So did the deep and darksome pass
Devour the battle's mingled mass:
None linger now upon the plain,
Save those who ne'er shall fight again.

XIX

Now westward rolls the battle's din,
That deep and doubling pass within.—

487 *Bracklinn*: see p. 168, II. 270n.

Minstrel, away, the work of fate
Is bearing on: its issue wait,
Where the rude Trossachs' dread defile
Opens on Katrine's lake and isle.—
Grey Benvenue I soon repassed,
Loch Katrine lay beneath me cast.
  The sun is set; the clouds are met,
    The lowering scowl of heaven
  An inky hue of livid blue
    To the deep lake has given;
Strange gusts of wind from mountain glen
Swept o'er the lake, then sunk again.
I heeded not the eddying surge,
Mine eye but saw the Trossachs' gorge,
Mine ear but heard the sullen sound,
Which like an earthquake shook the ground,
And spoke the stern and desperate strife
That parts not but with parting life,
Seeming, to minstrel ear, to toll
The dirge of many a passing soul.
Nearer it comes: the dim-wood glen
The martial flood disgorged again,
  But not in mingled tide;
The plaided warriors of the North
High on the mountain thunder forth
  And overhang its side;
While by the lake below appears
The darkening cloud of Saxon spears.
At weary bay each shattered band,
Eyeing their foemen, sternly stand;
Their banners stream like tattered sail,
That flings its fragments to the gale,
And broken arms and disarray
Marked the fell havoc of the day.

XX

Viewing the mountain's ridge askance,
The Saxon stood in sullen trance,
Till Moray pointed with his lance,
  And cried—'Behold yon isle!

See! none are left to guard its strand,
But women weak, that wring the hand:
'Tis there of yore the robber band
  Their booty wont to pile;
My purse, with bonnet-pieces store,
To him will swim a bow-shot o'er,
And loose a shallop from the shore.
Lightly we'll tame the war-wolf then,
Lords of his mate, and brood, and den.'
Forth from the ranks a spearman sprung,
On earth his casque and corslet rung,
  He plunged him in the wave:
All saw the deed, the purpose knew,
And to their clamours Benvenue
  A mingled echo gave;
The Saxons shout, their mate to cheer,
The helpless females scream for fear,
And yells for rage the mountaineer.
'Twas then, as by the outcry riven,
Poured down at once the lowering heaven;
A whirlwind swept Loch Katrine's breast,
Her billows reared their snowy crest.
Well for the swimmer swelled they high,
To mar the Highland marksman's eye;
For round him showered, 'mid rain and hail,
The vengeful arrows of the Gael.
In vain. He nears the isle—and lo!
His hand is on a shallop's bow.—
Just then a flash of lightning came,
It tinged the waves and strand with flame—
I marked Duncraggan's widowed dame,
Behind an oak I saw her stand,
A naked dirk gleamed in her hand:
It darkened—but, amid the moan
Of waves, I heard a dying groan;
Another flash!—the spearman floats
A weltering corse beside the boats,
And the stern Matron o'er him stood,
Her hand and dagger streaming blood.

539 *bonnet-pieces*: gold coins of the reign of James V on which the king is represented as wearing a bonnet.
539 *store*: crammed full. 565 *widowed dame*: see III. sts. XV–XVI.

XXI

"Revenge! revenge!" the Saxons cried,
The Gaels' exulting shout replied.
Despite the elemental rage,
Again they hurried to engage;
But, ere they closed in desperate fight,
Bloody with spurring came a knight,
Sprung from his horse, and, from a crag,
Waved 'twixt the hosts a milk-white flag.
Clarion and trumpet by his side
Rung forth a truce-note high and wide,
While, in the Monarch's name, afar
An herald's voice forbade the war,
For Bothwell's lord, and Roderick bold,
Were both, he said, in captive hold.'

But here the lay made sudden stand!
The harp escaped the Minstrel's hand!
Oft had he stolen a glance, to spy
How Roderick brooked his minstrelsy:
At first the Chieftain, to the chime,
With lifted hand kept feeble time;
That motion ceased—yet feeling strong
Varied his look as changed the song;
At length, no more his deafened ear
The minstrel melody can hear;
His face grows sharp—his hands are clenched,
As if some pang his heart-strings wrenched;
Set are his teeth, his fading eye
Is sternly fixed on vacancy;
Thus, motionless, and moanless, drew
His parting breath, stout Roderick Dhu!
Old Allan-Bane looked on aghast,
While grim and still his spirit passed:
But when he saw that life was fled,
He poured his wailing o'er the dead:

XXII

LAMENT

'And art thou cold and lowly laid,
Thy foeman's dread, thy people's aid,

576 *elemental*: here, of the element of air.

Breadalbane's boast, Clan-Alpine's shade!
For thee shall none a requiem say?
For thee, who loved the minstrel's lay,
For thee, of Bothwell's house the stay,
The shelter of her exiled line,
E'en in this prison-house of thine,
I'll wail for Alpine's honoured Pine!

What groans shall yonder valleys fill!
What shrieks of grief shall rend yon hill!
What tears of burning rage shall thrill,
When mourns thy tribe thy battles done,
Thy fall before the race was won,
Thy sword ungirt ere set of sun!
There breathes not clansman of thy line,
But would have given his life for thine.
O woe for Alpine's honoured Pine!

Sad was thy lot on mortal stage!
The captive thrush may brook the cage,
The prisoned eagle dies for rage.
Brave spirit, do not scorn my strain!
And, when its notes awake again,
Even she, so long beloved in vain,
Shall with my harp her voice combine,
And mix her woe and tears with mine,
To wail Clan-Alpine's honoured Pine.'

XXIII

Ellen the while with bursting heart
Remained in lordly bower apart,
Where played with many-coloured gleams,
Through storied pane the rising beams.
In vain on gilded roof they fall,
And lightened up a tapestried wall,
And for her use a menial train
A rich collation spread in vain.
The banquet proud, the chamber gay,
Scarce drew one curious glance astray;
Or, if she looked, 'twas but to say,
With better omen dawned the day

610 *Breadalbane*: see II. 416.
638 *storied*: depicting historical scenes.

In that lone isle where waved on high
The dun-deer's hide for canopy;
Where oft her noble father shared
The simple meal her care prepared,
While Lufra, crouching by her side,
Her station claimed with jealous pride,
And Douglas, bent on woodland game,
Spoke of the chase to Malcolm Græme,
Whose answer, oft at random made,
The wandering of his thoughts betrayed.—
Those who such simple joys have known,
Are taught to prize them when they're gone.
But sudden, see, she lifts her head!
The window seeks with cautious tread.
What distant music has the power
To win her in this woeful hour!
'Twas from a turret that o'erhung
Her latticed bower, the strain was sung:

XXIV

LAY OF THE IMPRISONED HUNTSMAN[n]

'My hawk is tired of perch and hood,
My idle greyhound loathes his food,
My horse is weary of his stall,
And I am sick of captive thrall.

I wish I were, as I have been,
Hunting the hart in forest green,
With bended bow and bloodhound free,
For that's the life is meet for me.

I hate to learn the ebb of time
From yon dull steeple's drowsy chime,
Or mark it as the sunbeams crawl,
Inch after inch, along the wall.

The lark was wont my matins ring,
The sable rook my vespers sing;
These towers, although a king's they be,
Have not a hall of joy for me.

668 *thrall*: thraldom.

No more at dawning morn I rise
And sun myself in Ellen's eyes,
Drive the fleet deer the forest through
And homeward wend with evening dew;

A blithesome welcome blithely meet
And lay my trophies at her feet,
While fled the eve on wing of glee—
That life is lost to love and me!'

XXV

The heart-sick lay was hardly said,
The listener had not turned her head;
It trickled still, the starting tear,
When light a footstep struck her ear,
And Snowdoun's graceful knight was near.
She turned the hastier, lest again
The prisoner should renew his strain.
'O welcome, brave Fitz-James!' she said;
'How may an almost orphan maid
Pay the deep debt'— 'O say not so!
To me no gratitude you owe.
Not mine, alas! the boon to give,
And bid thy noble father live;
I can but be thy guide, sweet maid,
With Scotland's king thy suit to aid.
No tyrant he, though ire and pride
May lay his better mood aside.
Come, Ellen, come! 'tis more than time,
He holds his court at morning prime.'
With beating heart, and bosom wrung,
As to a brother's arm she clung.
Gently he dried the falling tear,
And gently whispered hope and cheer;
Her faltering steps half led, half stayed,
Through gallery fair and high arcade,
Till, at his touch, its wings of pride
A portal arch unfolded wide.

XXVI

Within 'twas brilliant all and light,
A thronging scene of figures bright;
It glowed on Ellen's dazzled sight,

As when the setting sun has given
Ten thousand hues to summer even,
And from their tissue fancy frames
Aerial knights and fairy dames.
Still by Fitz-James her footing stayed;
A few faint steps she forward made,
Then slow her drooping head she raised,
And fearful round the presence gazed;
For him she sought, who owned this state,
The dreaded prince whose will was fate!
She gazed on many a princely port,
Might well have ruled a royal court;
On many a splendid garb she gazed,
Then turned bewildered and amazed,
For all stood bare; and in the room,
Fitz-James alone wore cap and plume.
To him each lady's look was lent;
On him each courtier's eye was bent;
Midst furs and silks and jewels sheen,
He stood, in simple Lincoln green,
The centre of the glittering ring—
And Snowdoun's Knight[n] is Scotland's King!

XXVII

As wreath of snow on mountain-breast,
Slides from the rock that gave it rest,
Poor Ellen glided from her stay,
And at the Monarch's feet she lay;
No word her choking voice commands;
She showed the ring—she clasped her hands.
O! not a moment could he brook,
The generous prince, that suppliant look!
Gently he raised her; and, the while,
Checked with a glance the circle's smile;
Graceful, but grave, her brow he kissed,
And bade her terrors be dismissed:
'Yes fair, the wandering poor Fitz-James
The fealty of Scotland claims.
To him thy woes, thy wishes, bring;
He will redeem his signet ring.

726 *presence*: i.e., presence-chamber.
743 *stay*: support.

Ask nought for Douglas; yester even,
His prince and he have much forgiven.
Wrong hath he had from slanderous tongue,
I, from his rebel kinsmen, wrong.
We would not, to the vulgar crowd,
Yield what they craved with clamour loud;
Calmly we heard and judged his cause,
Our council aided, and our laws.
I stanched thy father's death-feud stern
With stout De Vaux and grey Glencairn;
And Bothwell's Lord henceforth we own
The friend and bulwark of our Throne.
But, lovely infidel, how now?
What clouds thy misbelieving brow?
Lord James of Douglas, lend thine aid;
Thou must confirm this doubting maid.'

XXVIII

Then forth the noble Douglas sprung,
And on his neck his daughter hung.
The Monarch drank, that happy hour,
The sweetest, holiest draught of Power,
When it can say, with godlike voice,
Arise, sad Virtue, and rejoice!
Yet would not James the general eye
On Nature's raptures long should pry;
He stepped between—'Nay, Douglas, nay,
Steal not my proselyte away!
The riddle 'tis my right to read,
That brought this happy chance to speed.
Yes, Ellen, when disguised I stray
In life's more low but happier way,
'Tis under name which veils my power,
Nor falsely veils—for Stirling's tower
Of yore the name of Snowdoun claims,
And Normans call me James Fitz-James.
Thus watch I o'er insulted laws,
Thus learn to right the injured cause.'
Then, in a tone apart and low—
'Ah, little traitress! none must know

779 *general*: of the company.

What idle dream, what lighter thought,
What vanity full dearly bought,
Joined to thine eye's dark witchcraft, drew
My spell-bound steps to Benvenue,
In dangerous hour, and all but gave
The Monarch's life to mountain glaive!'—
Aloud he spoke—'Thou still dost hold
That little talisman of gold,
Pledge of my faith, Fitz-James's ring —
What seeks fair Ellen of the King?'

XXIX

Full well the conscious maiden guessed
He probed the weakness of her breast;
But, with that consciousness, there came
A lightening of her fears for Græme,
And more she deemed the Monarch's ire
Kindled 'gainst him, who, for her sire,
Rebellious broadsword boldly drew;
And, to her generous feeling true,
She craved the grace of Roderick Dhu.—
'Forbear thy suit: the King of kings
Alone can stay life's parting wings:
I know his heart, I know his hand,
Have shared his cheer, and proved his brand:
My fairest earldom would I give
To bid Clan-Alpine's Chieftain live!
Hast thou no other boon to crave?
No other captive friend to save?'
Blushing, she turned her from the King,
And to the Douglas gave the ring,
As if she wished her sire to speak
The suit that stained her glowing cheek.—
'Nay, then, my pledge has lost its force,
And stubborn justice holds her course.
Malcolm, come forth!' And at the word,
Down kneeled the Græme to Scotland's Lord.
'For thee, rash youth, no suppliant sues,
From thee may Vengeance claim her dues,
Who, nurtured underneath our smile,
Hast paid our care by treacherous wile,

And sought, amid thy faithful clan,
A refuge for an outlawed man,
Dishonouring thus thy loyal name.—
Fetters and warder for the Græme!'
His chain of gold the King unstrung,
The links o'er Malcolm's neck he flung,
Then gently drew the glittering band,
And laid the clasp on Ellen's hand.

HARP of the North, farewell! The hills grow dark,
  On purple peaks a deeper shade descending;
In twilight copse the glow-worm lights her spark,
  The deer, half-seen, are to the covert wending.
Resume thy wizard elm! the fountain lending,
  And the wild breeze, thy wilder minstrelsy;
Thy numbers sweet with nature's vespers blending,
  With distant echo from the fold and lea,
And herd-boy's evening pipe, and hum of housing bee.

Yet once again farewell, thou Minstrel Harp!
  Yet once again forgive my feeble sway,
And little reck I of the censure sharp
  May idly cavil at an idle lay.
Much have I owed thy strains on life's long way,
  Through secret woes the world has never known,
When on the weary night dawned wearier day,
  And bitterer was the grief devoured alone.
That I o'erlive such woes, Enchantress! is thine own.

Hark! as my lingering footsteps slow retire,
  Some Spirit of the Air has waked thy string!
'Tis now a seraph bold, with touch of fire,
  'Tis now the brush of Fairy's frolic wing.
Receding now, the dying numbers ring
  Fainter and fainter down the rugged dell,
And now the mountain breezes scarcely bring
  A wandering witch-note of the distant spell—
And now, 'tis silent all!—Enchantress, fare thee well!

END OF THE LADY OF THE LAKE

846 *wizard*: based on misconception of 'witch-elm', from 'wych', pliant.

Notes

I. Ballads, Lyrics, and Shorter Pieces

p. 3 'Jamie Telfer of the Fair Dodhead' is Scott's presentation of an account of a border raid of the late 16th or early 17th century (*Minstrelsy* 1802, I. 80 ff.). The raid involved both Scotts and Elliots, but the ballad is based on Scott family tradition. James Hogg the Ettrick Shepherd stated that his mother knew a very different ballad (*Letters*, I. No. 44), and an Elliot version, in which the Scotts were denigrated, was printed by Child from the MSS. of C. K. Sharpe (Child, V. 249–51). How many lines of the *Minstrelsy* ballad were written by Scott is not certain, but lines 133–6, 141–4 and 149–52 are probably Scott's own (Henderson, II. 9).

lines 157–60: 'The Editor has used some freedom with the original.... The account of the Captain's disaster (teste laevo vulnerato) is rather too naïve for literal publication' (S).

p. 10 'Kinmont Willie' narrates an exploit of one of Scott's ancestors, Sir Walter Scott of Branxholm, Laird of Buccleuch, on 13 Apr. 1596. Printed in *Minstrelsy* 1802, I. 111 ff. it 'is preserved by tradition in the West Borders, but mangled by reciters, so that some conjectural emendations have been absolutely necessary to render it intelligible' (S). Child comments (III. 472): 'It is to be suspected that a great deal more emendation was done than the mangling of reciters rendered absolutely necessary. One would like, for example, to see Stanzas 10–12 and 31 (lines 37–48 and 121–4) in their mangled condition.' Henderson (II. 57) thought that these stanzas, and stanza ix (lines 33–6) as well, were wholly by Scott. The ballad can be regarded as an example of 'creative editing', as much deserving the credit of original composition as many of the songs of Burns.

p. 16 'The Eve of Saint John' was first published at Kelso in 1800. The Feast of St. John the Baptist because of its date (24 June) became linked with certain customs connected with the summer solstice. The folk-source is 'a well-known Irish tradition' (S), and Scott mingles the themes of 'the demon lover, ethical warning, supernaturally intensified punishment for sexual sin' (Parsons, p. 35).

line 1: Smailholm Tower 'is situated in the northern boundary of Roxburghshire, among a cluster of wild rocks, called Sandiknow Crags' (S). The neighbouring farmhouse of Sandyknowe was regularly visited by Scott between his third and his eighth year.

line 123: The original canons regular of Dryburgh Abbey were Premonstratensians from Alnwick in Northumberland. They wore a coarse black cassock covered by a white woollen cope, from which was derived their popular title—White Friars.

p. 22 'Lochinvar' forms stanza xii of *Marmion*, Canto V. It is sung in Holyrood Palace by James IV's mistress, Lady Heron of Ford, and is modelled on the ballad of 'Katherine Janfarie' (Child 221: IV. 216–30, *Minstrelsy* 1833, III. 122–7). Lockhart glosses 'Lochinvar' as 'Gordon of Lochinvar, head of a powerful branch of that name, afterwards Viscount of Lochinvar' (*Minstrelsy*, III. 123, n.).

p. 24 The song is sung by the aged Elspeth Mucklebackit in *The Antiquary*, Chap. XL, after her fisher grandson is drowned. Elspeth's maiden name was Cheyne, and she claims to be descended from the Roland of the ballad. Harlaw is some eighteen miles NW. of Aberdeen, where on 24 July 1411 Donald of the

Isles was defeated by the men of Mar, Garioch, Angus, and the Mearns under the leadership of Alexander Stewart, Earl of Mar. A ballad on the fight, mentioned in *The Complaynt of Scotland* 1549 (ed. J. A. H. Murray, *Early English Text Society*, Extra series 17 and 18, London 1872, p. 65) has been lost; a poem on the battle was printed by Allan Ramsay in *The Ever Green*, 2 vols., Edinburgh 1724, I. 28; and a traditional ballad circulates orally in Scotland at the present time, whose earliest recorded versions date from the 19th century (Child 163: III. 316–20). Elspeth's song bears little resemblance to any of these.

p. 25 'Law versus Love', From *New Love-Poems By Sir Walter Scott, Discovered in the Narrative of an Unknown Love Episode with Jessie—of Kelso*, ed. Davidson Cook, Oxford 1932, pp. 32–4.

p. 26 'Where shall the Lover rest', from *Marmion*, Canto III, of which it forms Stanzas x and xi, is sung in an inn by the squire Fitz-Eustace to a melancholy Highland air,

the lament of men
Who languished for their native glen;
And thought how sad would be such sound,
On Susquehana's swampy ground,
Kentucky's wood-encumbered brake,
Or wild Ontario's boundless lake,
Where heart-sick exiles, in the strain,
Recalled fair Scotland's hills again!
(St. ix, lines 11–18)

The words were in fact fitted to a Gaelic tune which Scott had 'literally picked up' from Highland harvesters in the Lowlands (*Letters*, I. 403, 15 Dec. 1807).

p. 28 'False Love, and hast thou played me this' from *Waverley*, Chap. IX, is sung at Tully-Veolan by the 'half-crazed simpleton' David Gellatley. These are genuinely traditional words slightly altered by Scott in exactly the same fashion as Burns altered folk material. The earliest text appears to be that in D. Herd, *Ancient and Modern Scottish Songs*, Edinburgh 1776, II. 6.

p. 28 'Young men will love thee more fair and more fast', from *Waverley*, Chap. XIV, is also sung by Gellatley. It is an oblique way of telling Waverley that his host, the aged Baron of Bradwardine, has fought the Laird of Balmawhapple on Waverley's behalf whilst the latter was asleep.

p. 28 'Birth Song' (or Charm), is sung in *Guy Mannering*, Chap. III by the gipsy, Meg Merrilies, at the lying-in of the Lady of Ellangowan.

p. 29 'Dirge' is sung in *Guy Mannering*, Chap. XXVII by Meg Merrilies in a gipsy's hide-out over a wretch dying 'upon a lair composed of straw, with a blanket stretched over it'.

p. 30 'Gin by Pailfuls' is sung in *Guy Mannering*, Chap. XXXIV by the scheming Justice, Glossin, to cap a German ditty of the smuggler, Dirk Hatteraick.

p. 30 'Jock of Hazeldean.' 'The first stanza of this Ballad is ancient' (S). The others were written for T. Campbell, *Albyn's Anthology*, Edinburgh 1816.

p. 31 'MacGregor's Gathering' was written to the air 'Thain' a Grigalach' ('The MacGregor is Come') for *Albyn's Anthology*, 1816. 'The severe treatment of the Clan, their outlawry, and the proscription of their very name, are alluded to in the Ballad' (S). For the proper names in this song, see below, the notes to *The Lady of the Lake*; for the clan history, see *Rob Roy*, Introduction and author's notes.

p. 32 'Pibroch of Donuil Dhu' was written to the air 'Piobair of Donuil Dhuidh' for *Albyn's Anthology*, 1816. A setting by Hummel (first engraved 1830)

appears in G. Thomson, *The Melodies of Scotland*, 5 vols London 1831, V. 242. The piece is based on 'a very ancient pibroch belonging to Clan MacDonald, and supposed to refer to the expedition of Donald Balloch, who, in 1413, launched from the Isles with a considerable force, invaded Lochaber, and at Inverlochy defeated and put to flight the earls of Mar and Caithness, though at the head of an army superior to his own' (S). The Gaelic original is thus translated:

The pipe-summons of Donald the Black,
The pipe-summons of Donald the Black,
The war-pipe and the pennon are on the
gathering-place at Inverlochy.

p. 33 'The Aged Carle' is from *The Antiquary*, Chap. X. Sung by Jonathan Oldbuck's niece, Mary, it awakens the hero, Lovel, after a night spent in the haunted chamber in Oldbuck's house.

p. 34 'Dredging Sang' from *The Antiquary*, Chap. XL, is sung by Elspeth Mucklebackit immediately before she gives her version of *The Battle of Harlaw* (above, p. 24).

p. 34 'I'm Madge of the Country' from *The Heart of Midlothian*, Chap. XXXI, is sung by the madwoman, Madge Wildfire, who says of it—'I like that the best o' a' my sangs, because *he* [i.e., George Staunton, her seducer] made it.'

p. 35 'The Fight of Grace' from *The Heart of Midlothian*, Chap. XL, is sung by Madge Wildfire on her workhouse deathbed, to a strain which 'resembled the music of the Methodist hymns'.

p. 35 'Proud Maisie' from *The Heart of Midlothian*, Chap. XL, is again sung by Madge Wildfire, to a tune 'wilder, less monotonous, and less regular. . . . Her voice died away with the last notes, and she fell into a slumber, from which the experienced attendant assured them that she never would wake at all, or only in the death agony.'

p. 36 'Look not thou on Beauty's charming' is from *The Bride of Lammermoor*, Chap. II. Sung by the heroine, Lucy Ashton, it is related to the novel's tragic theme and at the same time is an expression of her own passive character.

p. 36 'Rebecca's Hymn' from *Ivanhoe*, Chap. XXXIX, is sung in prison by the Jewess Rebecca, accused of sorcery and in imminent danger of death.

p. 37 'March, march, Ettrick and Teviotdale' from *The Monastery*, Chap. XXV, is sung at the command of Julian Avenel to Halbert Glendinning just before the latter is locked in his room in Avenel Castle. 'The song, rude as it was, had in it that warlike character which at any other time would have roused Halbert's spirit; but at present the charm of minstrelsy had no effect upon him.'

p. 38 'Donald Caird's come again' was written to the tune 'Malcolm Caird's come again' for Campbell, *Albyn's Anthology* (vol. II, 1818) and set by G. Thomson in his *Melodies of Scotland*, 5 vols. 1831, V. 224.

p. 40 *Epilogue to the Drama founded on* '*St. Ronan's Well*' (1824). Addressed by Meg Dodds, the innkeeper, to the Edinburgh audience, these lines—in the traditional Burns or 'Standard Habbie' stanza—celebrate the material progress of Edinburgh since the end of the 18th century.

p. 43 'Bonny Dundee' is from the play *The Doom of Devorgoil*, 1830, II, ii. Sung by Leonard, a Ranger, in 'a voice that's rough with hollowing to the hounds'. The occasion is 1689—in the words of another character in the play:

What time fierce Claver'se with his Cavaliers,
Abjuring the new change of government,
Forcing his fearless way through timorous friends,
And enemies as timorous, left the capital
To rouse in James's cause the distant Highlands.

II. Romances

The Lay of the Last Minstrel

p. 49 'The poem was inscribed to 'the Right Honourable Charles Earl of Dalkeith' and prefixed by the following brief foreword:

'The Poem, now offered to the Public, is intended to illustrate the customs and manners which anciently prevailed on the Borders of England and Scotland. The inhabitants, living in a state partly pastoral and partly warlike, and combining habits of constant depredation with the influence of a rude spirit of chivalry, were often engaged in scenes highly susceptible of poetical ornament. As the description of scenery and manners was more the object of the Author than a combined and regular narrative, the plan of the Ancient Metrical Romance was adopted, which allows greater latitude, in this respect, than would be consistent with the dignity of a regular Poem. The same model offered other facilities, as it permits an occasional alteration of measure, which, in some degree, authorises the change of rhythm in the text. The machinery, also, adopted from popular belief, would have seemed puerile in a Poem which did not partake of the rudeness of the old Ballad, or Metrical Romance.

For these reasons, the poem was put into the mouth of an ancient Minstrel, the last of the race, who, as he is supposed to have survived the Revolution, might have caught somewhat of the refinement of modern poetry, without losing the simplicity of his original model. The date of the Tale itself is about the middle of the sixteenth century, when most of the personages actually flourished. The time occupied by the action is Three Nights and Three Days.'

Introduction

lines 21–2: The minstrel sings his lay after the accession of William III (1688–1702); he had been persecuted during the convenanting and Commonwealth periods, 'the iron time'.

line 27: Anne, Duchess of Monmouth and Buccleuch, to whom the minstrel sings, had been brought up in Newark Castle. She was the descendant of the Lords of Buccleuch, hereditary chiefs of the Scott family, and widow of the Duke of Monmouth, the illegitimate son of Charles II, beheaded for treason in 1685.

Canto First

line 5: An echo of Coleridge's *Christabel.* See Intro., p. xi.

line 16: All would bear the surname Scott, as appears from the source, Walter Scot of Satchells', *A true History of Several Honourable Families of the Right Honourable Name of Scot*, Edinburgh 1688, where their number is given as twenty-four (pp. 45–6).

line 33: The armed men in Branxholm were perpetually ready for battle; they did not even raise their visors to drink, but drank through the bars.

line 49: Scroop, Howard, and Percy were leading families on the English side of the border, who resided in the fortresses of Carlisle, Naworth, and Warkworth respectively.

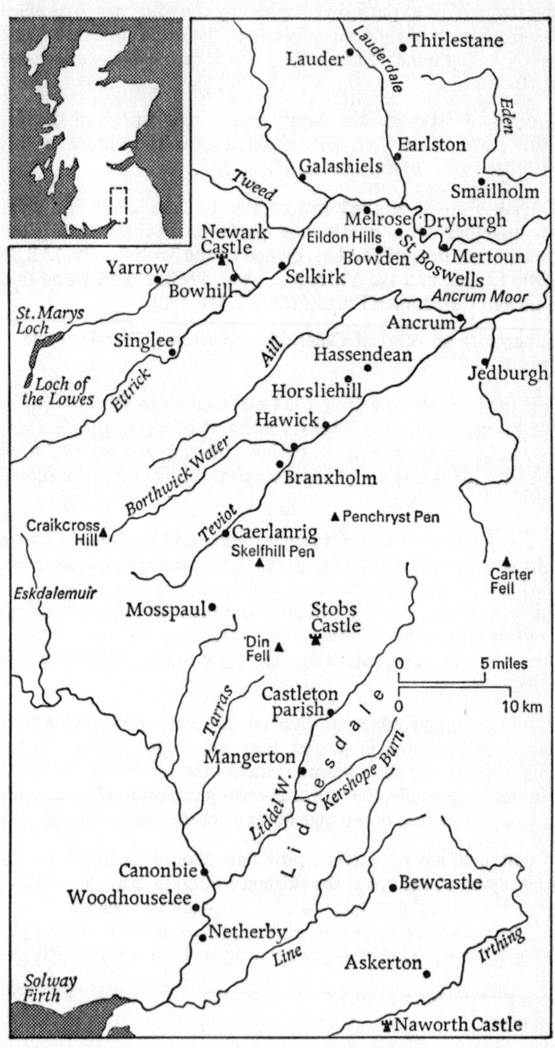

Map of the Border

line 58: Sir Walter Scott of Buccleuch, slain by his enemies the Kerrs in the streets of Edinburgh in 1552. The action of *The Lay* itself takes place shortly after this event.

line 70: 'Among other expedients resorted to for stanching the feud betwixt the Scotts and Kerrs, there was a bond executed in 1529, between the heads of each clan, binding themselves to perform reciprocally the four principal pilgrimages of Scotland, for the benefit of the souls of those of the opposite name who had fallen in the quarrel. . . . But either it never took effect, or the feud was renewed shortly afterwards' (S).

line 73: Cessford Castle was the family seat of the branch of the Kerrs whose head was the Duke of Roxburghe, 'situated near the village of Morebattle, within two or three miles of the Cheviot Hills' (S).

line 74: Ettrick Forest, applied historically to 'the whole or chief part of Selkirkshire, together with contiguous parts of Peebles and [Midlothian]'. Much of it was, at the time of *The Lay*, owned by the Scott family. 'All the country drained by the Ettrick and the Yarrow . . . was clothed with wood once, a remnant of the ancient Caledonian Forest' (*O.G.S.* III. 580).

line 86: apparently an echo of Coleridge, *Christabel*, Part II. 1. 85, 'words of high disdain'.

line 109: At the time of the action, the Cranstouns and Scotts were 'at feud. . . . The Lady of Buccleuch, in 1557, beset the Laird of Cranstoun, seeking his life. Nevertheless, the same Cranstoun, or perhaps his son, was married to a daughter of the same Lady' (S). There was, therefore, some basis in fact for Scott's Romeo-and-Juliet plot.

line 113: 'The Bethunes were of French origin, and derived their name from a small town in Artois. . . . Of this family was descended Dame Janet Beaton, Lady Buccleuch, widow of Sir Walter Scott at Branksome. She was a woman of masculine spirit, as appeared from her riding at the head of her son's clan, after her husband's murder. She also possessed the hereditary abilities of her family in such a degree, that the superstition of the vulgar imputed them to supernatural knowledge' (S).

lines 120–1: 'The vulgar conceive, that when a class of students have made a certain progress in their mystic studies, they are obliged to run through a subterraneous hall, where the devil literally catches the hindmost in the race, unless he crosses the hall so speedily, that the arch-enemy can only apprehend his shadow. In the latter case, the person of the sage never after throws any shade.' (S).

line 125: Scott justified his River Spirit and Mountain Spirit by noting that 'the Scottish vulgar . . . believe in the existence of an intermediate class of spirits, residing in the air, or in the waters; to whose agency they ascribe floods, storms, and all such phenomena as their own philosophy cannot readily explain'. But he suspected that they weakened 'the general tone of the romance' (*PW*, VI. 236–7).

lines 130–5: The rhetorical questions are further echoes of the style of Coleridge's *Christabel.*

line 214: 'William Scott, commonly called Cut-at-the-Black, who had the lands of Nether Deloraine for service' (Satchells, p. 46). These adjoined the Buccleuch estate in Ettrick Forest.

line 221: The river Esk in East Dumfriesshire flows for some distance along the English border before passing into Cumberland on the way to the Solway Firth. The Liddel is a border stream in Roxburgh and East Dumfriesshire.

line 258: The beginning of the 51st psalm, traditionally read by 'criminals claiming the benefit of clergy' (S). Haribee was where border outlaws were executed in Carlisle.

lines 287–8: Minto Crags, East of the Minto Hills in Roxburghshire, were crowned by Fatlips Castle, 'which is supposed to have been the stronghold of Turnbull of Barnhills, a noted freebooter. A small platform, a little way from the top, is called Barnhills' bed' (*O.G.S.* V. 36).

line 296: Pastoral song. The shepherd's pipe was made from a reed; Theocritus, founder of Greek pastoral poetry, wrote in a modification of the Doric dialect; and the term 'Doric' is often used as a euphemism for Scots vernacular speech.

line 297: An allusion to 'My sheep I neglected, I lost my sheep-hook', by Sir Gilbert Elliot of Minto (1722–77). The piece was printed in *The Charmer* (Edinburgh 1749), but by no stretch of the imagination can it be said to be written in the 'Doric' vernacular:

My sheep I neglected—I lost my sheep-hook,
And all the gay haunts of my youth I forsook;
No more for Amynta fresh garlands I wove;
For ambition, I said, would soon cure me of love.
  Oh, what had my youth with ambition to do?
  Why left I Amynta? Why broke I my vow?
  Oh give me my sheep, and my sheep-hook restore,
  And I'll wander from love and Amynta no more. (St. i)

The song was popular at concerts and in drawing-rooms throughout the 18th century.

line 300: The barony of Ryedale or Lilliesleaf in NW. Roxburghshire. Walter, the first Riddel, obtained a charter of Lilliesleaf, Whettunes, etc., in the 12th century: hence 'ancient Riddel'.

line 338: 'The first of the day-hours of the Church, the Psalms of which always end with Pss. cxlviii–cl, sung as one psalm and technically called *laudes*' (*O.E.D.*).

Canto Second

lines 53–4: Some such idea as 'has been tormented' must be understood between these two lines.

line 86: The *aurora borealis* or Northern Lights, 'a luminous atmospheric phenomenon, now ascribed to electricity, occurring near, or radiating from, the earth's northern or southern magnetic pole, and visible from time to time by night over more or less of the earth's surface' (*O.E.D.*).

line 91: The Spaniards and Moors had the reputation of piercing even chain mail with feathered darts.

line 103: James, Earl of Douglas, the leader of the Scots at the Battle of Otterburn (1388) was killed in the action and buried beneath the high altar at Melrose. The English leader, Sir Henry Percy (Hotspur), was taken prisoner.

line 110: William Douglas, who lived in the reign of David II (1329–71), murdered his former friend Sir Alexander Ramsay of Dalhousie because 'the King had conferred upon Ramsay the sheriffdom of Teviotdale, to which Douglas

pretended some claim' (S). Douglas was given the sheriffdom, but was later slain while hunting in Ettrick Forest.

lines 115–20: A reference to the theory of Gothic architecture put forward by Sir James Hall, which traces it back to 'an architectural imitation of wicker work' (S).

line 138: A 13th-century philosopher and writer on astrology and alchemy, who 'passed among his contemporaries as a magician' (S). By an intentional anachronism he is here placed in the early 16th century.

line 145: It was at Michael Scott's command that Eildon hill was split into the three hills which today dominate the parishes of Melrose and Bowden in Roxburghshire.

line 184: 'Baptista Porta and other authors who treat of natural magic, talk much of eternal lamps, pretended to be found burning in ancient sepulchres' (S).

line 223: 'The magical powers of wizards were supposed to be due to the devil; and the price of such powers was the soul of the wizard. But the calm appearance of Michael Scott's face gave reason to hope that he had escaped the natural doom of those who meddled with magic' (Stuart and Elliot, p. 132).

line 298 ff.: The repeated questions and the rhythm are again reminiscent of *Christabel.*

line 353: This malicious imp is drawn from a legendary 'being called Gilpin Horner, who appeared and made some stay, at a farm-house among the Border mountains' (S). On his first appearance he cried 'tint [lost]! tint! tint!', and vanished when his name was called three times by the devil who had lost him some weeks or months before. 'As much has been objected to Gilpin Horner on account of his being supposed rather a device of the author than a popular superstition, I can only say, that no legend which I ever heard seemed to be more universally credited' (S). In a letter to Scott of 4 June 1805, the antiquarian George Ellis defends the dwarf on the ground that his characteristics are perfectly in accord with folk tradition: 'It cannot fairly be required that, because the goblin is mischievous, all his tricks should be directed to the production of general evil. The old idea of goblins seems to have been that they were essentially active, & careless about the mischief they produced, rather than providently malicious' (quoted Parsons, p. 58, n.).

line 378: According to folk belief, a being of this sort was obliged to serve the first mortal he met.

line 382: All persons living on the Scottish side of the Border. Home Castle is in Berwickshire, to the NE. of the Border; Hermitage Castle is in Liddesdale in South Roxburghshire.

lines 390–402: It is a historical fact that on 25 June 1557 'Dame Janet Beatoune, Lady Buccleuch and a great number of the name of Scott' broke open the door of the Church of St. Mary of the Lowes 'in order to apprehend the Laird of Cranstoune for his destruction' (S).

line 393: One of the poet's ancestors, and a noted cattle-raider (see *Jamie Telfer of the Fair Dodhead*, line 101). Harden is in the Roxburghshire part of Roberton parish, 4 miles West of Hawick.

Canto Third

line 33: 'The crest of the Cranstouns, in allusion to their name, is a crane

dormant, holding a stone in his foot, with an emphatic Border motto, *Thou shalt want ere I want*' (S).

line 42: 'A distance between the warriors sufficient to enable them to obtain the necessary momentum for the charge' (Stuart and Elliot, p. 140).

line 100: This 'owed its efficacy to the fact that he had been christened, so that the spell by which the book remained closed had no effect against it' (Stuart and Elliot, p. 142).

line 119: The behaviour of the Goblin Page is an expansion of the oral tradition of Gilpin Horner mentioned in the end-note to II. 353, above. According to Scott's informant, 'It was real flesh and blood, and ate and drank, was fond of cream, and, when it could get at it would destroy a great deal. It seemed a mischievous creature; and any of the children whom it could master, it would beat and scratch without mercy. It was once abusing a child belonging to the same Moffat, who had been so frightened by its first appearance; and he, in a passion, struck it so violent a blow upon the side of the head, that it tumbled upon the ground; but it was not stunned; for it set up its head directly, and exclaimed, "Ah hah, Will o' Moffat, you strike sair"' (S).

line 155: A common folk-belief is that all magic is destroyed by living water. Cp. Burns, 'Tam o' Shanter', line 208—'A running stream they dare na cross'.

line 296: This refers to the superstition that 'weapon–salve', applied to a cleaned object that has been steeped in blood from a wound, would (through sympathetic magic) heal the wound itself.

line 345: 'The act of parliament of 1455, c. 48, directs, that one bale or fagot shall be warning of the approach of the English in any manner; two bales that they are *coming indeed*; four bales, blazing beside each other, that the enemy are in great force' (S).

line 395: Ringing the bell backwards is ringing a muffled peal, either to express sorrow or to give warning of danger.

Canto Fourth

line 20: John Graham of Claverhouse, Viscount Dundee, slain in the battle of Killiecrankie, 1689. See p. 279, note on 'Bonny Dundee.'

line 44: 11 June, 'in old style reckoned the longest day' (*O.E.D.*); the festival of St. Barnabas, an apostle and companion of St. Paul.

line 74: The third son of Thomas, Duke of Norfolk, and warden of the Western Marches. 'By a poetical anachronism, he is introduced into the romance a few years earlier than he actually flourished' (S).

line 75: A member of the Dacre family, reputedly of 'hot and obstinate character', was warden of the west marches in the reign of Edward VI.

line 85: Both these men are from the English side of the border. It seems strange that Scott should have bestowed the Scots fore-name Fergus upon one of the English Graemes.

lines 100–3: Added in the fourth edition, 1806.

line 105: An estate belonging to the Scotts of Thirlestane, 1¾ miles E. of Ettrick church. The 'dusky height' is 1,490 ft. above sea level.

line 110: A large area of peat-bog, near the spot, some 15 miles SE. of Edinburgh, where James V assembled his nobility for an invasion of England. Sir John Scott of Thirlestane 'alone declared himself ready to follow the King whereever he should lead' (S).

lines 122–3: A description of the armorial bearings of the Harden family. 'The family of Harden are descended from a younger son of the Laird of Buccleuch, who flourished before the estate of Murdieston was acquired by the marriage of one of these chieftains with the heiress in 1296. Hence they bear the cognizance of the Scotts upon the field [i.e., the surface of the shield]; whereas those of Buccleuch are disposed upon a bend dexter assumed in consequence of that marriage' (S).

line 125: Scott does not stress that Oakwood tower belonged in the 13th century to the wizard Michael Scott, who plays such a part in the poem.

line 135: Mary Scott, daughter of Philip Scott of Dryhope and wife to Walter Scott of Harden, was celebrated in traditional song. Though the original words of 'Mary Scott, the flower of Yarrow' have been lost, the tune survived, to be the inspiration of some rather insipid verses by Allan Ramsay in the early 18th century:

> With success crowned, I'll not envy
> The folks who dwell above the sky:
> When Mary Scott's become my marrow,
> We'll make a paradise in Yarrow.
> (St. ii, lines 5–8)

Many of Scott's original public would know Ramsay's words.

lines 145–223: Added in the fifth edition, 1806.

line 181: The tenant is habitually called by the name of his holding—here, Woodkerrick.

line 224: The occupant of Whitslaid, a seat of the Lauder family, 3 miles SSE. of Lauder town, Berwickshire.

lines 226–9: Added in the second edition, 1805.

line 258: Rankle Burn, 'a stream of Ettrick Parish, Selkirkshire, rising at an altitude of 1,350 feet within ¼ mile of Moodlaw Loch, at the meeting point of Selkirk, Dumfries and Roxburgh shires, and winding 9⅞ miles northward . . . till, after a total descent of 635 feet, it falls into Ettrick Water opposite Tushielaw Tower. It traverses first a widely moorish tract, afterwards a deeply sequestered pastoral glen' (*O.G.S.* VI. 236). 'Rangleburn' is a word of four syllables here, the 'r' being fully syllabic in general Scottish pronunciation.

line 365: 'A glove upon a lance was the emblem of faith among the ancient Borderers, who were wont when anyone broke his word, to expose this emblem, and proclaim him a faithless villain at the first Border meeting. This ceremony was much dreaded' (S).

line 437: 'In dubious cases the innocence of Border criminals was occasionally referred to their own oath' (S).

line 474: 'An elongated, rugged peaked hill on the mutual border of Hobkirk and Cavers parishes, Roxburghshire. Rising 1,392 feet above sea level and projecting boldly from the northern frontier masses of the Cheviots . . . it looks along a great extent of the Teviot's valley, and forms a conspicuous feature in one-half or more of all the picturesque landscape of Teviotdale; presents a bleak stern aspect . . . [and] contrasts strongly in peaked summit, ragged skyline,

sharp saliencies of contour, and rockiness or heathiness of surface, with the green, smooth, neighbouring Cheviots' (*O.G.S.* VI. 289).

line 484: 'A district on the Eastern part of the Scottish Border. In modern territorial arrangement it is the largest and the most southerly of the three divisions of Berwickshire...; in popular phraseology it is the whole of Berwickshire...; in proper topographical nomenclature, based on strict reference to geographical feature, it is all the low country between the Lammermuirs and the river Tweed...; and in ancient political designation it was the entire champaign country between the Lammermuirs and the Cheviots.... It forms, in any view, the eastern part of what were formerly termed 'the marches' [and] was anciently called March...' (*O.G.S.* V., 2nd section, p. 28).

line 492–5: 'The well-known name of Dacre is derived from the exploits of one of their ancestors at the siege of Acre or Ptolemais, under Richard Coeur de Leon' (S).

line 553: 'There are some weak points in the story here. If the Lady had a foreknowledge of the coming relief, why did she propose terms which made the fate of her son depend on the uncertain issue of a fight between Musgrave and Deloraine? Perhaps, it may be said, she had a foreknowledge here too of how the combat would terminate. Where then was the necessity for the strong emotion betrayed by her, and the conflict between her feeling as a mother and her sense of duty as chieftain of the clan? It is not easy to see, too, why the Lady should have "gainsaid" terms which were not very different from those which she herself had proposed' (Stuart and Elliot, p. 179).

line 570: 'The person here alluded to, is one of our ancient Border minstrels, called Rattling Roaring Willie. This *soubriquet* was probably derived from his bullying disposition; being, it would seem, such a roaring boy, as is frequently mentioned in old plays. While drinking at Newmill, upon Teviot, about five miles above Hawick, Willie chanced to quarrel with one of his own profession, who was usually distinguished by the odd name of Sweet Milk, from a place on Rule Water so called. They retired to a meadow on the opposite side of the Teviot, to decide the contest with their swords, and Sweet Milk was killed on the spot. A thorn-tree marks the scene of the murder, which is still called Sweet Milk Thorn. Willie was taken and executed at Jedburgh, bequeathing his name to the beautiful Scotch air, called "Rattling Roaring Willie"' (S).

Canto Fifth

lines 1–38: These two stanzas are directly related to the close of Canto IV and the Minstrel's memory of the 'jovial Harper' (IV. 570). The first stanza expresses the notion, traditional in the pastoral elegy, that Nature sympathizes with the dead poet who has sung her praises. But in the second stanza Scott shifts his ground. 'Inanimate things, it is admitted, cannot possibly mourn. It is therefore the spiritual world, not the natural world, that is thrown into grief when the poet dies; and the balmy dewdrops, the sighing winds, and the mountain rills are but the manifestations of that grief which is felt... by the spirits that haunt them,—the spirits of those whom the poet had celebrated in his verses, and who, now that he is dead, must be confined to hateful oblivion' (Stuart and Elliot, p. 181). These spirits are the ghosts of those who made a particular appeal to late 18th- and early 19th-century sensibilities—the betrayed maiden of traditional folksong who turns into a hawthorn or a briar; the Knight of the medieval revival; the Rhineland, Border or Highland chieftain in mountain mist. Thus Scott grafts 'romantic' emotions on a tradition that goes back to the ancient *Lament for Adonis*, the *Lament for Bion*, and Theocritus' first Idyll.

line 50: 'The governments of both countries (England and Scotland) in the

fourteenth century divided the frontier into the East, West and Middle Marches, over each of which divisions wardens were appointed by their respective sovereigns' (Stuart and Elliot, pp. 183–4).

line 51: 'The chief of this potent race of heroes, about the date of the poem, was Archibald Douglas, seventh Earl of Angus, a man of great courage and activity. The Bloody Heart was the well-known cognizance of the house of Douglas, assumed from the time of good Lord James, to whose care Robert Bruce committed his heart, to be carried to the Holy Land' (S).

lines 53–8: Added in the second edition, 1805.

lines 56–8: 'At the battle of Beaugé, in France (1421), Thomas, Duke of Clarence, brother to Henry V, was unhorsed by Sir John Swinton of Swinton, who distinguished him by a coronet set with precious stones, which he wore around his helmet' (S). Sir John Swinton was one of Scott's ancestors.

line 60: The Lammermuir hills, in E. Lothian and Berwickshire, 'a broad range of moorish heights, stretching eastward from the vale of Gala Water' to the North Sea at the promontories of Fast Castle and St. Abbs Head. 'In themselves the Lammermuirs are an extensive curvature of, for the most part, wild and cheerless heights' (*O.G.S.* IV. 453).

lines 62–5: 'The Earls of Home, as descendants of the Dunbars, ancient Earls of March, carried a lion rampant, argent' (S), and their traditional allies were the Hepburns. 'The slogan, or war-cry, of this powerful family was, "A Home! a Home!"' (pronounced Hume).

line 152: Added in the second edition, 1805.

line 178: Borrowed from the style of *Christabel.*

line 193: A castle in Liddesdale, S. Roxburghshire, on the left bank of Hermitage Water. At one time a Douglas stronghold, it passed into the hands of the first Earl of Bothwell in 1492, and into those of Sir Walter Scott of Buccleuch in 1594.

lines 292–3: Added in the second edition, 1805.

lines 319–24: These six lines were added in the second edition of 1805, for the single couplet of the first edition:

> At the last words with deadly blows
> The ready warriors fiercely close.

line 333: 'Possibly the Minstrel refers here to that same battle of Killiecrankie in which his son was slain, and where, if he had been present at it, he must have seen the Highlanders armed with their claymores or broadswords engage in a hand-to-hand struggle with the English soldiers, armed with musket and bayonet' (Stuart and Elliot, p. 194).

line 490: Scott himself notes the source:

> The lands, that over Ouse to Berwick forth do bear,
> Have for their blazon had, the snaffle, spur, and spear.
> Drayton, *Poly-Olbion*, Song 13

line 495: 'The pursuit of Border marauders was followed by the injured party and his friends with blood-hounds and bugle-horn, and was called the *hot-trod.* He was entitled, if his dog could trace the scent, to follow the invaders into the opposite kingdom; a privilege which often occasioned bloodshed' (S).

Canto Sixth

line 34: Added in the second edition, 1805.

line 68: The Lady was a magician, with command over evil spirits—not a 'romancer, or wizard', subjected or allied to them (S).

line 90: 'The peacock, it is well known, was considered, during the times of chivalry, not merely as an exquisite delicacy, but as a dish of peculiar solemnity. After being roasted, it was again decorated with plumage, and a sponge, dipped in lighted spirits of wine, was placed in its bill' (S).

line 91: Perhaps 'surrounded with little banners displaying the colours and achievements' of the Scotts of Buccleuch (John Pinkerton, *History of Scotland*, 2 vols., London 1797, I. 432, quoted S).

line 120: 'The Rutherfords of Hunthill were an ancient race of Border Lairds, whose names occur in history, sometimes as defending the frontier against the English, sometimes as disturbing the peace of their own country. Dickon Draw-the-sword was son to the ancient warrior, called in tradition the Cock of Hunthill, remarkable for leading into battle nine sons, gallant warriors, all sons of the aged champion' (S).

line 128: 'To bite the thumb, or the glove, seems not to have been considered, upon the Border, as a gesture of contempt, though so used by Shakespeare, but as a pledge of mortal revenge' (S).

line 144: 'The person bearing this redoubtable *nom de guerre* was an Elliot, and resided at Thorleshope, in Liddesdale. He occurs in the list of Border riders, in 1597' (S). As an Elliot, Arthur belonged to the party of the Kerrs, enemies to the Scotts; and it follows therefore that Watt Tinlinn deliberately laid aside all hostility in drinking Arthur's health.

line 155: According to legend, the first Buccleuch got his name from seizing a buck in a cleugh (ravine with steep sides) after the King (Kenneth MacAlpine, *regn.* A.D. 844–60) and his party were unable to pursue it farther. He was made ranger of the royal forest for this feat.

line 162: The battle of Solway Moss, 1542, where it is said that ten thousand Scots were routed by three hundred Englishmen—a disgrace which is alleged to have broken James V's heart.

lines 162–3: It is clear from IV. l. 40–71 that Watt Tinlinn—one of the Scott family—was a brave man who would be deeply ashamed of his part in the rout of Solway Moss. At the same time the 'hardy partner' (IV. 71) who was in the habit of carrying his bows and arrows seems the last woman who would yield to the attentions of a neighbour, let alone a member of another clan like the Armstrongs. In his malice, the goblin page cunningly mingles truth and falsehood.

line 192: 'This burden is adopted, with some alteration, from an old Scottish song, beginning thus:

> She leaned her back against a thorn,
> The sun shines fair on Carlisle wa':
> And there she has her young babe born,
> And the lyon shall be lord of a'.' (S)

line 248: Henry VIII. 'The charge against Surrey was that he had quartered the royal arms, the arms of Edward the Confessor, on his shield. It was pretended that this indicated a treasonable design; but, as a fact, the royal arms had been borne by Surrey's ancestors, and they were assumed now in furtherance of a scheme to prevent the regency from falling into the hands of the Seymours, and to secure it for the Howards, Henry being at this time on his deathbed' (Stuart and Elliot, p. 218).

line 257: 'The song of the supposed bard is founded on an incident said to

have happened to the Earl on his travels. Cornelius Agrippa, the celebrated alchemist (1486–1535), showed him, in a looking glass, the lovely Geraldine, to whose service he had devoted his pen and his sword. The vision represented her as indisposed, and reclining upon a couch, reading her lover's verses by the light of a waxen taper' (S). The song is of course in Spenserian stanzas.

line 282: A couch lined with Indian silk. 'Agra rose to importance in the beginning of the 16th century and was the capital of the Mogul Empire down to the year 1658. As such, its fame must have become known to the people of Europe, who would naturally regard costly articles of Indian manufacture, wheresoever they may have been made, as coming from Agra' (Stuart and Elliot, p. 221).

lines 304–5: Logically and grammatically, 'these' should refer to the 'Southern chiefs', the nearer of the two nouns, and 'those' to the Scots. Yet Scott's meaning is unclear. In any case, both the Northern Lords and the Scots were still Catholic at this period (*c.* 1550).

line 315: Kirkwall Castle and the Orkney and Shetland Isles were confiscated from the St. Clairs by James III. But Scott is also thinking of the later loyalty of the St. Clair family to the House of Stuart.

line 336: The *jormungandr*, or Snake of the Ocean of Norse mythology, whose folds surround the earth. 'It was very nearly caught by the god Thor, who went to fish for it with a hook baited with a bull's head. In the battle betwixt the evil demons and the divinities of Odin, which is to precede the *Ragnarockr*, or Twilight of the Gods, this Snake is to act as a conspicuous part' (S).

line 338: 'These were the *Valcyriur* [Valkyrie], or Selectors of the Slain, despatched by Odin from Valhalla, to choose who were to die, and to distribute the contest. They are well known to the English reader, as Gray's Fatal Sisters' (S)—i.e., in the Ode so titled.

lines 340–5: 'The northern warriors were usually entombed with their arms, and their other treasures. . . . Indeed, the ghosts of the northern warriors were not wont tamely to suffer their tombs to be plundered; and hence the mortal heroes had an additional temptation to attempt such adventures; for they held nothing more worthy of their valour than to encounter supernatural beings' (S, who cites Bartholinus *De causis contemptae a Danis mortis*, Copenhagen 1689, lib. i. cap. 2, 9, 10, 13).

line 358: 'A large and strong castle, now ruinous, situated betwixt Kirkcaldy and Dysart, on a steep crag, washed by the Firth of Forth. It was conferred on Sir William St. Clair, as a slight compensation for the earldom of Orkney, by a charter of King James III dated in 1471. . . . It was long a principal residence of the Barons of Roslin' (S).

line 372: Riding at the ring 'was a favourite pastime with knights in late feudal times. . . . A ring was suspended from a beam, and those who took part in the sport were required to show their skill by thrusting their lances through the ring, riding at full speed, and bearing it off on their lance point' (Stuart and Elliot, p. 229).

line 384: The chapel was supposed to seem ablaze before the death of a St. Clair of Roslin. 'This superstition . . . is probably of Norwegian derivation, and may have been imported by the Earls of Orkney into their Lothian dominions. The tomb-fires of the north are mentioned in most of the Sagas' (S).

line 393: 'Among the profuse carving on the pillars and buttresses, the rose is frequently introduced, in allusion to the name, with which, however, the flower

has no conexion; the etymology being Rosslinnhe, the promontory of the linn, or waterfall' (S).

line 455: This refers to a legend about a soldier in the Isle of Man who lost the power of speech after addressing a supernatural dog, and died in agony three days later.

line 476: Loch of the Lowes, 'in the extreme NW. of Ettrick Parish, Selkirk; separated by only a narrow neck of land from St. Mary's Loch' (*O.G.S.* V. 561).

line 477: Lisle has been identified, most implausibly, with Edinburgh. In Dr. J. D. Corson's opinion, Lille in N. France is meant. It is curious that neither Scott nor Lockhart annotated the line.

line 478: St. Mary's Isle, 'the seat of the Earl of Selkirk, in Kirkcudbright parish . . . 1¼ miles SSW. of the town. . . . It stands on a finely-wooded peninsula, projecting 1⅛ miles SSW. into the head of Kirkcudbright Bay. . . . The sea, in former times, made the place literally an isle,' which was the site of an Augustinian priory dedicated to the Virgin Mary (*O.G.S.* VI. 314).

line 533: 'It is not very clear what hymn the poet refers to. It may be the intercessional prayer, *Requiem aeternam dona eis, Domine; et lux perpetua luceat eis* (Eternal rest give to them, O Lord; and let perpetual light shine on them), which is frequently and regularly repeated at the close,—not of the "office",—but of each division of the office. The same prayer is found in . . . the Responsory, which is sung after Solemn Mass for the Dead' (Stuart and Elliot, pp. 238–9).

The Lady of the Lake

p. 140 The title derives from Malory, *Morte Darthur*, Bk I ch. xxiii; Malory's Lady was the damsel from whom King Arthur obtained his sword Excalibur. The first edition was prefaced by the dedication 'To the most noble John James Marquis of Abercorn this Poem is inscribed by the Author' and by the following note: 'The scene of the following Poem is laid chiefly in the vicinity of Loch Katrine, in the Western Highlands of Perthshire. The time of Action includes Six Days, and the transactions of each Day occupy a Canto.'

Canto First

line 2: 7th-century abbot of Kilmund in Argyll, who later lived at Glendarshy in Fife. Many wells supposed to cure madness were dedicated to him, 'particularly in Perthshire' (S, note on *Marmion*, I. xxix. 12).

line 31: The valley of the Ruchill water, a tributary of the Earn, in Perthshire. The hunt begins in this glen, and 'sweeps past Callander, up the valley of the Teith, towards the Trossachs—some twenty miles westward from the starting-point' (A.L.).

line 145: Gael, 'bristled territory'. 'A romantic mountain defile of SW. Perthshire, on the southern boundary of Callander parish, extending one mile westward from the head of Loch Achray to the foot of Loch Katrine, and forming a portal of the Western Highlands. . . . The Trossachs are a contracted vale, whose sides are soaring eminences wildly and irregularly feathered all over with hazels, oaks, birches, hawthorns and mountain ashes, and whose central space is "a tumultuous confusion of little rocky eminences, all of the most fantastic and extraordinary forms, everywhere shagged with trees and shrubs" and presenting "an aspect of roughness and wildness, of tangled and inextricable boskiness, totally unexampled, it is supposed, in the world". Thus the discoverer of the Trossachs' beauties, the Rev. Dr. Robertson (d. 1812), who was presented to the parish of Callander in 1768' (*O.G.S.* VI. 453). After the early 19th century it became fashionable for romantically-minded tourists to visit the area; Dorothy Wordsworth and Nathaniel Hawthorne are among the many who have described the Trossachs.

line 218–19: Many readers wrote to Scott asking him to explain these lines, which he generally did as follows: 'I incline to think that I have confused the night-shade with hemlock, used you know, for the execution of criminals, and so far therefore an emblem of punishment; and that the foxglove from its determined erect figure and decisive colour, might be no bad emblem of pride' (To Lionel Thomas Bergner, 20 Oct. 1812, in *Letters*, III. 180).

line 258: 'Until the present road was made through the romantic pass which I have presumptuously attempted to describe in the preceding stanzas, there was no mode of issuing out of the defile called the Trossachs, excepting by a sort of ladder composed of the branches and roots of trees' (S).

line 481: This line, and indeed the whole description of the island which follows, has a curiously ironic relation to Spenser, *Faerie Queene*, II. vi. sts. 5 ff. Spenser's Phaedria is a 'wanton Damzell', not the chaste daughter of a noble house; her 'little frigot' (st. 7) is not propelled by oars but by a magic 'pin' (st. 5); and her luxuriant floating island merely helps her to feed Cymochles' eyes and senses 'with false delights . . . and pleasures vaine' (st. 14). Ellen, in contrast, has much more in common with Una, or even Britomart—'My hope, my heaven, my trust must be, My gentle guide, in following thee' (lines 534–5).

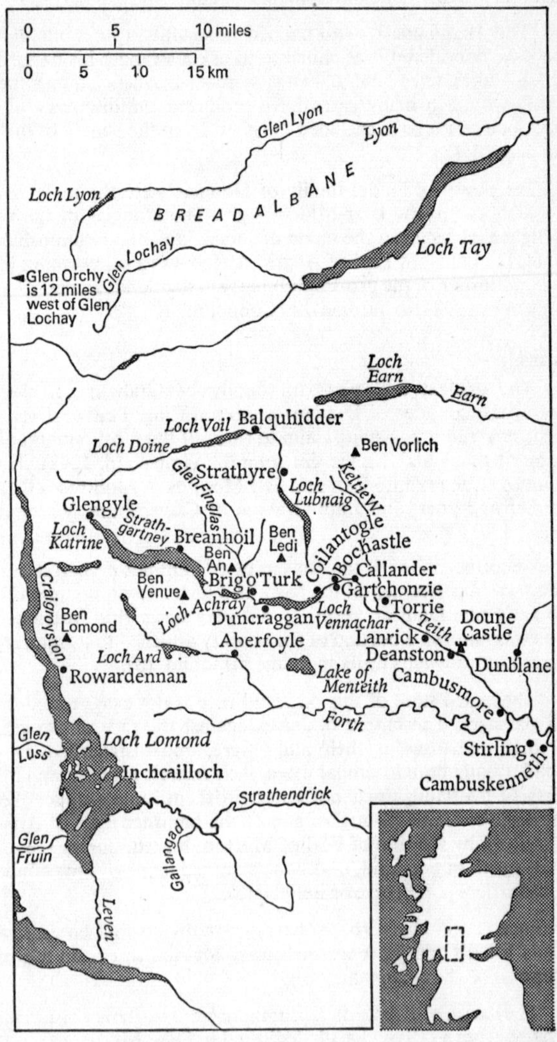

Map of the Trossachs

line 505: 'The Celtic chieftains, whose lives were continually exposed to peril, had usually in the most retired spot of their domains, some place of retreat for the hour of necessity, which, as circumstances would admit, was a tower, a cavern, or a rustic hut, in a strong and secluded situation' (S). Scott had in mind a particular hut, which 'gave refuge to the unfortunate Charles Edward, in his perilous wanderings after the battle of Culloden', and quotes a detailed description of it from John Home, *History of the Rebellion*, London 1802, p. 381.

line 585: 'The Highlanders, who carried hospitality to a punctilious excess, are said to have considered it as churlish, to ask a stranger his name or lineage, before he had taken refreshment. Feuds were so frequent among them, that a contrary rule would in many cases have produced the discovery of some circumstance which might have excluded the guest from the benefit of the assistance he stood in need of' (S).

line 731: The powerful feudal family of Douglas were the main rivals of the Stewart royal house in the later Middle Ages. The Douglas of the poem is an imaginary figure. He is given the name of James, and the relationship of uncle to Archibald, the banished Earl of Angus. Angus was a supporter of Henry VIII of England and leader of the pro-English party in Scotland; James V had escaped from his tutelage in 1528, to become the 'Commons' King'.

Canto Second

line 109: 'The ancient and powerful family of Graham . . . held extensive possessions in the counties of Dunbarton and Stirling. Few families can boast of more historical renown, having claim to three of the most remarkable characters in the Scottish annals' (S), viz. Sir John the Graeme (d. 1298), the friend of Wallace; James Graham, fifth Earl and first Marquis of Montrose (1612–50), the royalist soldier and poet; and John Graham of Claverhouse, Viscount Dundee (?1649–89).

line 131: A Scottish abbot of the 7th century. 'I am not prepared to show that Saint Modan was a performer on the harp. It was, however, no unsaintly accomplishment; for Saint Dunstan certainly did play upon that instrument, which retaining, as was natural, a portion of the sanctity attached to its master's character, announced future events by its spontaneous sound' (S).

line 229: 'The exiled state of this powerful race is not exaggerated in this and subsequent passages. The hatred of James against the race of Douglas was so inveterate, that numerous as their allies were, and disregarded as the regal authority had usually been in similar cases, their nearest friends, even in the most remote parts of Scotland, durst not entertain them, unless under the strictest and closest disguise. James Douglas, son of the banished Earl of Angus, afterwards well known by the title of Earl of Morton, lurked, during the exile of his family, in the north of Scotland, under the assumed name of James Innes, otherwise *James the Grieve* [*i.e.*, Reeve or Bailiff]' (S).

line 236: Since canon law forbade marriages between first cousins, and since Roderick was Ellen's cousin, it was necessary for him to obtain a dispensation from the Pope before he could marry her.

line 260: 'The parish of Kilmaronock, at the eastern extremity of Loch Lomond, derives its name from a cell or chapel, dedicated to Saint Maronock, or Marnock, or Maronnan' (S).

line 306: Archibald, third Earl of Douglas, was called 'Tine-man' because he 'tined', or lost, his followers in every battle which he fought. 'He was vanquished, as every reader must remember, in the bloody battle of Homildon-hill near Wooler (1402), where he himself lost an eye, and was made prisoner by Hotspur.

He was no less unfortunate when allied with Percy, being wounded and taken at the battle of Shrewsbury' (S). The qualification 'as every reader must remember' is an interesting gloss on Scott's ideal reader—an educated Scotsman familiar with his country's history and with ballad lore.

line 356: A particular style of classical bagpipe music characterized by complex variations. 'The connoisseurs in pipe-music affect to discover in a well-composed pibroch, the imitative sounds of march, conflict, fight, pursuit and all the "current of a heady fight"' (S). But a pibroch is not necessarily a martial piece; it may be a dirge. The source of Scott's description in st. xvii is a note in James Beattie, *Essay on Laughter and Ludicrous Composition*, Edinburgh 1776, chap. III.

line 399: 'The song itself is intended as an imitation of the *jorrams*, or boat songs of the Highlanders, which were usually composed in honour of a favourite chief. They are so adapted as to keep time with the sweep of the oars, and it is easy to distinguish between those intended to be sung to the oars of a galley, where the stroke is lengthened and doubled, as it were, and those which were timed to the rowers of an ordinary boat' (S). This note shows Scott as aware as any modern folklorist of the nature and prosody of a work-song.

line 408: 'Besides his ordinary name and surname, which were chiefly used in the intercourse with the Lowlands, every Highland chief had an epithet expressive of his patriarchal dignity as head of the clan, and which was common to all his predecessors and successors, as Pharaoh to the kings of Egypt, or Arsaces to those of Parthia. This name was usually a patronymic, expressive of his descent from the founder of the family. . . . But besides this title, which belonged to his office and dignity, the chieftain had usually another peculiar to himself, which distinguished him from the chieftains of the same race. This was sometimes derived from the complexion, as *dhu* [black] or *roy* [red]; sometimes from size, as *beg* [little] or *more* [great]; at other times, from some peculiar exploit, or from some peculiarity of habit or appearance. The line of the text therefore signifies,

Black Roderick, the descendant of Alpine' (S).

line 497: 'Won by the Earl Douglas in a skirmish before the walls of Newcastle, 1388. The attempt to recover it led to the . . . battle of Otterbourne, in which Douglas was slain, and Percy (not Earl Percy, but his son Hotspur), was taken prisoner. This battle is celebrated in the ballad . . . of the *Battle of Otterbourne*. . . . The pennon remained in possession of the Douglasses; and Scott either represents it as being carried before them in subsequent times as a sort of trophy or refers to some later capture of a pennon' (Stuart, p. 189).

line 616: 'In 1529 James V made a convention in Edinburgh for the purpose of considering the best mode of quelling the Border robbers who, during the license of his minority, and the troubles which followed, had committed many exorbitancies. Accordingly he assembled a flying army of ten thousand men, consisting of his principal nobility and their followers, who were directed to bring their hawks and dogs with them, that the monarch might refresh himself with sport during the intervals of military execution. With this array he swept through Ettrick forest, where he hanged over the gate of his own castle Piers Cockburn of Henderland, who had prepared, according to tradition, a feast for his reception' (S). Other malefactors were put down and hanged, including the famous John Armstrong of the ballad and of John Arden's play, *John Armstrong's Last Goodnight*. When the Borders were tamed, James turned his attention to the Highlands.

line 634: 'James was in fact equally attentive to restrain rapine and feudal oppression in every part of his dominions' (S).

line 809: A personal attendant on the chief. 'This officer is a sort of secretary, and is to be ready, upon all occasions, to venture his life in defence of his master

and at drinking-bouts, he stands behind his seat . . . and watches the conversation, to see if any one offends his patron.' (E. Burt, *Letters from Scotland*, 2 vols., London 1754, II. 157, quoted by Scott).

Canto Third

line 18: A cross of light wood whose ends were seared in fire then dipped in goat's blood to put out the glow. It was passed on, at the chieftain's instructions, from one hamlet to another, 'with a single word, implying the place of rendezvous.' Every man from sixteen to sixty was bound to go there 'in his best arms and accoutrements. . . . He who failed to appear suffered the extremities of fire and sword, which were emblematically denounced to the disobedient by the bloody and burnt marks upon this warlike signal' (S).

line 65: The idea for this character came (i) from priests and friars who accompanied English border outlaws in the early 16th century; (ii) from friars who served with Irish guerilla septs in Elizabeth's reign; and (iii) from an 18th-century description of a lay capuchin on the Hebridean island of Benbecula, from whom the 'naked arms and legs' are derived (S). But the associations of 'Druid's' (l. 76) and 'human sacrifice' are from Scott, not his sources.

line 91: The folk-tale on which the story of the seer's birth is founded was taken from 'the geographical collections made by the laird of Macfarlane' II, 188, where he reports how a certain 'maid or wench' of Unnatt warmed herself before a fire made from the bones of slain soldiers and 'tooke up her cloaths above her knees, or thereby, to warm her; a wind did come and caste the ashes upon her, and she was conceived of ane man-chyld'. The child was named, in Gaelic, 'Black Child, Son to the Bones', was given an education and became 'a good schollar, and godlie' (S).

line 114: Ribbon worn by maidens in Scotland to confine their hair, replaced by the 'curch' or coif on marriage. If a girl lost her virginity yet did not marry, she was allowed to wear neither snood nor curch.

line 154: River-horse ('kelpie' in the Scottish Lowlands,) 'an evil and malicious spirit, delighting to forebode and to witness calamity' (S).

line 156: 'A tall, emaciated, gigantic female figure' who was 'supposed in particular to haunt the district of Knoidart. . . . A goblin, dressed in antique armour, and having one hand covered with blood, called from that circumstance . . . Red-hand, is a tenant of the forests of Glenmore and Rothiemurchus' (S).

line 205: 'The Highlanders are as zealous of their rights of sepulture, as may be expected from a people whose whole laws and government, if clanship can be called so, turned upon the single principle of family descent. "May his ashes be scattered on the water," was one of the deepest and most solemn imprecations which they used against an enemy' (S).

line 300: 'The present *brogue* of the Highlanders is made of half-dried leather, with holes to admit and let out the water; for walking the moors dry-shod is a matter altogether out of question. The ancient buskin was still ruder, being made of undressed deer's hide, with the hair outwards, a circumstance which procured the Highlanders the well-known epithet of *Red-shanks*' (S).

line 545: This song was translated into German by P. A. Storck as *Normans Gesang* and set by Schubert, D.846. There is a fine recording by Dietrich Fischer-Dieskau, *Schubert Lieder Recital No. 4*, H.M.V., ALP 1827. Storck's translation uses a twelve-syllable line instead of Scott's eight syllables.

line 622: Coir-nan-Uriskin 'is a very steep and most romantic hollow in the mountain of Benvenue, overhanging the south-eastern extremity of Loch Katrine. It is surrounded with stupendous rocks, and overshadowed with birch-trees,

mingled with oaks. . . . The name literally implies the Corri, or Den, of the Wild or Shaggy men. . . . But tradition has ascribed to the *Urisk*, who gives name to the cavern, a figure between a goat and a man . . . precisely that of the Grecian Satyr' (S). According to Patrick Graham, *Scenery on the Southern Confines of Perthshire*, 1806, p. 19, quoted in Scott's note, 'The *Urisks* were a set of lubberly supernaturals who, like the Brownies, could be gained over, by kind attention, to perform the drudgery of the farm, and it was believed that many of the families in the Highlands had one of the order attached to it. They were supposed to be dispersed over the Highlands, each in his own wild recess, but the solemn stated meetings of the order were regularly held in this Cave of Benvenue.'

Canto Fourth

line 63: A mode of divination whereby 'a person was wrapped up in the skin of a newly-slain bullock, and deposited beside a waterfall, or at the bottom of a precipice, or in some other strange, wild and unusual situation, where the scenery around him suggested nothing but objects of horror. In this situation, he revolved in his mind the question proposed; and whatever was impressed upon him by his exalted imagination, passed for the inspiration of the disembodied spirits, who haunt the desolate recesses' (S).

lines 65–78: 'This passage is taken almost literally from the mouth of an old Highland Kern or Ketteran, as they were called. He used to narrate the merry doings of the good old time when he was follower of Rob Roy MacGregor. This leader, on one occasion, thought proper to make a descent upon the lower part of the Loch Lomond district, and summoned all the heritors and farmers to meet at the Kirk of Drymen, to pay him blackmail, i.e., tribute for forbearance and protection. As this invitation was supported by a band of thirty or forty stout fellows, only one gentleman . . . ventured to decline compliance. Rob Roy instantly swept his land of all he could drive away, and among the spoil was a bull of the old Scottish wild breed, whose ferocity occasioned great plague to the Ketterans. 'But ere we had reached the Row of Dennan,' said the old man, 'a child might have scratched his ears' (S). The circumstance, as Scott says, 'is a minute one', but it illustrates how oral tradition helps to create the poem's density of reference.

lines 132–3: 'Though this be in the text described as a response of the Taghairm, or Oracle of the Hide, it was of itself an augury frequently attended to. The fate of the battle was often anticipated in the imagination of the combatants, by observing which party first shed blood. It is said that the Highlanders under Montrose were so deeply imbued with this notion, that on the morning of the battle of Tippermoor (1644) they murdered a defenceless herdsman, whom they found in the fields, merely to secure an advantage of so much consequence to their party' (S).

lines 152–3: The coat of arms of the Earls of Moray had three silver stars; the Mar coat of arms had a black band across it—in heraldic language a 'sable pale'.

line 261: 'Alice Brand' is typical of Scott's ballad imitations and of the influence upon him of continental traditions. 'This little fairy-tale is founded upon a very curious Danish ballad which occurs in the *Kaempe Viser*, a collection of heroic songs first published in 1591, and reprinted in 1695, inscribed by Anders Sofrensen, the collector and editor, to Sophia Queen of Denmark. . . . The story will remind readers of the Border Minstrelsy of the tale of young Tamlane' (S). Scott got a literal translation of the original from the antiquarian and ballad-collector Robert Jamieson.

line 308: 'The Elves were supposed greatly to envy the privileges acquired by Christian initiation, and they gave to those mortals who had fallen into their power, a certain precedence . . .' (S).

line 578–81: In the MS., the song read:

Sweet William was a woodsman true,
He stole poor Blanche's heart away!
His coat was of the forest hue,
And sweet he sung the Lowland lay.
(*PW*, viii. 191–2, nn.)

The alteration is in the direction of irregularity, towards a rhythm which seems to imitate that of a typical broadside-type tune.

line 762: This was prepared by compressing the raw venison 'between two batons of wood, so as to force out the blood and render it extremely hard' (S). It was then dried and eaten without further cooking.

Canto Fifth

lines 136–69: Scott supports Roderick's racial nationalism by means of the following anecdote: 'Sir James Grant of Grant is in possession of a letter of apology from Cameron of Lochiel, whose men had committed some depredation upon a farm called Moines, occupied by one of the Grants. Lochiel assures Grant that, however the mistake had happened, his instructions were precise, that the party should foray the province of Moray (a lowland district), where, as he coolly observes, "all men take their prey."'

line 380: 'A round target of light wood, covered with strong leather, and studded with brass or iron, was a necessary part of a Highlander's equipment. In charging regular troops, they received the thrust of the bayonet in this buckler, twisted it aside, and used the broadsword against the encumbered soldier ... A person thus armed had a considerable advantage in private fray' (S).

lines 443–4: 'The good faith and valour displayed by Roderick will be rewarded with praise if he live, which praise will be lost to him, if he die. This is what the words seem to mean as they stand; but the sentiment intended to be expressed appears to be that whether Roderick lives or dies, his faith and valour deserve praise. Faith and valour are personified, and give praise to Roderick for the observance that he has paid to them' (Stuart, p. 230).

lines 494–502: '... the Poet marks the progress of the King by naming in succession places familiar and dear to his own early recollections—Blair-Drummond, the seat of the Homes of Kaimes; Kier, that of the principal family of the name of Stirling; Ochtertyre, that of John Ramsay, the well-known antiquary, and correspondent of Burns; and Craigforth, that of the Callanders of Craigforth, almost under the walls of Stirling Castle;—all hospitable roofs, under which he had spent many of his younger days' (L).

line 614: 'The exhibition of this renowned outlaw and his band was a favourite frolic at such festivals as we are describing. This sporting, in which kings did not disdain to be actors, was prohibited in Scotland upon the Reformation, by a statute of the 6th Parliament of Queen Mary, c. 61, A.D. 1555, which ordered, under heavy penalties, that 'na manner of person be chosen Robert Hude, nor Little John, Abbot of Unreason, Queen of May, nor otherwise' (S).

lines 629–31: 'The King's behaviour during an unexpected interview with the Laird of Kilspindie, one of the banished Douglasses, under circumstances similar to those in the text, is imitated from a real story told by Hume of Godscroft' (S).

line 641: 'The usual prize of a wrestling was a ram and a ring, but the animal would have embarrassed my story' (S). But Scott's sources are both English ones —*The Cokes Tale of Gamelyn*, and *The Litil Geste of Robin Hood.*

lines 659–60: 'In the Castle-hill is a hollow called "the Valley", comprehending

about an acre, and having the appearance of an artificial work, for justings and tournaments, with other feats of chivalry. Closely adjoining to this valley, on the south, is a small rocky pyramidical mount, called "The Ladies' Hill", where the fair ones of the court took their station to behold these feats.'—W. Nimmo, *A General History of Stirlingshire*, Edinburgh 1777, p. 222, quoted Stuart, p. 235.

line 768: 'There was a Sir John Carmichael of Hyndford who was Warden of the Borders between England and Scotland in the reign of Queen Mary of Scotland: see "The Raid of the Reidswire", *Minstrelsy of the Scottish Border*, 1833, II. 18, n. The Sir John in the poem may be supposed to be the ancestor of the Warden' (Stuart, p. 236). This supposition is typical of the link between Scott's imaginative world and Scottish social history, for Hyndford estate remained in the possession of the Carmichael family right up to Sir Walter's own day.

lines 828–35: Cp. *Coriolanus*, I. i. 186–8:

> With every minute you do change a mind,
> And call him noble that was now your hate,
> Him vile that was your garland.

Canto Sixth

lines 43–64: 'James V seems to have first introduced, in addition to the militia furnished from [feudal and clan] sources, the service of a small number of mercenaries, who formed a bodyguard called the Foot-Band' (S). In lines 43–5 Scott distinguishes between the feudal tenant who gives military service to his superior in return for the use of his land and the Highlander's service to a chief who was, in theory at least, regarded as the father of his clan; whose dependants were bound to follow him in war, and to render him the sort of obedience due from child to father, while the chief gave them his fatherly protection.

lines 130–1: 'The jongleurs, or jugglers . . . used to call in the aid of various assistants. . . . The glee-maiden was a necessary attendant. Her duty was tumbling and dancing. . . . In Scotland, these poor creatures seem, even at a late period, to have been bondswomen to their masters' (S).

line 369: 'A skirmish actually took place at a pass thus called in the Trossachs, and closed with the remarkable incident mentioned in the text. It was greatly posterior in date to the reign of James V' (S)—actually, during the Cromwellian period.

line 665: Like the song at III. 545, this lyric was translated into German by P. A. Storck, and set to music by Schubert, D.843. It, too, has been recorded by Dietrich Fischer-Dieskau on H.M.V., ALP 1827.

line 740: 'William of Worcester, who wrote about the middle of the fifteenth century, calls Stirling Castle Snowdoun. . . . It appears that the real name by which James was actually distinguished in his private excursions, was the Goodman of Ballenguich; derived from a steep pass leading up to the Castle of Stirling. . . . But the epithet would not have suited poetry, and would besides at once, and prematurely, have announced the plot to many of my countrymen' (S).

First Line Index